NO LONGER PROPERTY OF
ANYTHINK LIBRARIES/
RANGEVIEW LIBRARY DISTRICT

JAMES PATTERSON

WITCH & WIZARD

OPERATION ZERO

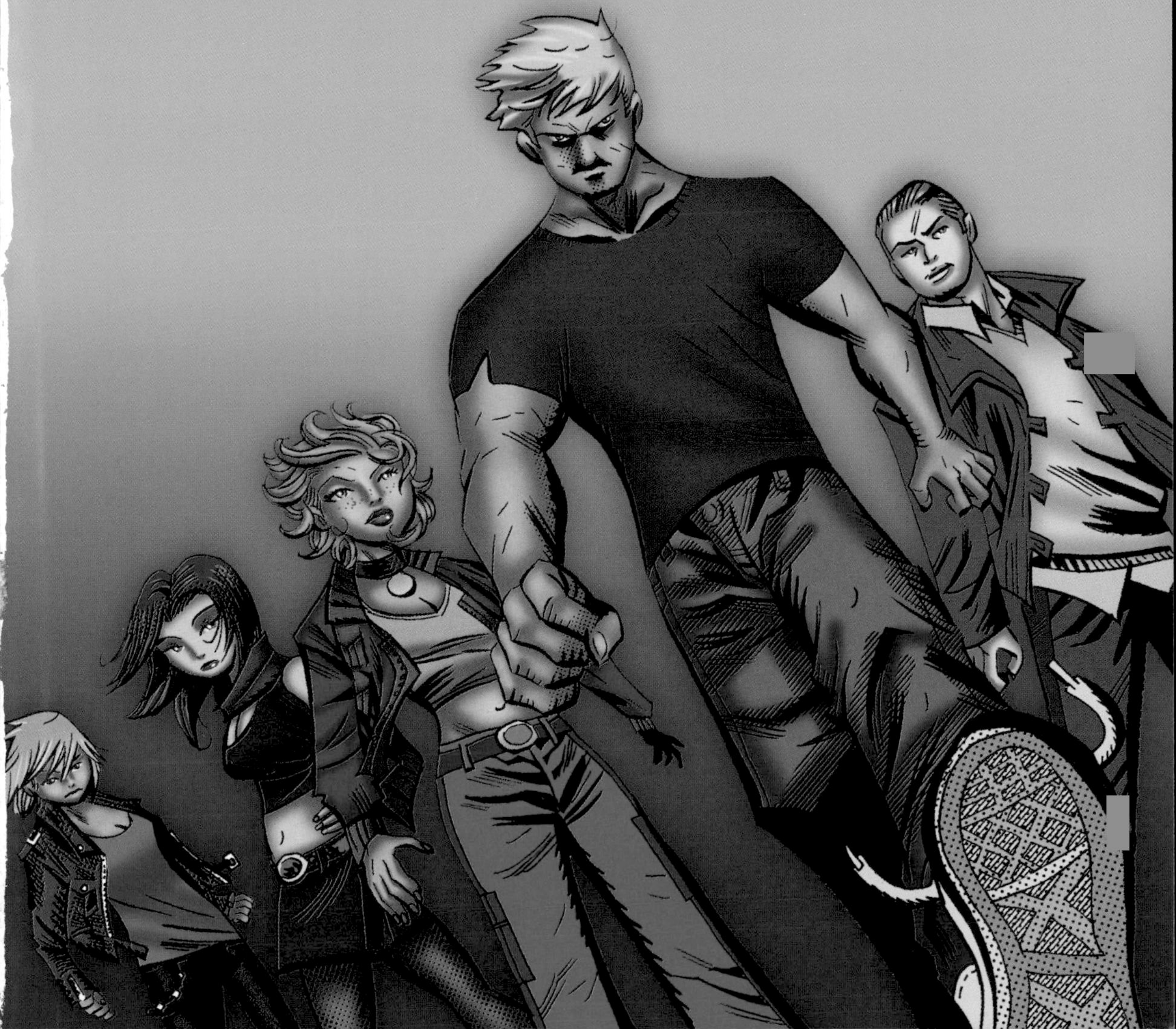

JAMES PATTERSON
WITCH & WIZARD
* OPERATION ZERO *

Special thanks to Leopoldo Gout, Steve Bowen, Gabrielle Charbonnet, and James Patterson.

www.IDWPUBLISHING.com   ISBN: 978-1-60010-890-7   14 13 12 11   1 2 3 4

IDW Publishing is: Operations: Ted Adams, CEO & Publisher • Greg Goldstein, Chief Operating Officer • Matthew Ruzicka, CPA, Chief Financial Officer • Alan Payne, VP of Sales • Lorelei Bunjes, Director of Digital Services • Jeff Webber, Director of ePublishing • AnnaMaria White, Dir., Marketing and Public Relations • Dirk Wood, Dir., Retail Marketing • Marci Hubbard, Executive Assistant • Alonzo Simon, Shipping Manager • Angela Loggins, Staff Accountant • Cherrie Go, Assistant Web Designer • Editorial: Chris Ryall, Chief Creative Officer, Editor-In-Chief • Scott Dunbier, Senior Editor, Special Projects • Andy Schmidt, Senior Editor • Justin Eisinger, Senior Editor, Books • Kris Oprisko, Editor/Foreign Lic. • Denton J. Tipton, Editor • Tom Waltz, Editor • Mariah Huehner, Editor • Carlos Guzman, Assistant Editor • Bobby Curnow, Assistant Editor • Design: Robbie Robbins, EVP/Sr. Graphic Artist • Neil Uyetake, Senior Art Director • Chris Mowry, Senior Graphic Artist • Amauri Osorio, Graphic Artist • Gilberto Lazcano, Production Assistant • Shawn Lee, Graphic Artist

WITCH & WIZARD, VOLUME 2: OPERATION ZERO. MARCH 2011. FIRST PRINTING. © 2011 James Patterson. All Rights Reserved. © 2011 Idea and Design Works, LLC. IDW Publishing, a division of Idea and Design Works, LLC. Editorial offices: 5080 Santa Fe St., San Diego, CA 92109. Any similarities to persons living or dead are purely coincidental. With the exception of artwork used for review purposes, none of the contents of this publication may be reprinted without the permission of Idea and Design Works, LLC. Printed in Korea. IDW Publishing does not read or accept unsolicited submissions of ideas, stories, or artwork.

Originally published as JAMES PATTERSON'S WITCH & WIZARD Issues #5–8.

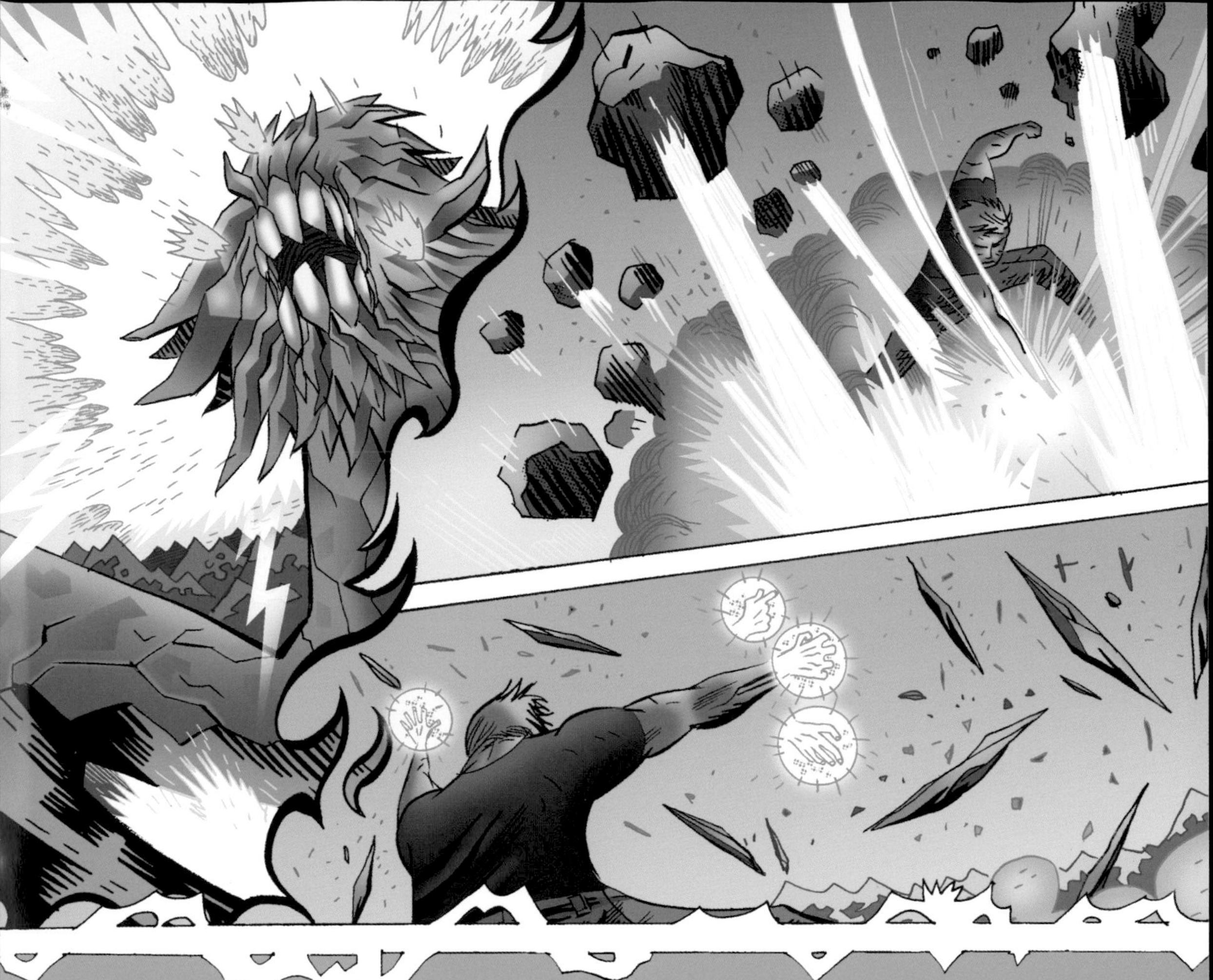

WRITERS
JAMES PATTERSON
AND DARA NARAGHI

ARTIST
VICTOR SANTOS

COLORIST
JAMIE GRANT

LETTERERS
SHAWN LEE & NEIL UYETAKE

SERIES EDITOR
BOB SCHRECK

ASSISTANT EDITOR
BOBBY CURNOW

COLLECTION EDITOR
JUSTIN EISINGER

COLLECTION DESIGNER
NEIL UYETAKE

WITCH & WIZARD CREATED BY JAMES PATTERSON

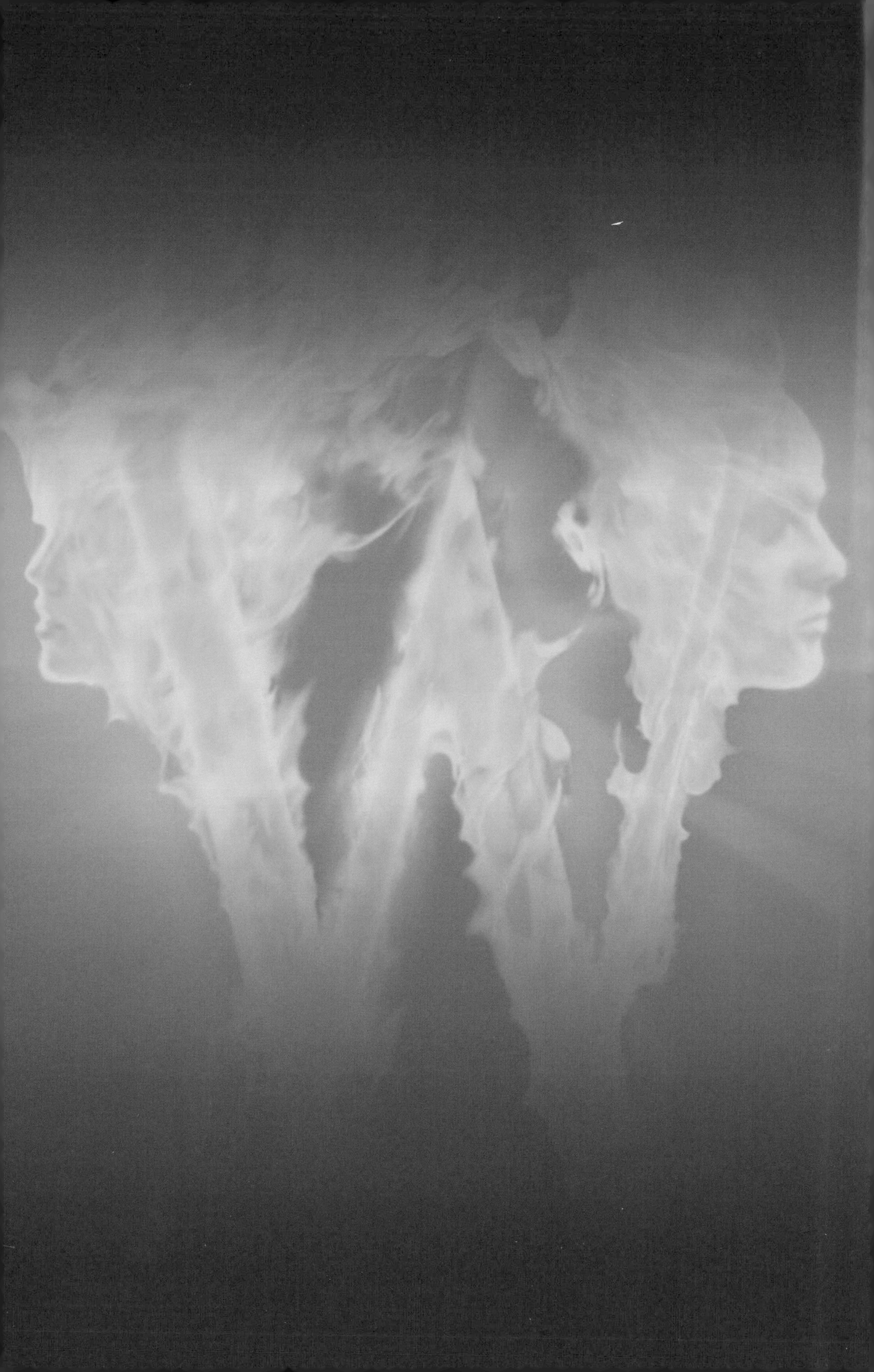

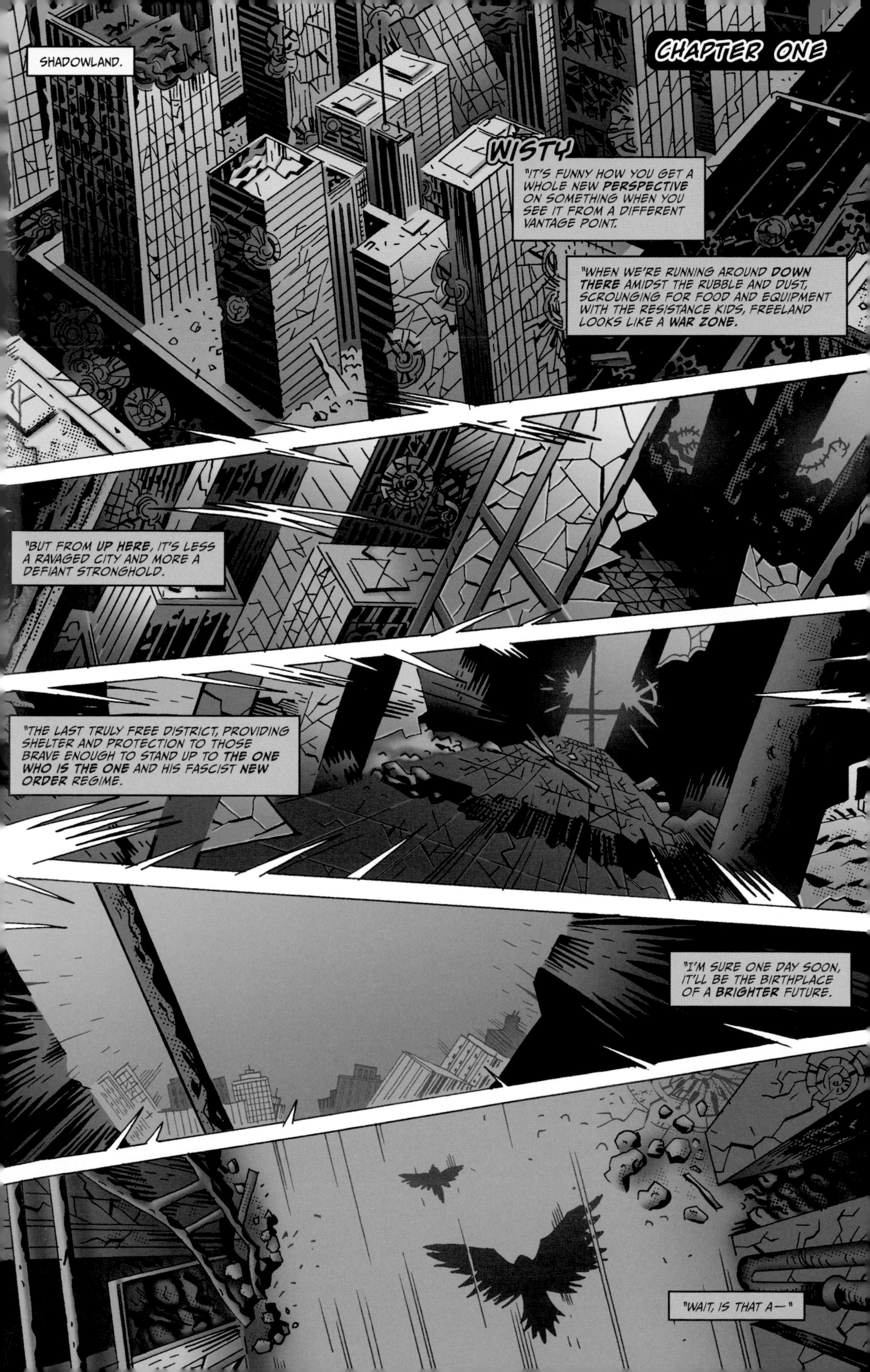
SHADOWLAND.
CHAPTER ONE
WISTY
"IT'S FUNNY HOW YOU GET A WHOLE NEW PERSPECTIVE ON SOMETHING WHEN YOU SEE IT FROM A DIFFERENT VANTAGE POINT.
"WHEN WE'RE RUNNING AROUND DOWN THERE AMIDST THE RUBBLE AND DUST, SCROUNGING FOR FOOD AND EQUIPMENT WITH THE RESISTANCE KIDS, FREELAND LOOKS LIKE A WAR ZONE.
"BUT FROM UP HERE, IT'S LESS A RAVAGED CITY AND MORE A DEFIANT STRONGHOLD.
"THE LAST TRULY FREE DISTRICT, PROVIDING SHELTER AND PROTECTION TO THOSE BRAVE ENOUGH TO STAND UP TO THE ONE WHO IS THE ONE AND HIS FASCIST NEW ORDER REGIME.
"I'M SURE ONE DAY SOON, IT'LL BE THE BIRTHPLACE OF A BRIGHTER FUTURE.
"WAIT, IS THAT A—"

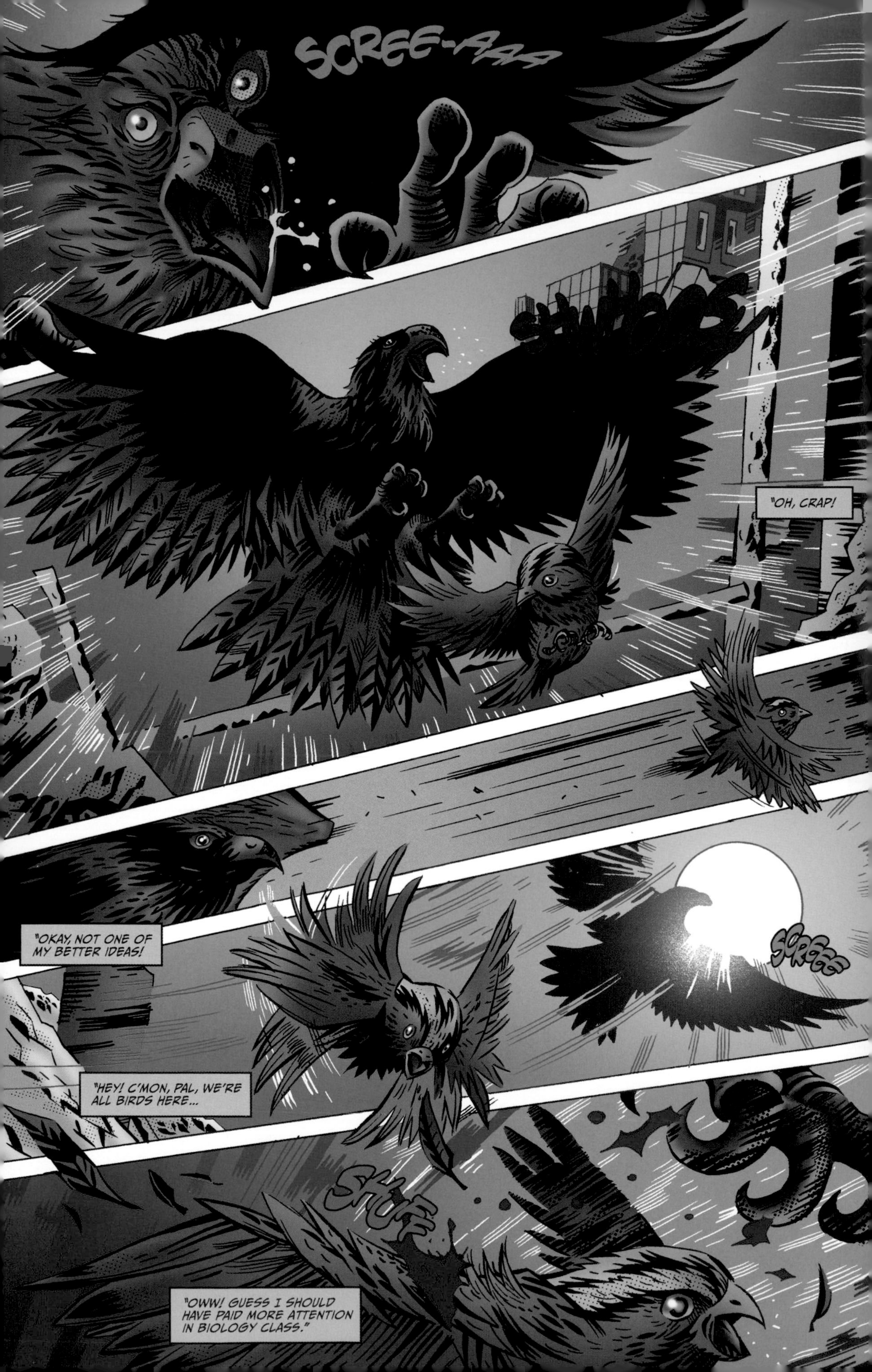
SCREE-AAA
SHWOOSH
"OH, CRAP!
"OKAY, NOT ONE OF MY BETTER IDEAS!
SCREEE
"HEY! C'MON, PAL, WE'RE ALL BIRDS HERE...
SHUFF
"OWW! GUESS I SHOULD HAVE PAID MORE ATTENTION IN BIOLOGY CLASS."

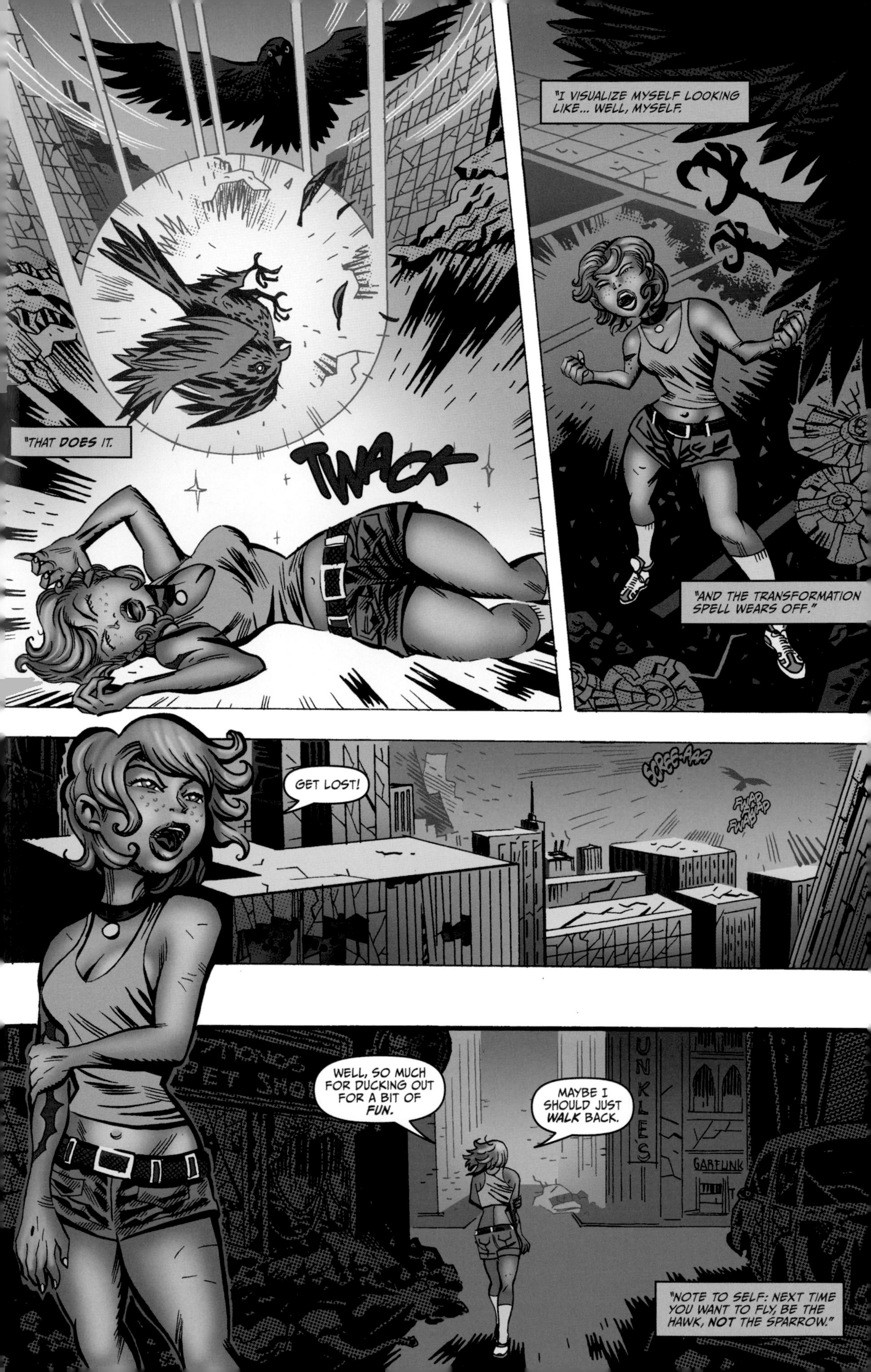
"THAT DOES IT.
TWACK
"I VISUALIZE MYSELF LOOKING LIKE... WELL, MYSELF.
"AND THE TRANSFORMATION SPELL WEARS OFF."
GET LOST!
SCREE-AAA
FWAP FWAP FWAP
WELL, SO MUCH FOR DUCKING OUT FOR A BIT OF FUN.
MAYBE I SHOULD JUST WALK BACK.
UNKLE'S
GARFUNK
"NOTE TO SELF: NEXT TIME YOU WANT TO FLY, BE THE HAWK, NOT THE SPARROW."

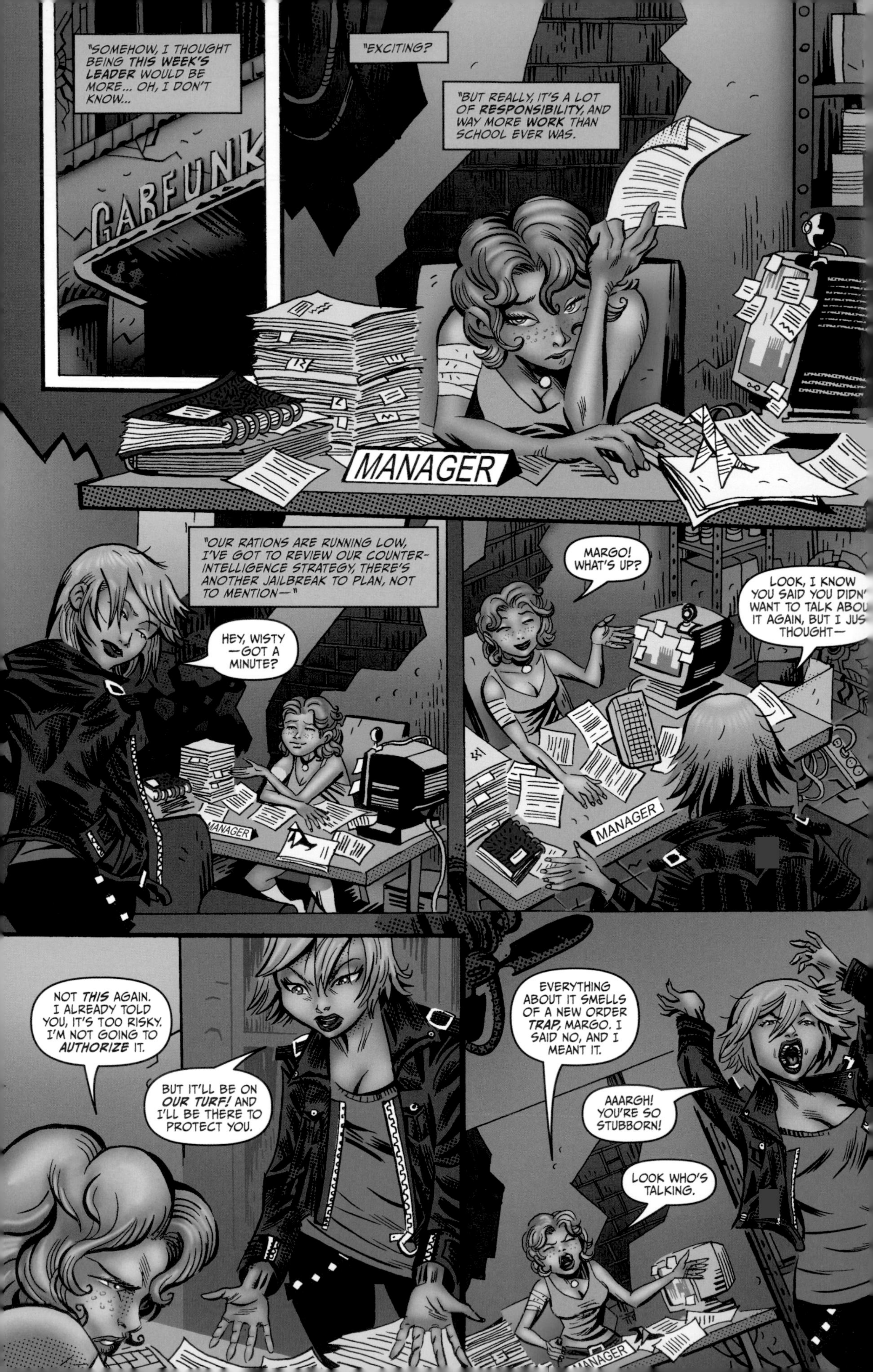
"SOMEHOW, I THOUGHT BEING THIS WEEK'S LEADER WOULD BE MORE... OH, I DON'T KNOW...
"EXCITING?
"BUT REALLY, IT'S A LOT OF RESPONSIBILITY, AND WAY MORE WORK THAN SCHOOL EVER WAS.
GARFUNK
MANAGER
"OUR RATIONS ARE RUNNING LOW, I'VE GOT TO REVIEW OUR COUNTER-INTELLIGENCE STRATEGY, THERE'S ANOTHER JAILBREAK TO PLAN, NOT TO MENTION—"
HEY, WISTY —GOT A MINUTE?
MANAGER
MARGO! WHAT'S UP?
LOOK, I KNOW YOU SAID YOU DIDN' WANT TO TALK ABOU IT AGAIN, BUT I JUS THOUGHT—
MANAGER
NOT THIS AGAIN. I ALREADY TOLD YOU, IT'S TOO RISKY. I'M NOT GOING TO AUTHORIZE IT.
BUT IT'LL BE ON OUR TURF! AND I'LL BE THERE TO PROTECT YOU.
EVERYTHING ABOUT IT SMELLS OF A NEW ORDER TRAP, MARGO. I SAID NO, AND I MEANT IT.
AAARGH! YOU'RE SO STUBBORN!
LOOK WHO'S TALKING.
MANAGER

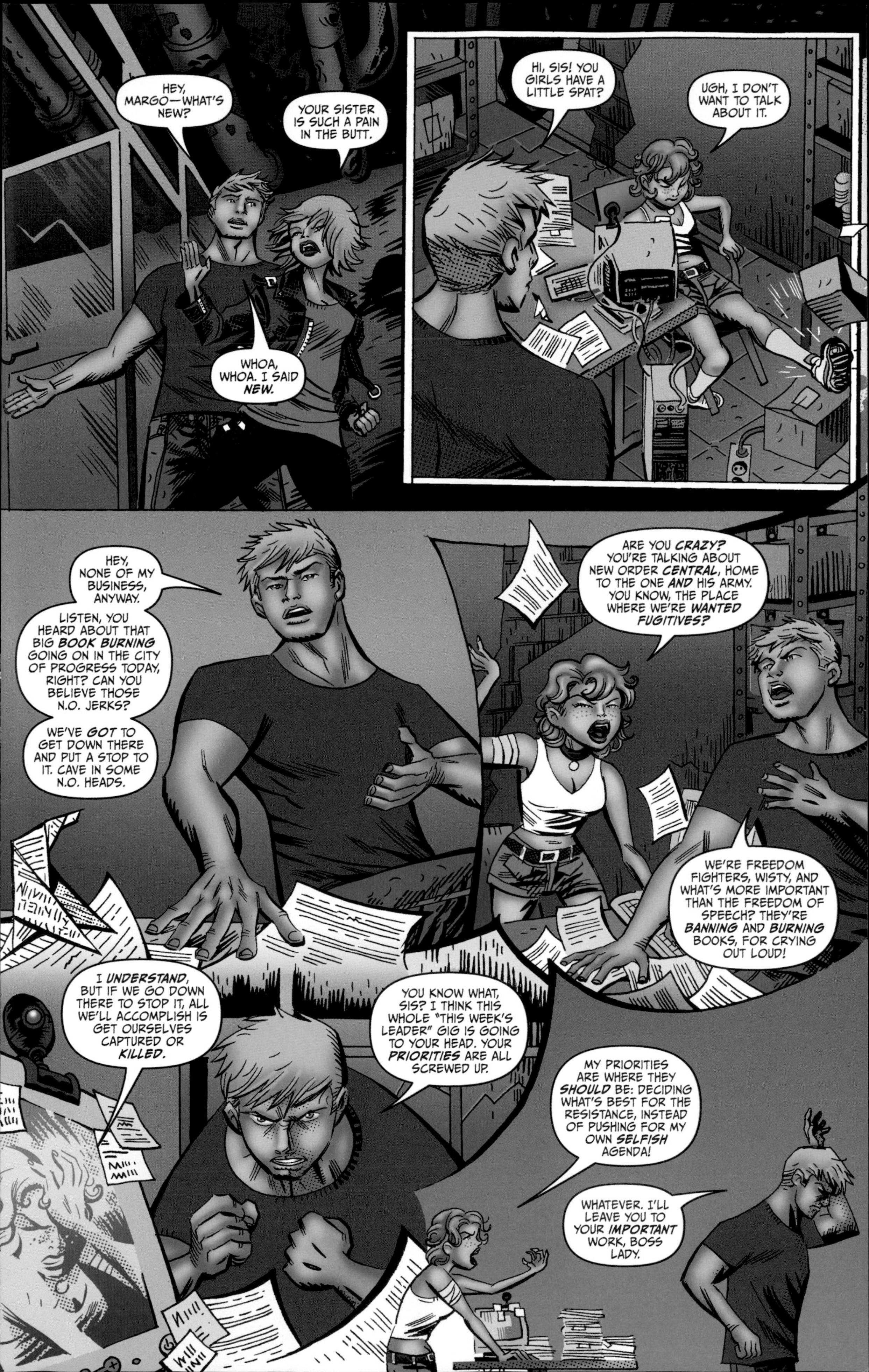
HEY, MARGO—WHAT'S NEW?
YOUR SISTER IS SUCH A PAIN IN THE BUTT.
WHOA, WHOA. I SAID NEW.
HI, SIS! YOU GIRLS HAVE A LITTLE SPAT?
UGH, I DON'T WANT TO TALK ABOUT IT.
HEY, NONE OF MY BUSINESS, ANYWAY.
LISTEN, YOU HEARD ABOUT THAT BIG BOOK BURNING GOING ON IN THE CITY OF PROGRESS TODAY, RIGHT? CAN YOU BELIEVE THOSE N.O. JERKS?
WE'VE GOT TO GET DOWN THERE AND PUT A STOP TO IT. CAVE IN SOME N.O. HEADS.
ARE YOU CRAZY? YOU'RE TALKING ABOUT NEW ORDER CENTRAL, HOME TO THE ONE AND HIS ARMY. YOU KNOW, THE PLACE WHERE WE'RE WANTED FUGITIVES?
WE'RE FREEDOM FIGHTERS, WISTY, AND WHAT'S MORE IMPORTANT THAN THE FREEDOM OF SPEECH? THEY'RE BANNING AND BURNING BOOKS, FOR CRYING OUT LOUD!
I UNDERSTAND, BUT IF WE GO DOWN THERE TO STOP IT, ALL WE'LL ACCOMPLISH IS GET OURSELVES CAPTURED OR KILLED.
YOU KNOW WHAT, SIS? I THINK THIS WHOLE "THIS WEEK'S LEADER" GIG IS GOING TO YOUR HEAD. YOUR PRIORITIES ARE ALL SCREWED UP.
MY PRIORITIES ARE WHERE THEY SHOULD BE: DECIDING WHAT'S BEST FOR THE RESISTANCE, INSTEAD OF PUSHING FOR MY OWN SELFISH AGENDA!
WHATEVER. I'LL LEAVE YOU TO YOUR IMPORTANT WORK, BOSS LADY.

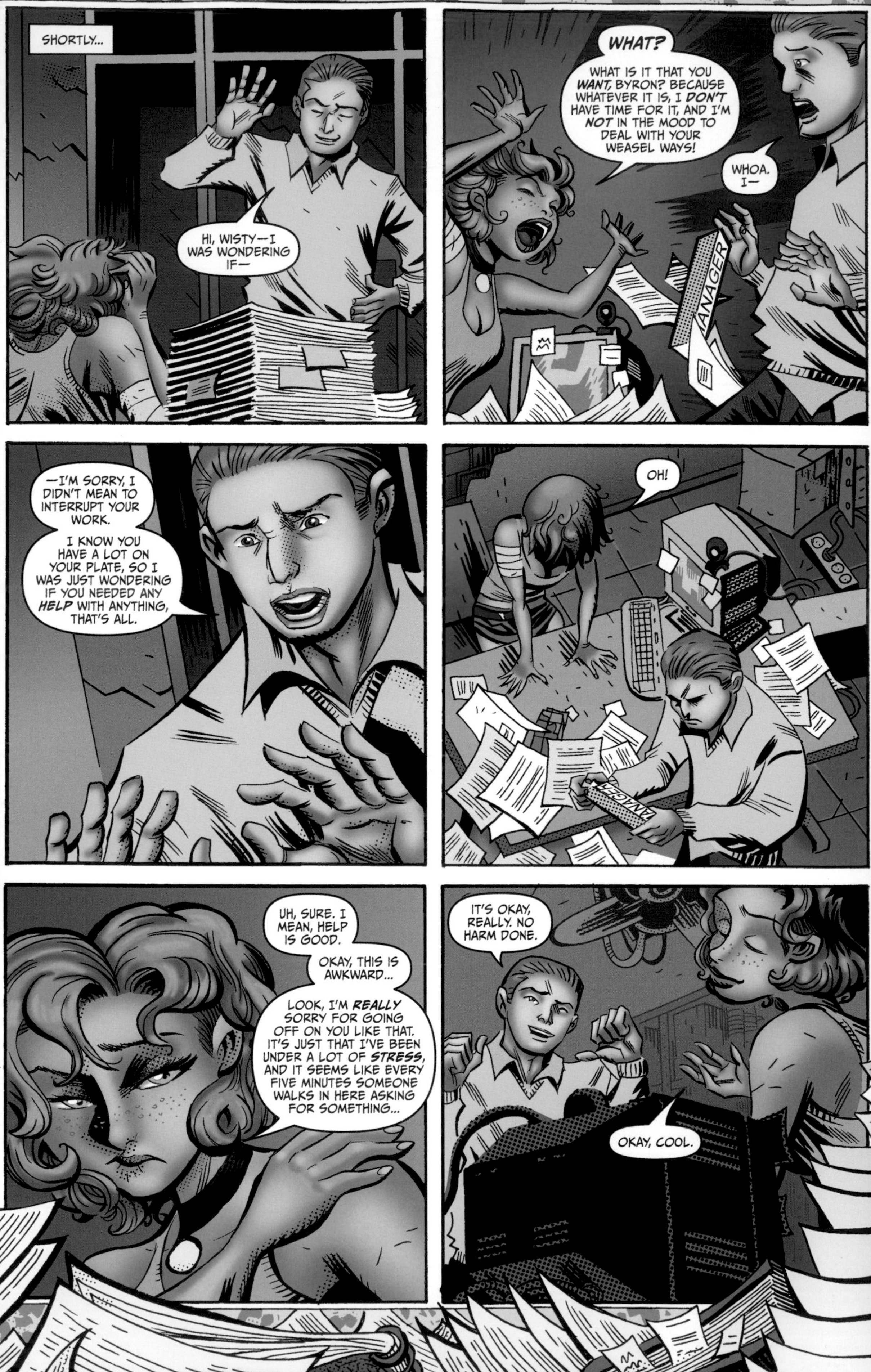
SHORTLY...
HI, WISTY—I WAS WONDERING IF—
WHAT?
WHAT IS IT THAT YOU WANT, BYRON? BECAUSE WHATEVER IT IS, I DON'T HAVE TIME FOR IT, AND I'M NOT IN THE MOOD TO DEAL WITH YOUR WEASEL WAYS!
WHOA. I—
—I'M SORRY, I DIDN'T MEAN TO INTERRUPT YOUR WORK.
I KNOW YOU HAVE A LOT ON YOUR PLATE, SO I WAS JUST WONDERING IF YOU NEEDED ANY HELP WITH ANYTHING, THAT'S ALL.
OH!
UH, SURE. I MEAN, HELP IS GOOD.
OKAY, THIS IS AWKWARD...
LOOK, I'M REALLY SORRY FOR GOING OFF ON YOU LIKE THAT. IT'S JUST THAT I'VE BEEN UNDER A LOT OF STRESS, AND IT SEEMS LIKE EVERY FIVE MINUTES SOMEONE WALKS IN HERE ASKING FOR SOMETHING...
IT'S OKAY, REALLY. NO HARM DONE.
OKAY, COOL.

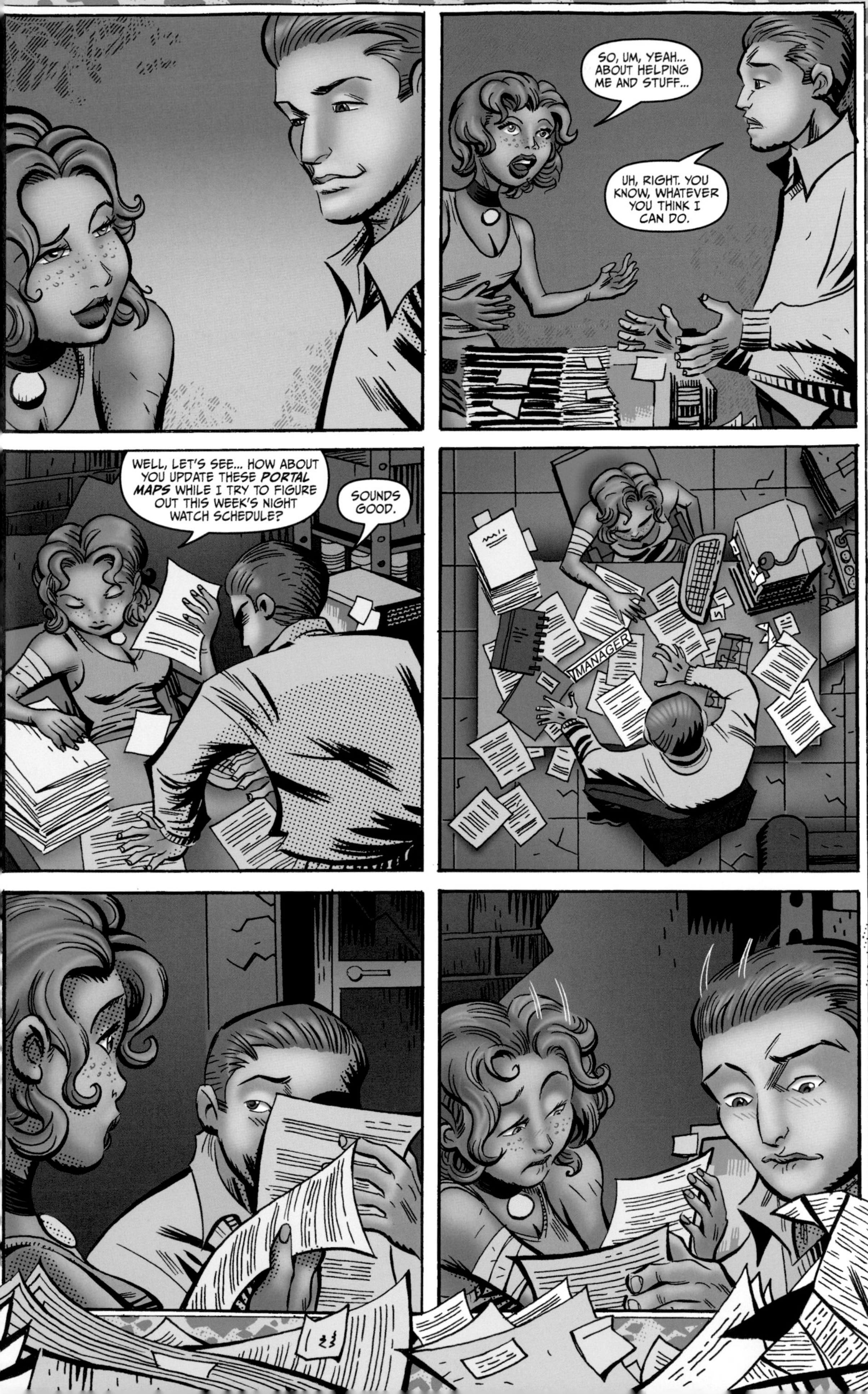

SO, UM, YEAH... ABOUT HELPING ME AND STUFF...
UH, RIGHT. YOU KNOW, WHATEVER YOU THINK I CAN DO.
WELL, LET'S SEE... HOW ABOUT YOU UPDATE THESE PORTAL MAPS WHILE I TRY TO FIGURE OUT THIS WEEK'S NIGHT WATCH SCHEDULE?
SOUNDS GOOD.
MANAGER

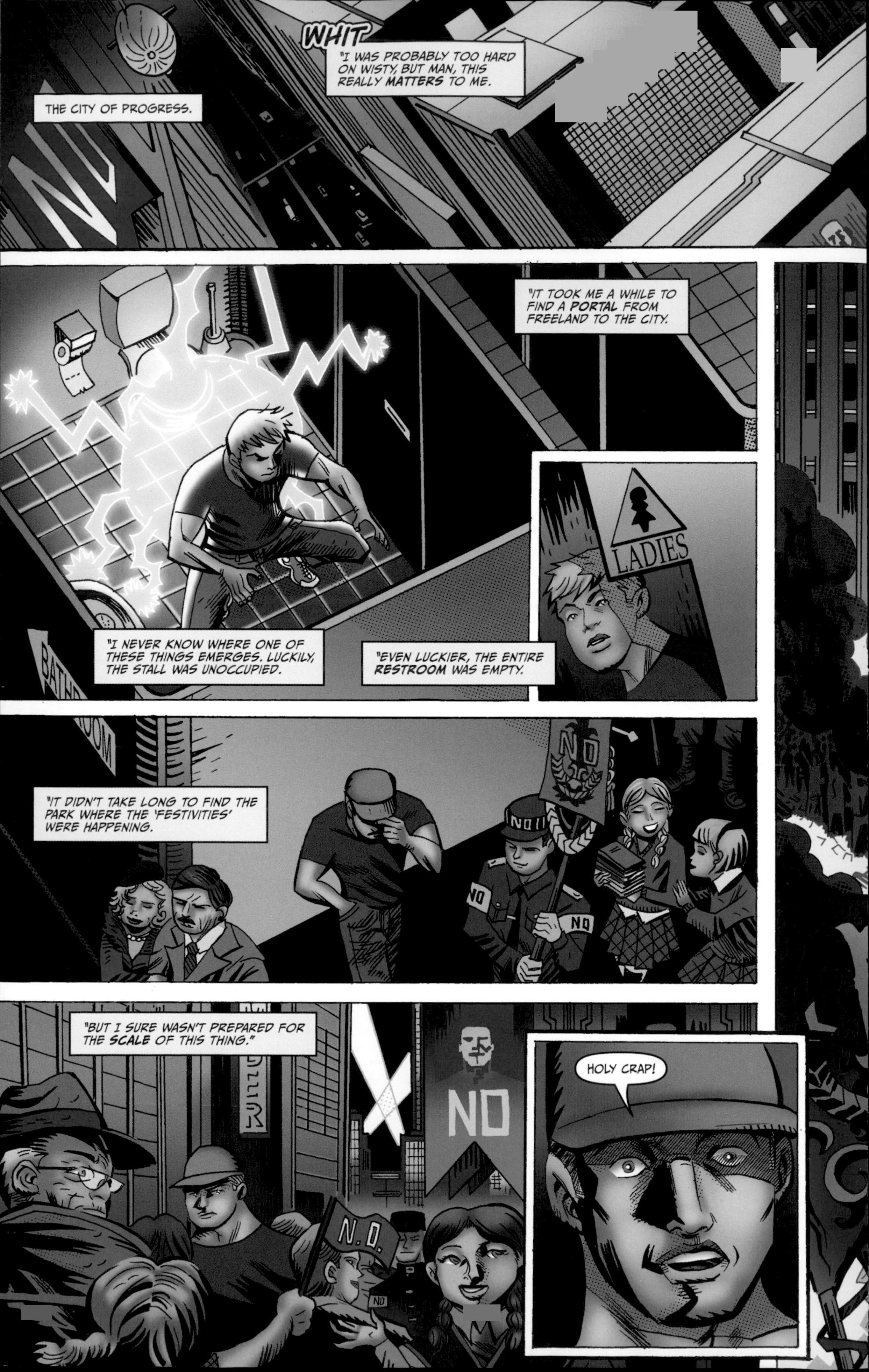
WHIT
"I WAS PROBABLY TOO HARD ON WISTY, BUT MAN, THIS REALLY MATTERS TO ME.
THE CITY OF PROGRESS.
"IT TOOK ME A WHILE TO FIND A PORTAL FROM FREELAND TO THE CITY.
LADIES
"I NEVER KNOW WHERE ONE OF THESE THINGS EMERGES. LUCKILY, THE STALL WAS UNOCCUPIED.
"EVEN LUCKIER, THE ENTIRE RESTROOM WAS EMPTY.
"IT DIDN'T TAKE LONG TO FIND THE PARK WHERE THE 'FESTIVITIES' WERE HAPPENING.
"BUT I SURE WASN'T PREPARED FOR THE SCALE OF THIS THING."
NO
N.O.
HOLY CRAP!

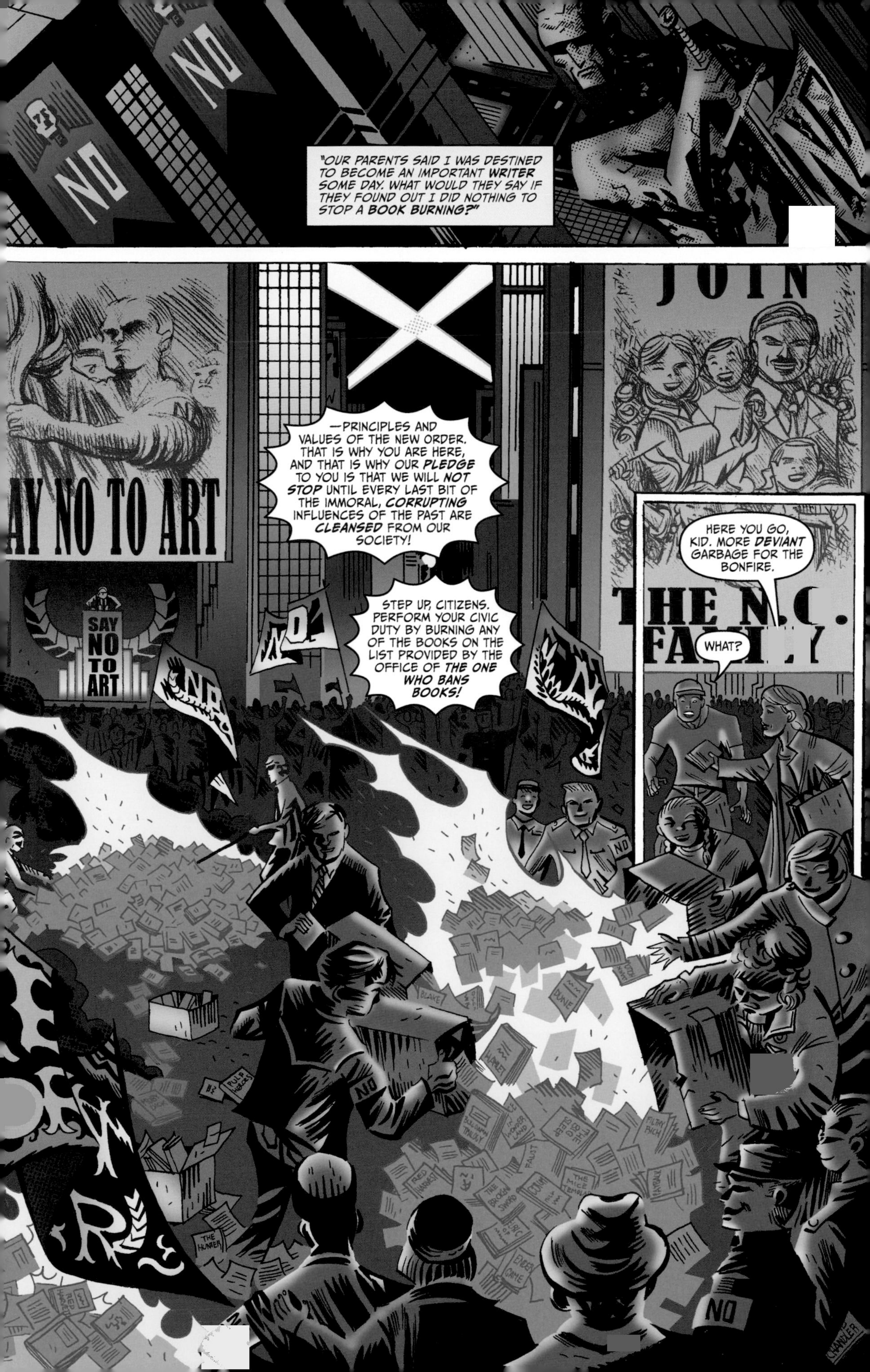
"OUR PARENTS SAID I WAS DESTINED TO BECOME AN IMPORTANT WRITER SOME DAY. WHAT WOULD THEY SAY IF THEY FOUND OUT I DID NOTHING TO STOP A BOOK BURNING?"
AY NO TO ART
JOIN
—PRINCIPLES AND VALUES OF THE NEW ORDER. THAT IS WHY YOU ARE HERE, AND THAT IS WHY OUR PLEDGE TO YOU IS THAT WE WILL NOT STOP UNTIL EVERY LAST BIT OF THE IMMORAL, CORRUPTING INFLUENCES OF THE PAST ARE CLEANSED FROM OUR SOCIETY!
HERE YOU GO, KID. MORE DEVIANT GARBAGE FOR THE BONFIRE.
SAY NO TO ART
STEP UP, CITIZENS. PERFORM YOUR CIVIC DUTY BY BURNING ANY OF THE BOOKS ON THE LIST PROVIDED BY THE OFFICE OF THE ONE WHO BANS BOOKS!
WHAT?

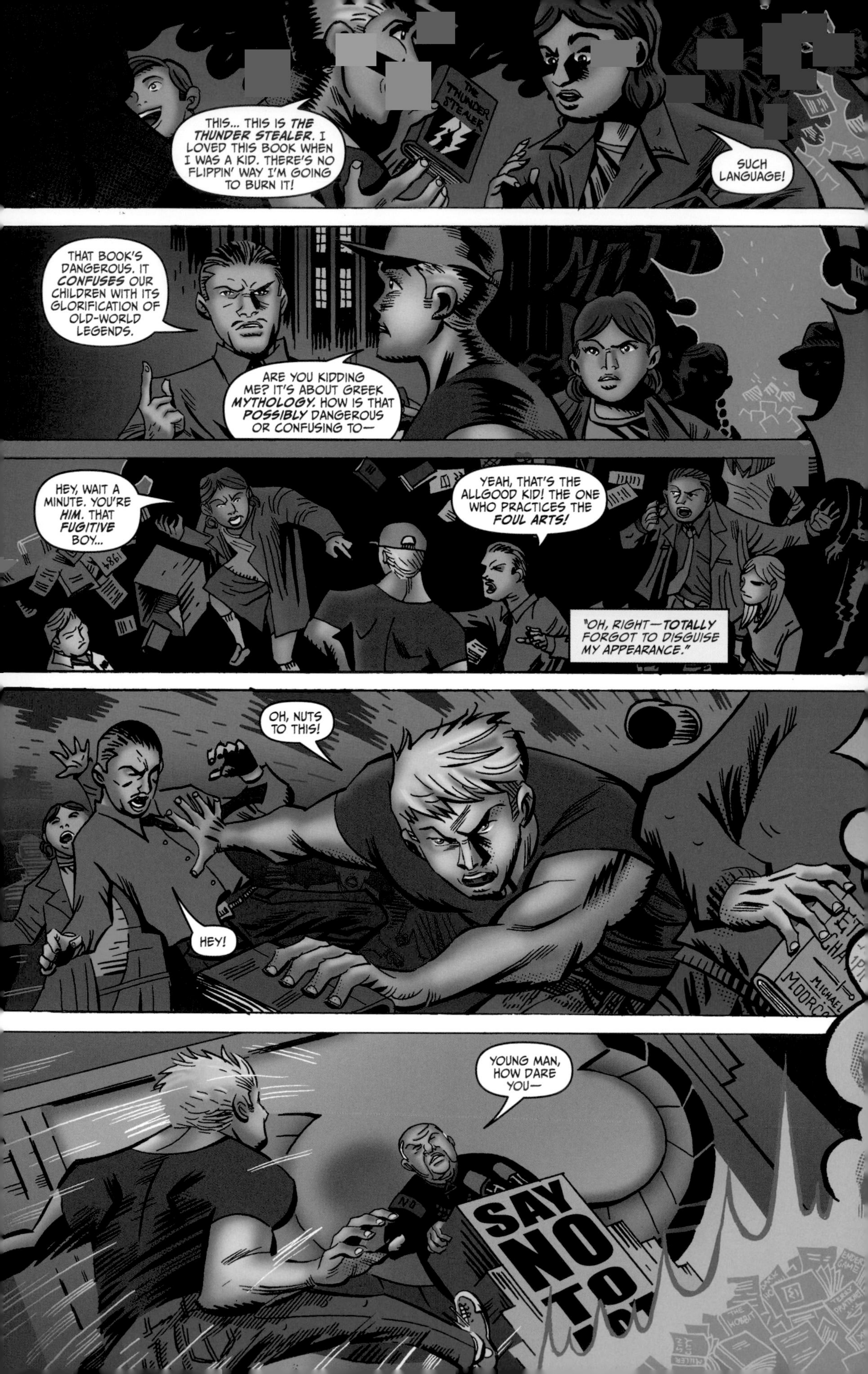
THIS... THIS IS THE THUNDER STEALER. I LOVED THIS BOOK WHEN I WAS A KID. THERE'S NO FLIPPIN' WAY I'M GOING TO BURN IT!
THE THUNDER STEALER
SUCH LANGUAGE!
THAT BOOK'S DANGEROUS. IT CONFUSES OUR CHILDREN WITH ITS GLORIFICATION OF OLD-WORLD LEGENDS.
ARE YOU KIDDING ME? IT'S ABOUT GREEK MYTHOLOGY. HOW IS THAT POSSIBLY DANGEROUS OR CONFUSING TO—
HEY, WAIT A MINUTE. YOU'RE HIM. THAT FUGITIVE BOY...
YEAH, THAT'S THE ALLGOOD KID! THE ONE WHO PRACTICES THE FOUL ARTS!
"OH, RIGHT—TOTALLY FORGOT TO DISGUISE MY APPEARANCE."
OH, NUTS TO THIS!
HEY!
YOUNG MAN, HOW DARE YOU—
SAY NO TO

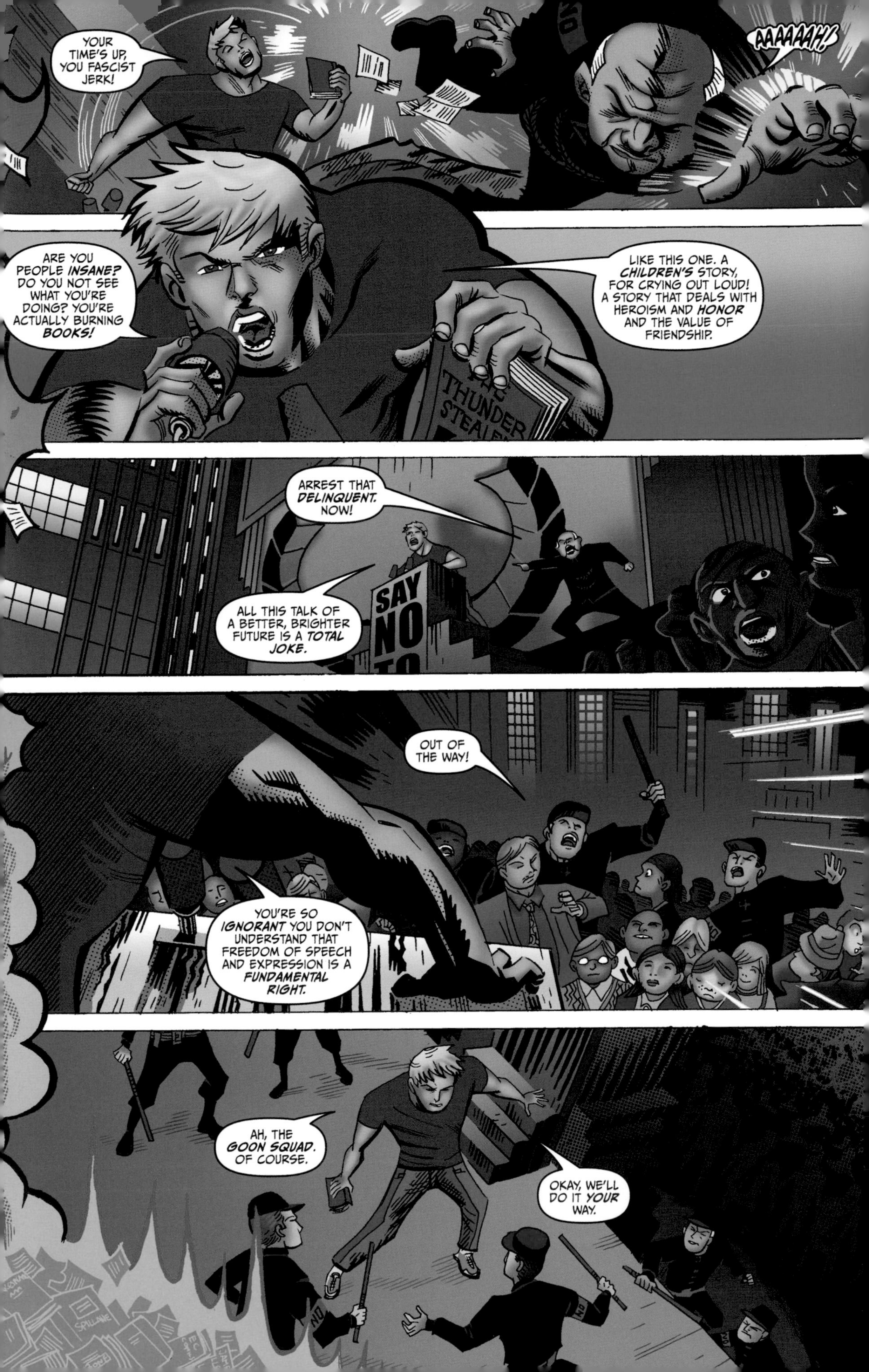
YOUR TIME'S UP, YOU FASCIST JERK!
AAAAAAH!
ARE YOU PEOPLE INSANE? DO YOU NOT SEE WHAT YOU'RE DOING? YOU'RE ACTUALLY BURNING BOOKS!
LIKE THIS ONE. A CHILDREN'S STORY, FOR CRYING OUT LOUD! A STORY THAT DEALS WITH HEROISM AND HONOR AND THE VALUE OF FRIENDSHIP.
THE THUNDER STEALER
ARREST THAT DELINQUENT. NOW!
ALL THIS TALK OF A BETTER, BRIGHTER FUTURE IS A TOTAL JOKE.
SAY NO TO
OUT OF THE WAY!
YOU'RE SO IGNORANT YOU DON'T UNDERSTAND THAT FREEDOM OF SPEECH AND EXPRESSION IS A FUNDAMENTAL RIGHT.
AH, THE GOON SQUAD. OF COURSE.
OKAY, WE'LL DO IT YOUR WAY.

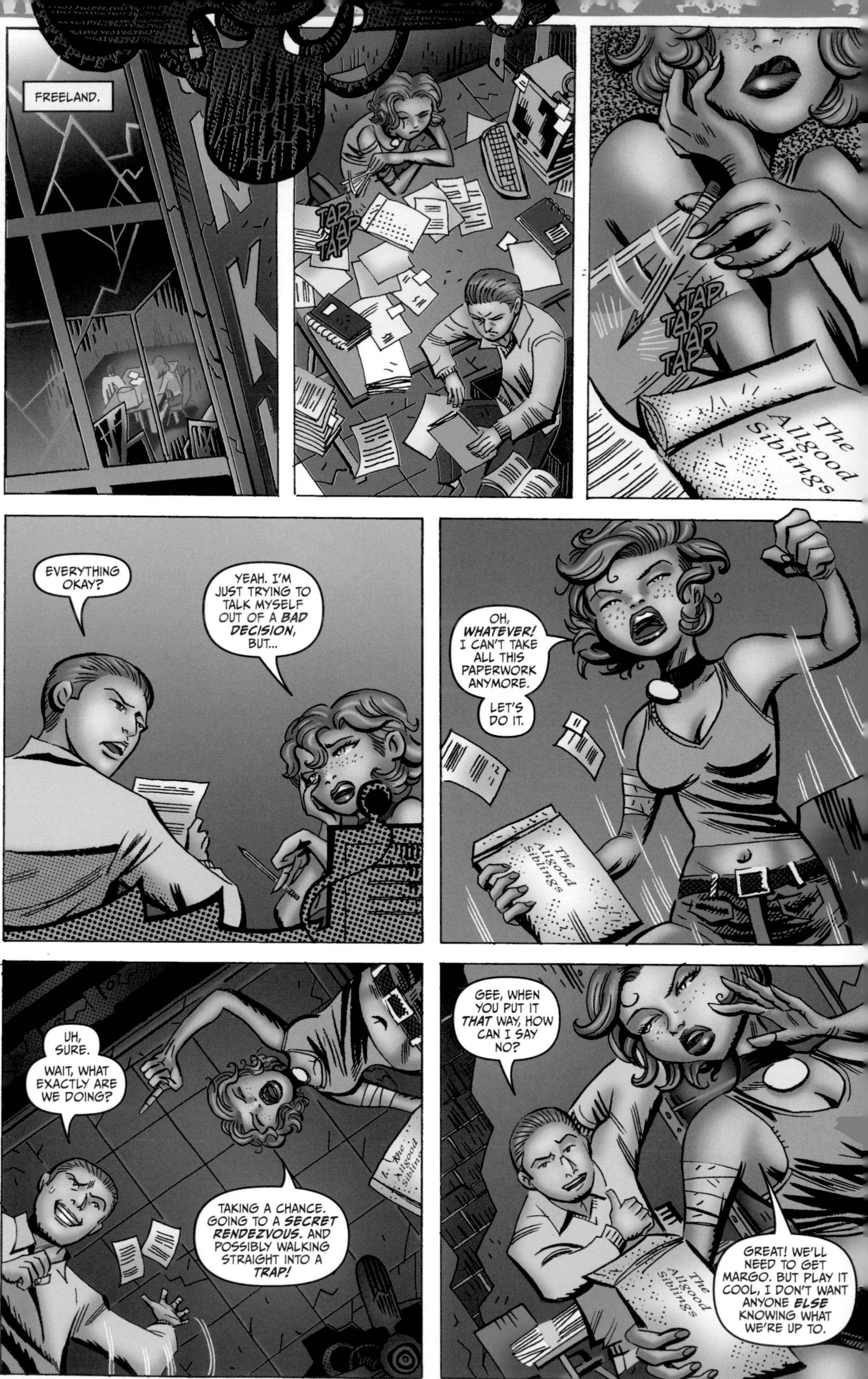
FREELAND.
TAP TAP TAP
TAP TAP TAP TAP
The Allgood Siblings
EVERYTHING OKAY?
YEAH. I'M JUST TRYING TO TALK MYSELF OUT OF A *BAD DECISION*, BUT...
OH, *WHATEVER!* I CAN'T TAKE ALL THIS PAPERWORK ANYMORE.
LET'S DO IT.
The Allgood Siblings
UH, SURE.
WAIT, WHAT EXACTLY ARE WE DOING?
TAKING A CHANCE. GOING TO A *SECRET RENDEZVOUS.* AND POSSIBLY WALKING STRAIGHT INTO A *TRAP!*
GEE, WHEN YOU PUT IT *THAT* WAY, HOW CAN I SAY NO?
GREAT! WE'LL NEED TO GET MARGO. BUT PLAY IT COOL, I DON'T WANT ANYONE *ELSE* KNOWING WHAT WE'RE UP TO.
The Allgood Siblings

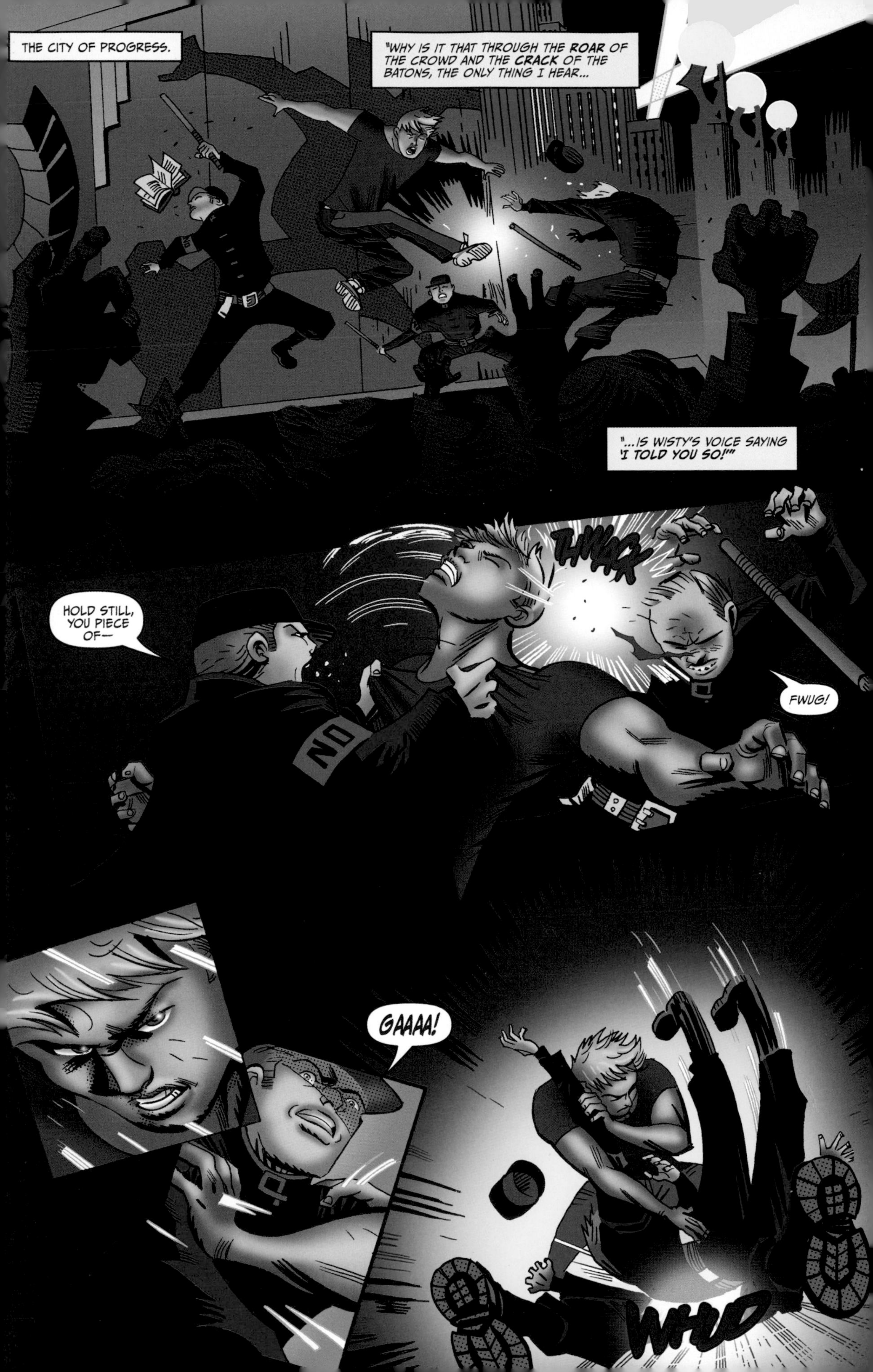

THE CITY OF PROGRESS.
"WHY IS IT THAT THROUGH THE ROAR OF THE CROWD AND THE CRACK OF THE BATONS, THE ONLY THING I HEAR...
"...IS WISTY'S VOICE SAYING 'I TOLD YOU SO!'"
THWAK
HOLD STILL, YOU PIECE OF—
FWUG!
GAAAA!
WHUD

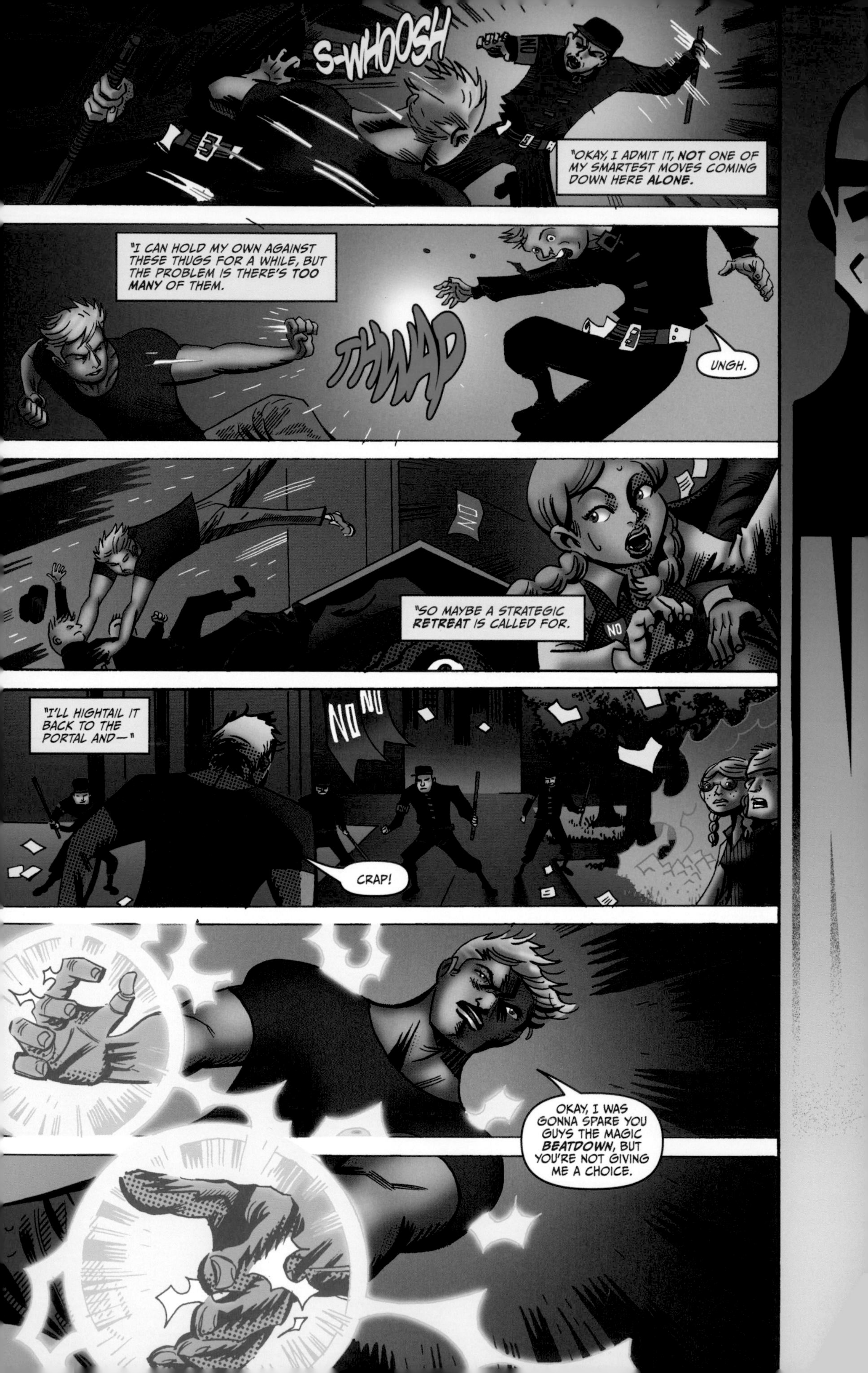
S-WHOOSH
"OKAY, I ADMIT IT, NOT ONE OF MY SMARTEST MOVES COMING DOWN HERE ALONE.
"I CAN HOLD MY OWN AGAINST THESE THUGS FOR A WHILE, BUT THE PROBLEM IS THERE'S TOO MANY OF THEM.
THWAP
UNGH.
"SO MAYBE A STRATEGIC RETREAT IS CALLED FOR.
"I'LL HIGHTAIL IT BACK TO THE PORTAL AND—"
CRAP!
OKAY, I WAS GONNA SPARE YOU GUYS THE MAGIC BEATDOWN, BUT YOU'RE NOT GIVING ME A CHOICE.

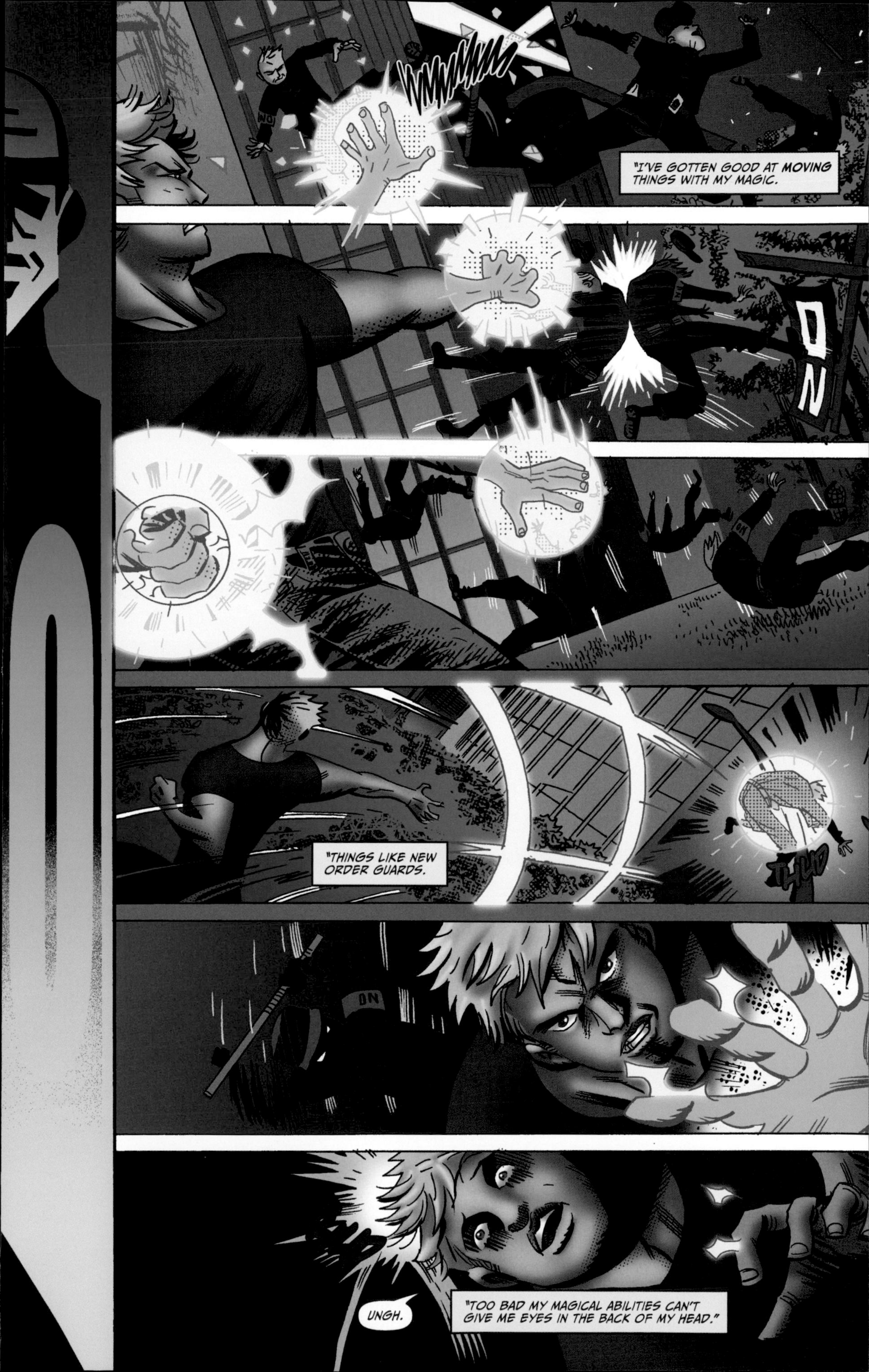
WMMMMMMM
"I'VE GOTTEN GOOD AT MOVING THINGS WITH MY MAGIC.
"THINGS LIKE NEW ORDER GUARDS.
THUD
UNGH.
"TOO BAD MY MAGICAL ABILITIES CAN'T GIVE ME EYES IN THE BACK OF MY HEAD."

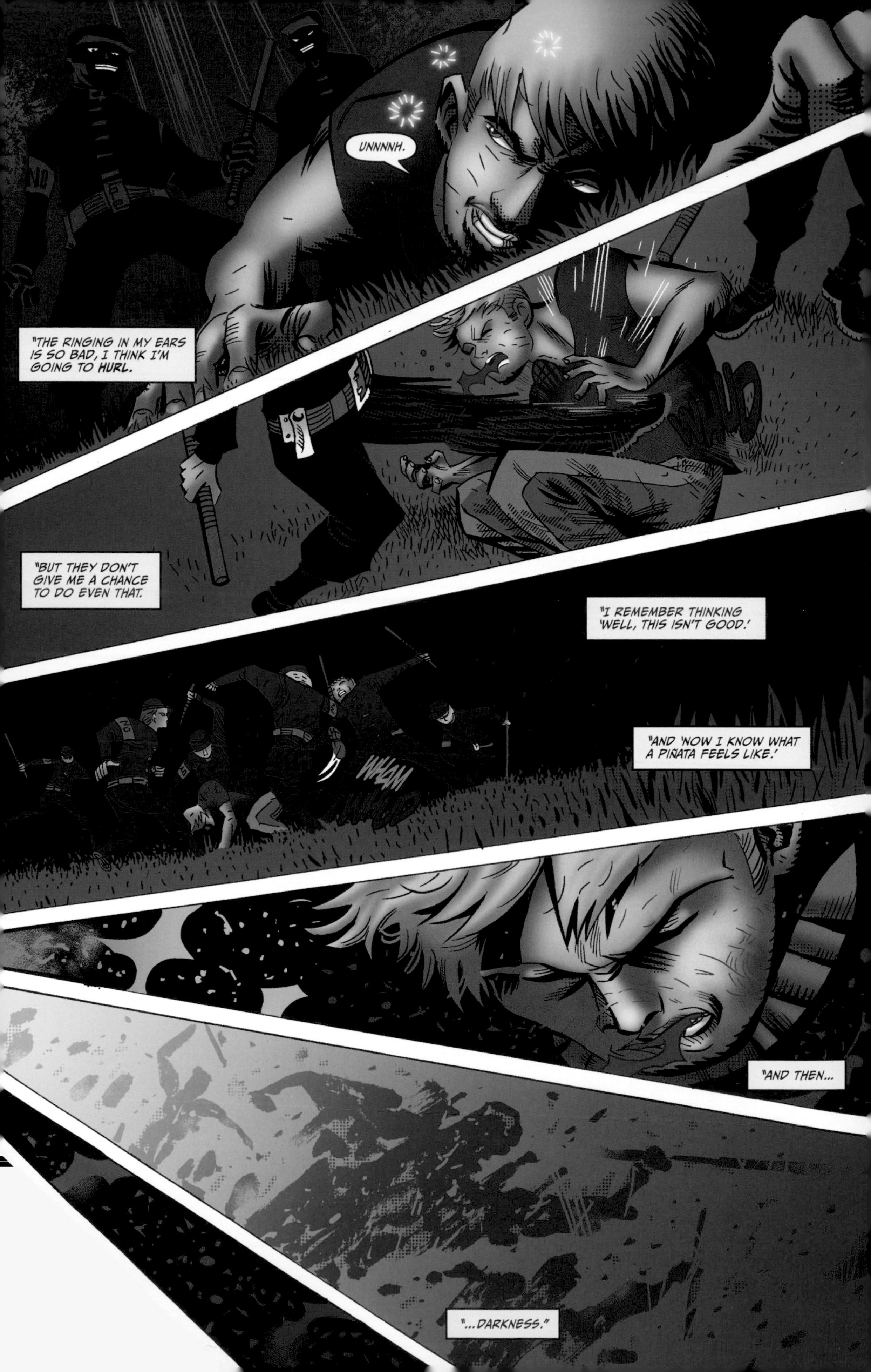
UNNNNH.
"THE RINGING IN MY EARS IS SO BAD, I THINK I'M GOING TO HURL.
WHUD
"BUT THEY DON'T GIVE ME A CHANCE TO DO EVEN THAT.
"I REMEMBER THINKING 'WELL, THIS ISN'T GOOD.'
"AND 'NOW I KNOW WHAT A PIÑATA FEELS LIKE.'
WHAM
"AND THEN...
"...DARKNESS."

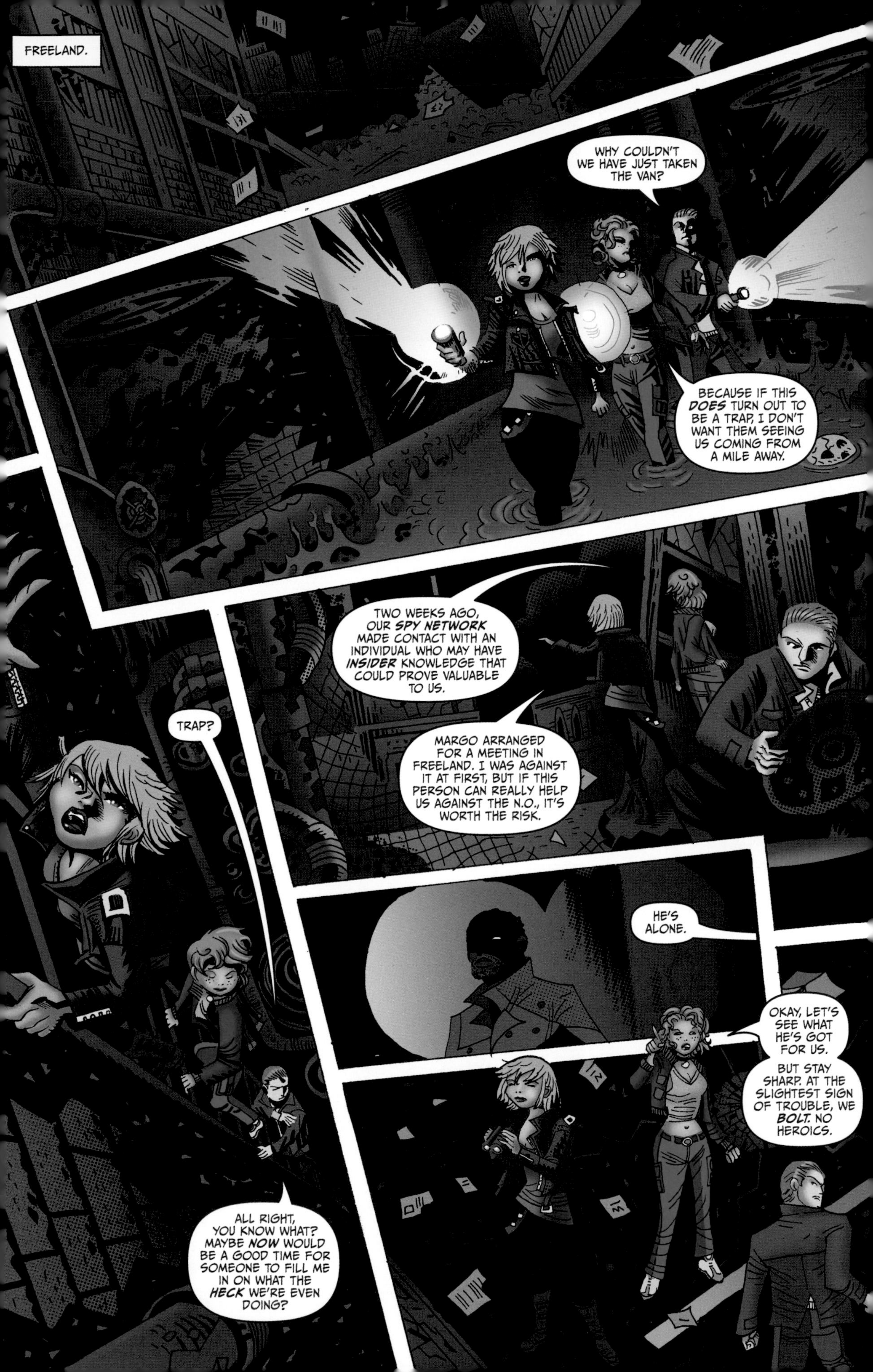
FREELAND.
WHY COULDN'T WE HAVE JUST TAKEN THE VAN?
BECAUSE IF THIS DOES TURN OUT TO BE A TRAP, I DON'T WANT THEM SEEING US COMING FROM A MILE AWAY.
TRAP?
ALL RIGHT, YOU KNOW WHAT? MAYBE NOW WOULD BE A GOOD TIME FOR SOMEONE TO FILL ME IN ON WHAT THE HECK WE'RE EVEN DOING?
TWO WEEKS AGO, OUR SPY NETWORK MADE CONTACT WITH AN INDIVIDUAL WHO MAY HAVE INSIDER KNOWLEDGE THAT COULD PROVE VALUABLE TO US.
MARGO ARRANGED FOR A MEETING IN FREELAND. I WAS AGAINST IT AT FIRST, BUT IF THIS PERSON CAN REALLY HELP US AGAINST THE N.O., IT'S WORTH THE RISK.
HE'S ALONE.
OKAY, LET'S SEE WHAT HE'S GOT FOR US.
BUT STAY SHARP. AT THE SLIGHTEST SIGN OF TROUBLE, WE BOLT. NO HEROICS.

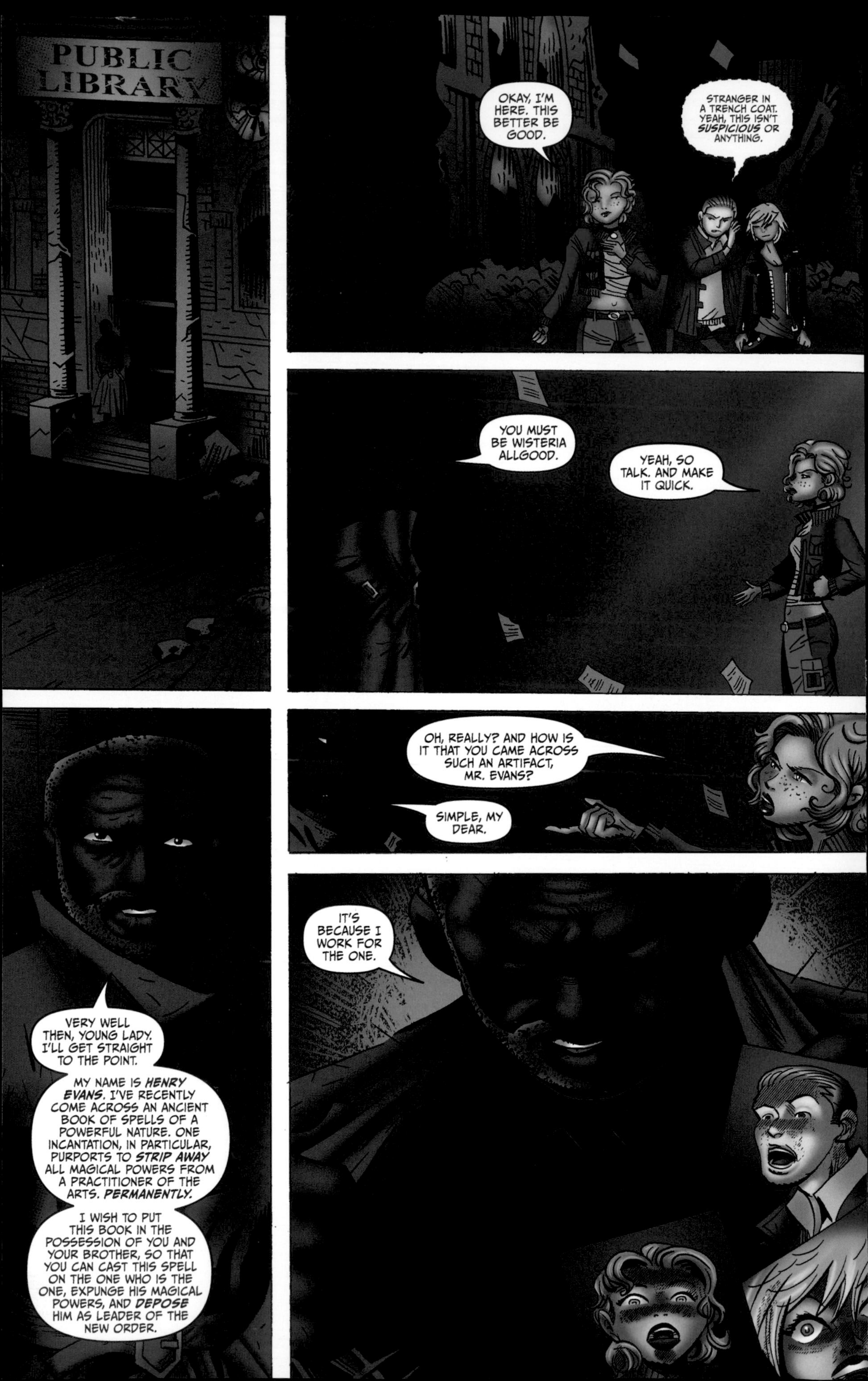
PUBLIC LIBRARY
OKAY, I'M HERE. THIS BETTER BE GOOD.
STRANGER IN A TRENCH COAT. YEAH, THIS ISN'T SUSPICIOUS OR ANYTHING.
YOU MUST BE WISTERIA ALLGOOD.
YEAH, SO TALK. AND MAKE IT QUICK.
VERY WELL THEN, YOUNG LADY. I'LL GET STRAIGHT TO THE POINT.
MY NAME IS HENRY EVANS. I'VE RECENTLY COME ACROSS AN ANCIENT BOOK OF SPELLS OF A POWERFUL NATURE. ONE INCANTATION, IN PARTICULAR, PURPORTS TO STRIP AWAY ALL MAGICAL POWERS FROM A PRACTITIONER OF THE ARTS. PERMANENTLY.
I WISH TO PUT THIS BOOK IN THE POSSESSION OF YOU AND YOUR BROTHER, SO THAT YOU CAN CAST THIS SPELL ON THE ONE WHO IS THE ONE, EXPUNGE HIS MAGICAL POWERS, AND DEPOSE HIM AS LEADER OF THE NEW ORDER.
OH, REALLY? AND HOW IS IT THAT YOU CAME ACROSS SUCH AN ARTIFACT, MR. EVANS?
SIMPLE, MY DEAR.
IT'S BECAUSE I WORK FOR THE ONE.

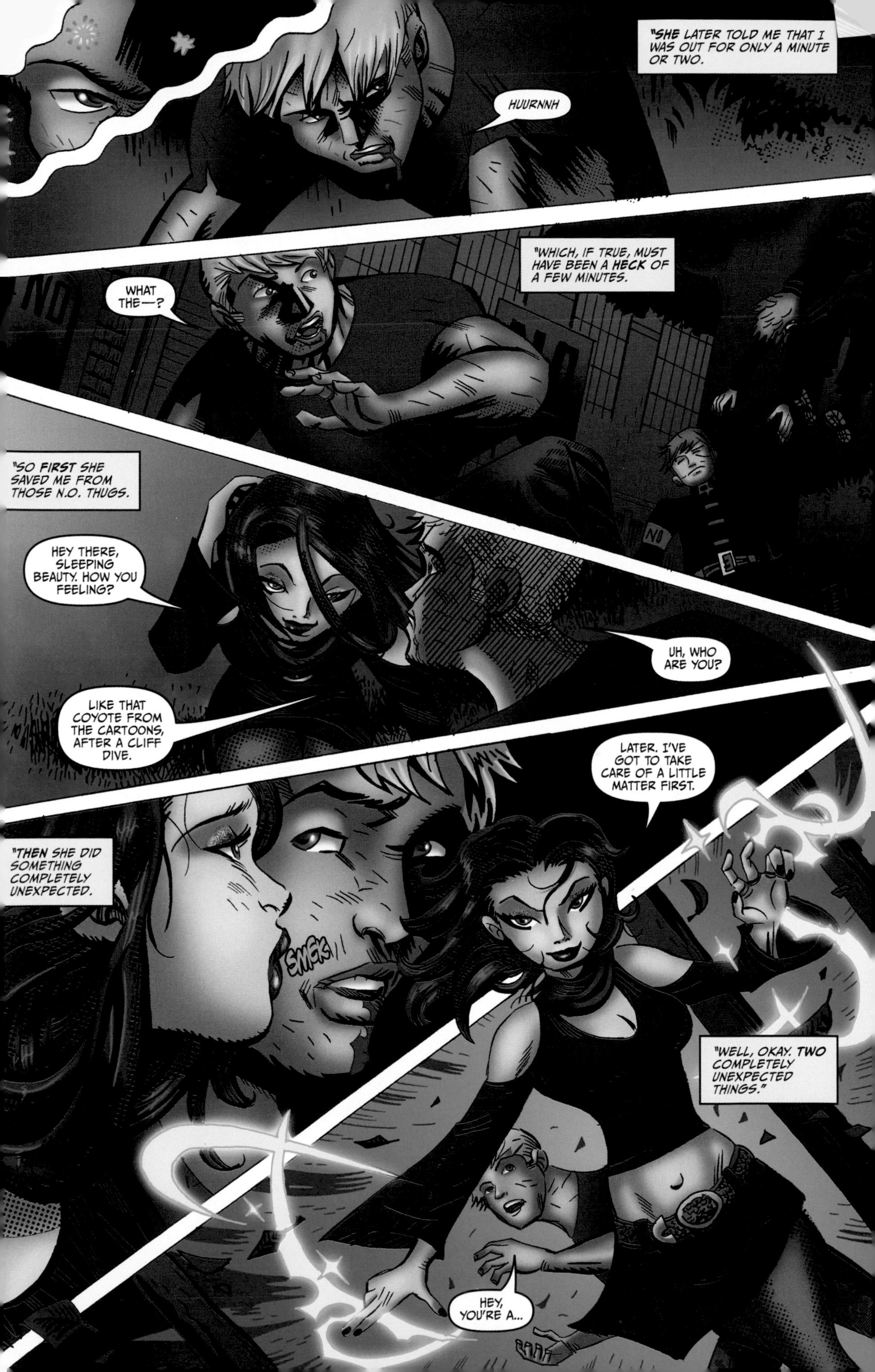

"SHE LATER TOLD ME THAT I WAS OUT FOR ONLY A MINUTE OR TWO.
HUURNNH
"WHICH, IF TRUE, MUST HAVE BEEN A HECK OF A FEW MINUTES.
WHAT THE---?
"SO FIRST SHE SAVED ME FROM THOSE N.O. THUGS.
HEY THERE, SLEEPING BEAUTY. HOW YOU FEELING?
UH, WHO ARE YOU?
LIKE THAT COYOTE FROM THE CARTOONS, AFTER A CLIFF DIVE.
LATER. I'VE GOT TO TAKE CARE OF A LITTLE MATTER FIRST.
"THEN SHE DID SOMETHING COMPLETELY UNEXPECTED.
SMEK
"WELL, OKAY. TWO COMPLETELY UNEXPECTED THINGS."
HEY, YOU'RE A...

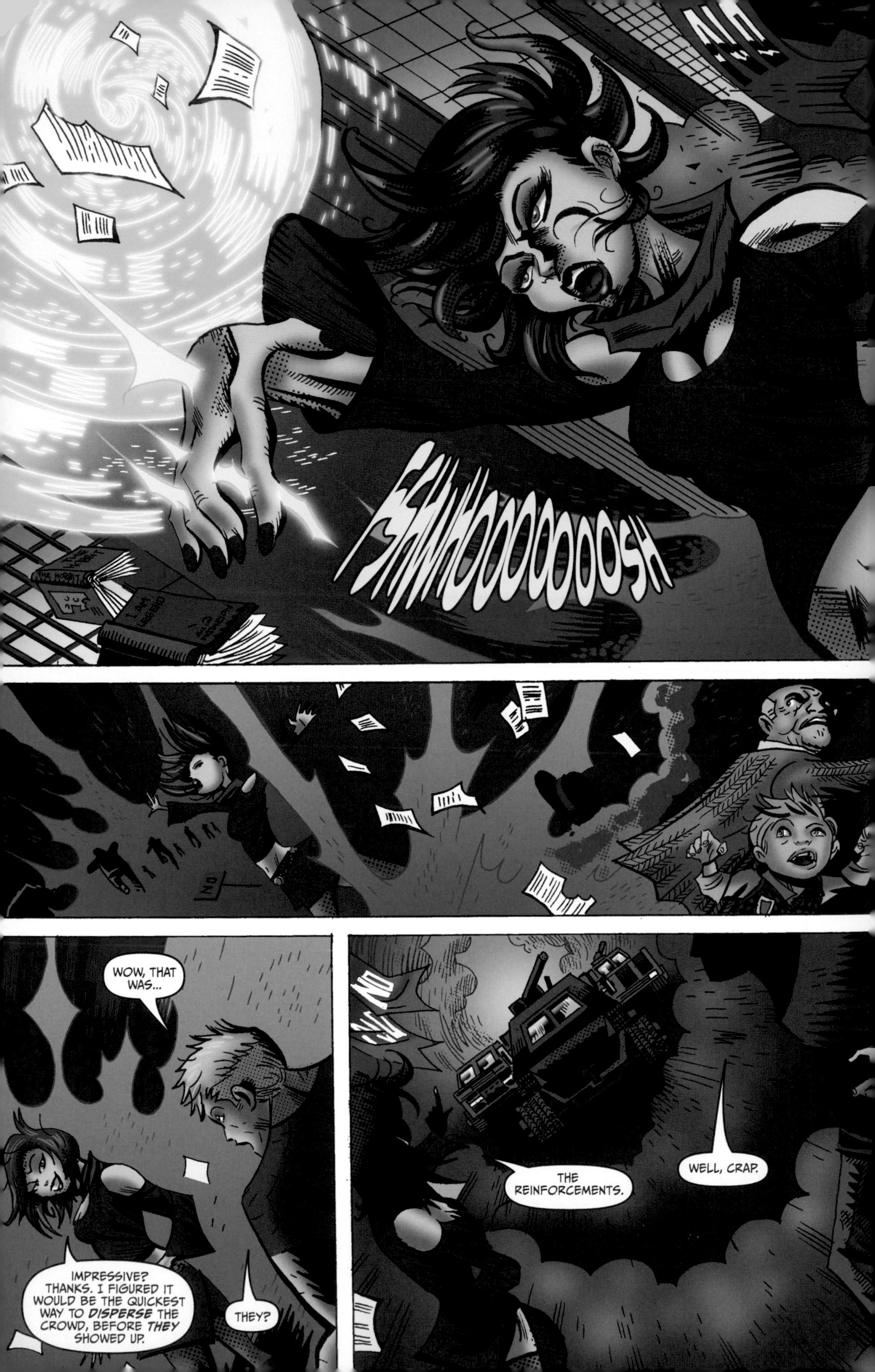
FSHWOOOOOOOOSH
WOW, THAT WAS...
IMPRESSIVE? THANKS. I FIGURED IT WOULD BE THE QUICKEST WAY TO DISPERSE THE CROWD, BEFORE THEY SHOWED UP.
THEY?
THE REINFORCEMENTS.
WELL, CRAP.

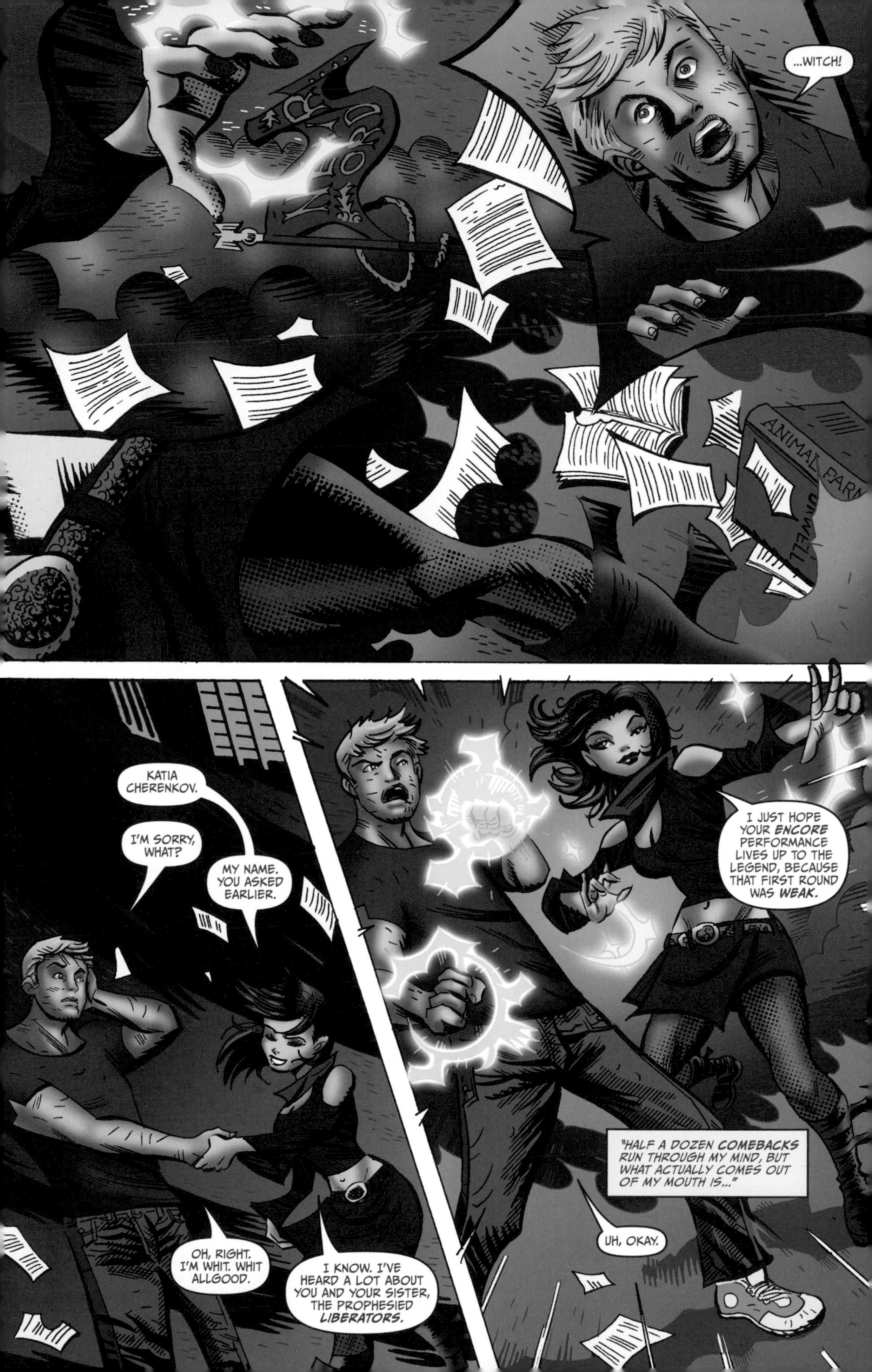
...WITCH!
KATIA CHERENKOV.
I'M SORRY, WHAT?
MY NAME. YOU ASKED EARLIER.
OH, RIGHT. I'M WHIT. WHIT ALLGOOD.
I KNOW. I'VE HEARD A LOT ABOUT YOU AND YOUR SISTER, THE PROPHESIED LIBERATORS.
I JUST HOPE YOUR ENCORE PERFORMANCE LIVES UP TO THE LEGEND, BECAUSE THAT FIRST ROUND WAS WEAK.
"HALF A DOZEN COMEBACKS RUN THROUGH MY MIND, BUT WHAT ACTUALLY COMES OUT OF MY MOUTH IS..."
UH, OKAY.

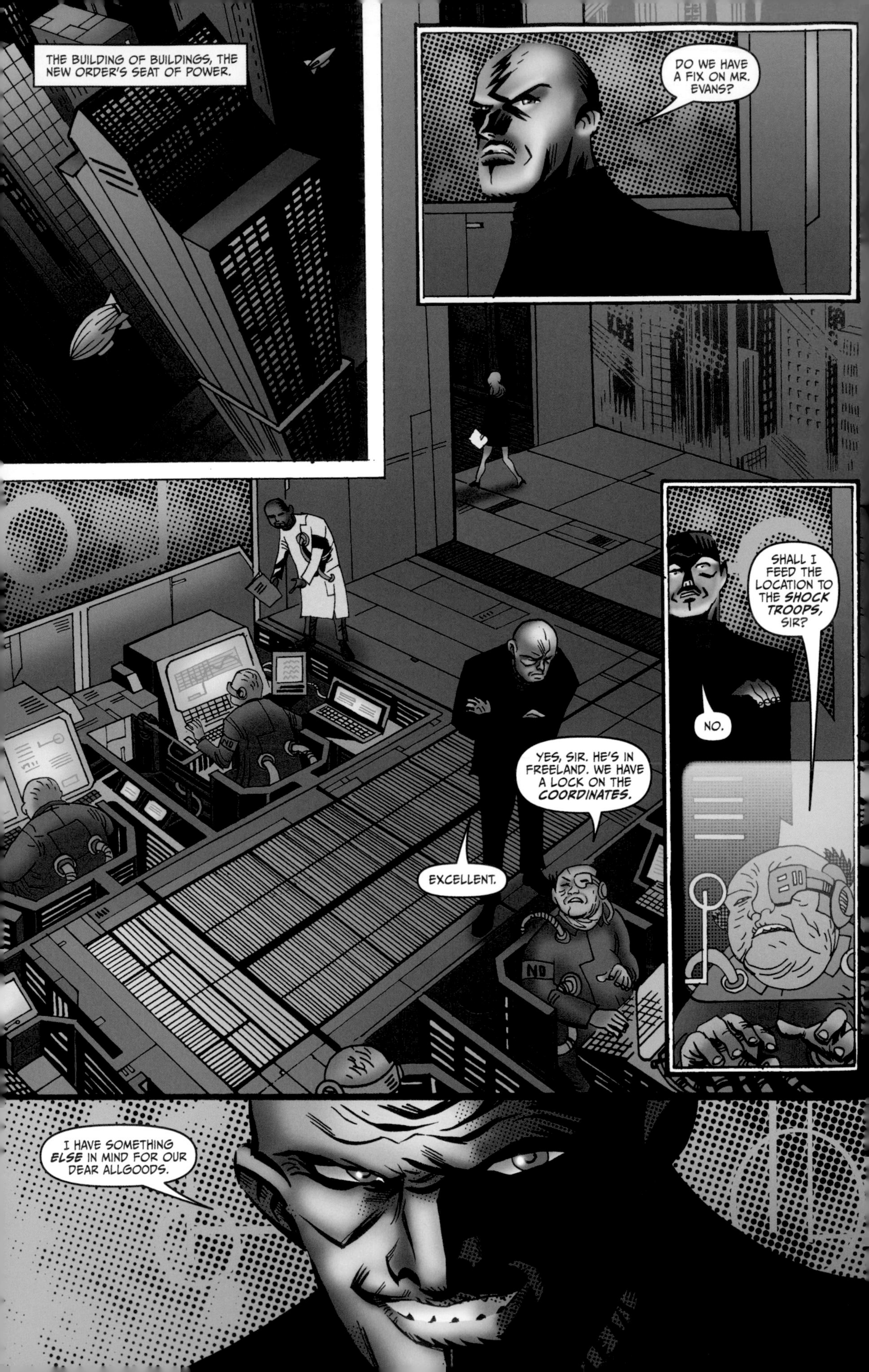

THE BUILDING OF BUILDINGS, THE NEW ORDER'S SEAT OF POWER.
DO WE HAVE A FIX ON MR. EVANS?
YES, SIR. HE'S IN FREELAND. WE HAVE A LOCK ON THE *COORDINATES.*
EXCELLENT.
SHALL I FEED THE LOCATION TO THE *SHOCK TROOPS,* SIR?
NO.
I HAVE SOMETHING *ELSE* IN MIND FOR OUR DEAR ALLGOODS.

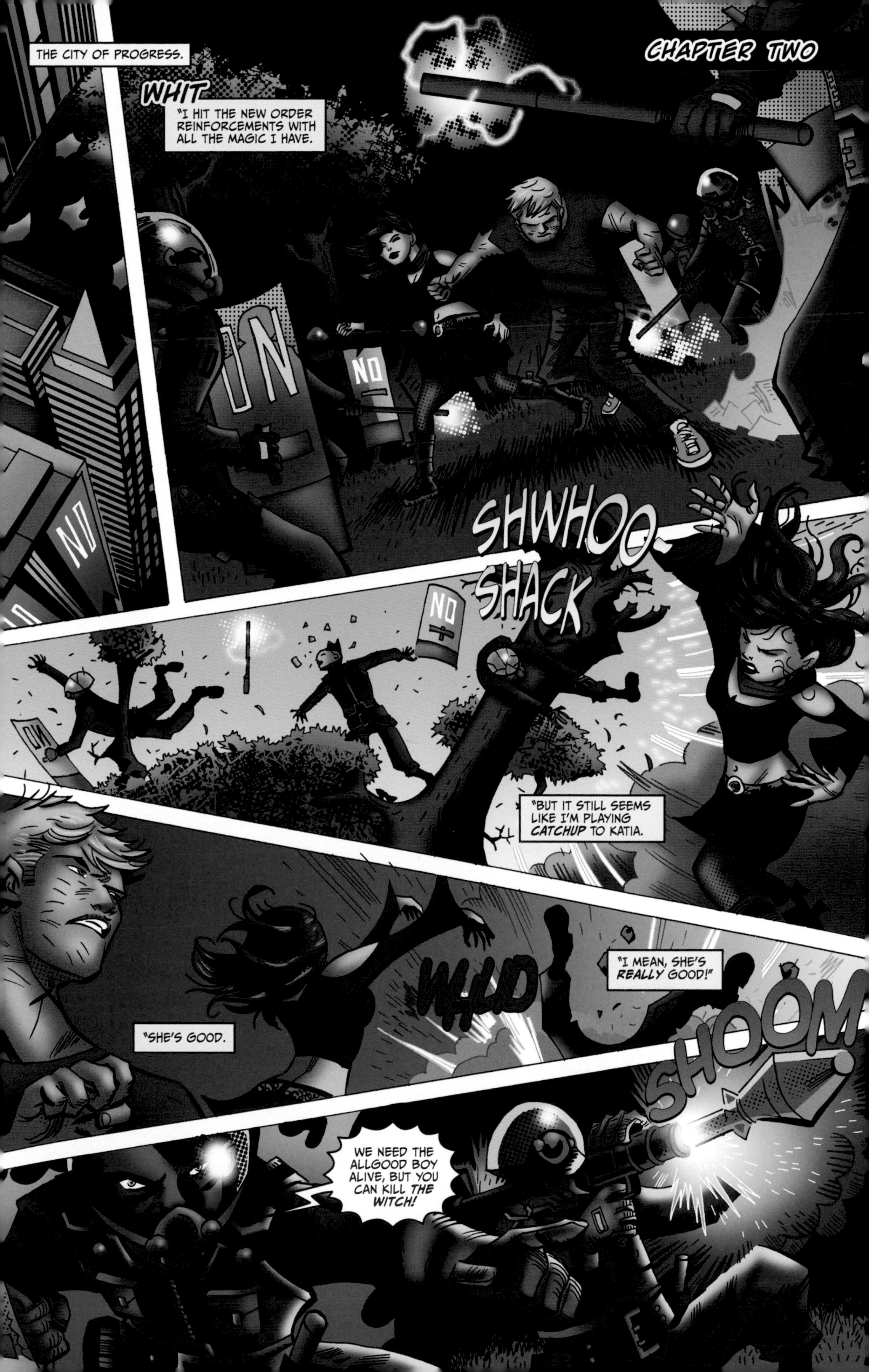
CHAPTER TWO
THE CITY OF PROGRESS.
WHIT
"I HIT THE NEW ORDER REINFORCEMENTS WITH ALL THE MAGIC I HAVE.
NO
SHWHOO-
SHACK
NO
"BUT IT STILL SEEMS LIKE I'M PLAYING CATCHUP TO KATIA.
WUD
"I MEAN, SHE'S REALLY GOOD!"
"SHE'S GOOD.
SHOOM
WE NEED THE ALLGOOD BOY ALIVE, BUT YOU CAN KILL THE WITCH!

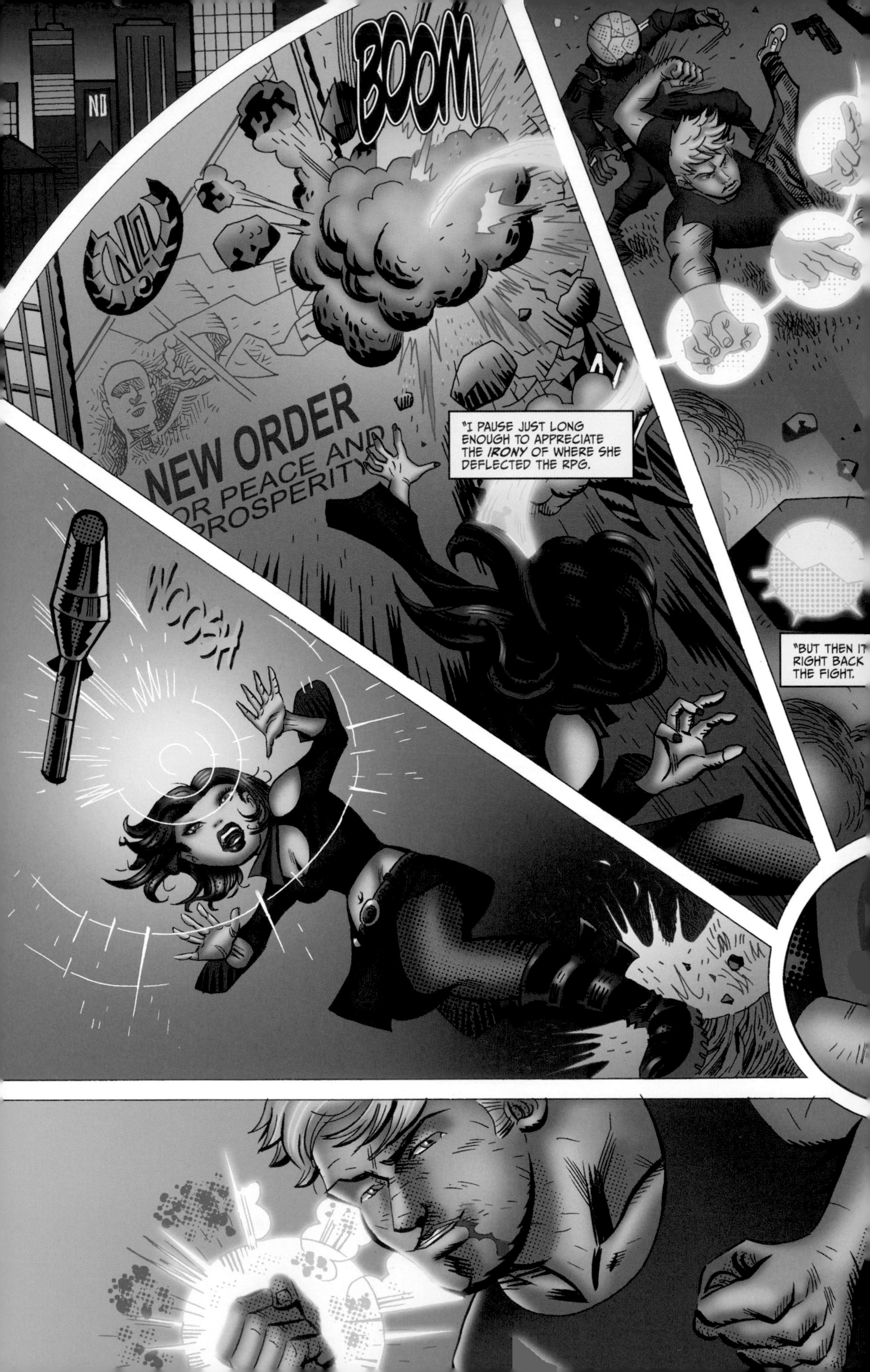

BOOM
NO
NEW ORDER
FOR PEACE AND PROSPERITY
"I PAUSE JUST LONG ENOUGH TO APPRECIATE THE *IRONY* OF WHERE SHE DEFLECTED THE RPG.
WOOSH
"BUT THEN IT RIGHT BACK THE FIGHT.

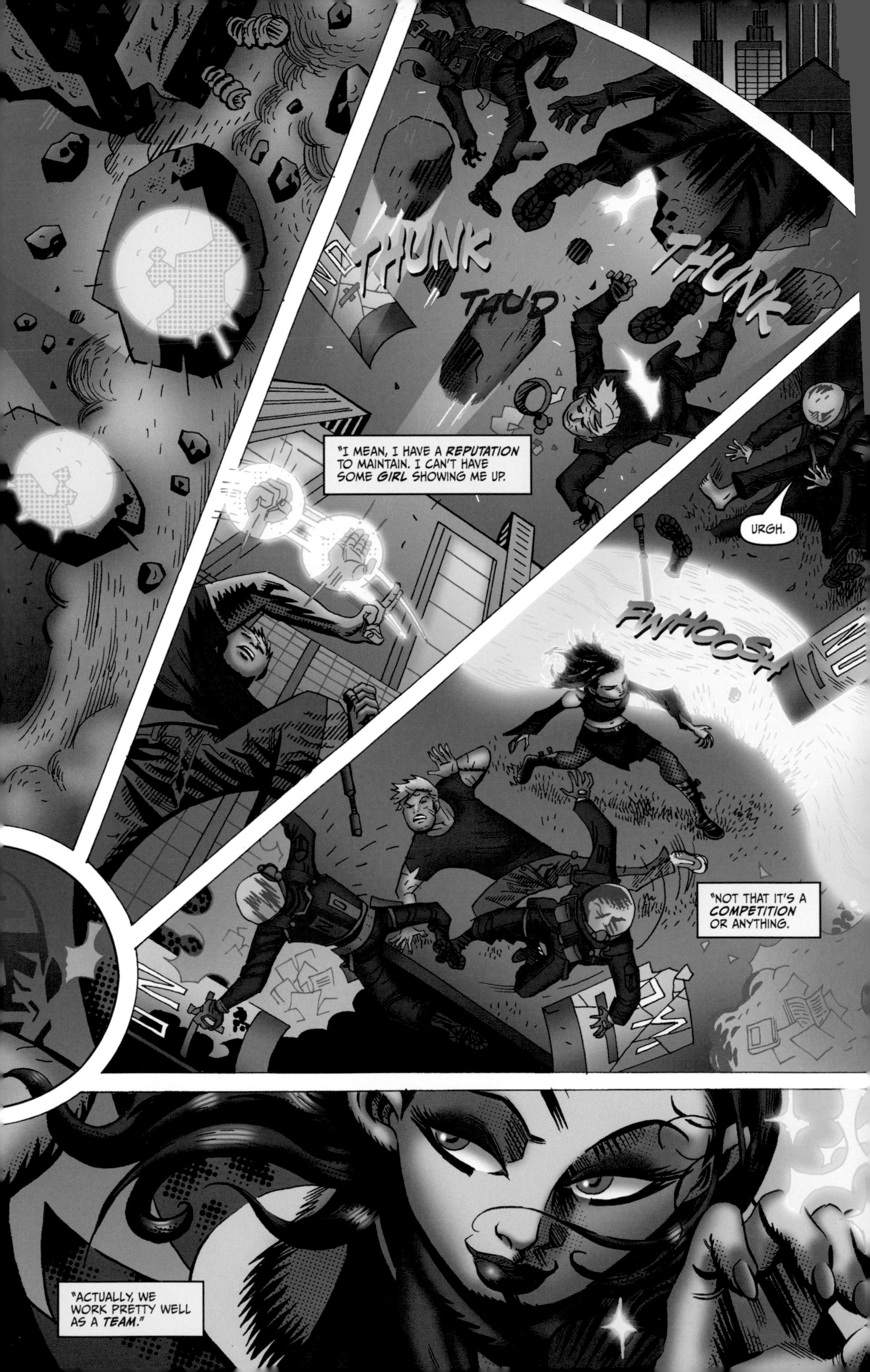
THUNK
THUNK
THUD
"I MEAN, I HAVE A *REPUTATION* TO MAINTAIN. I CAN'T HAVE SOME *GIRL* SHOWING ME UP.
URGH.
FWHOOSH
"NOT THAT IT'S A *COMPETITION* OR ANYTHING.
"ACTUALLY, WE WORK PRETTY WELL AS A *TEAM*."

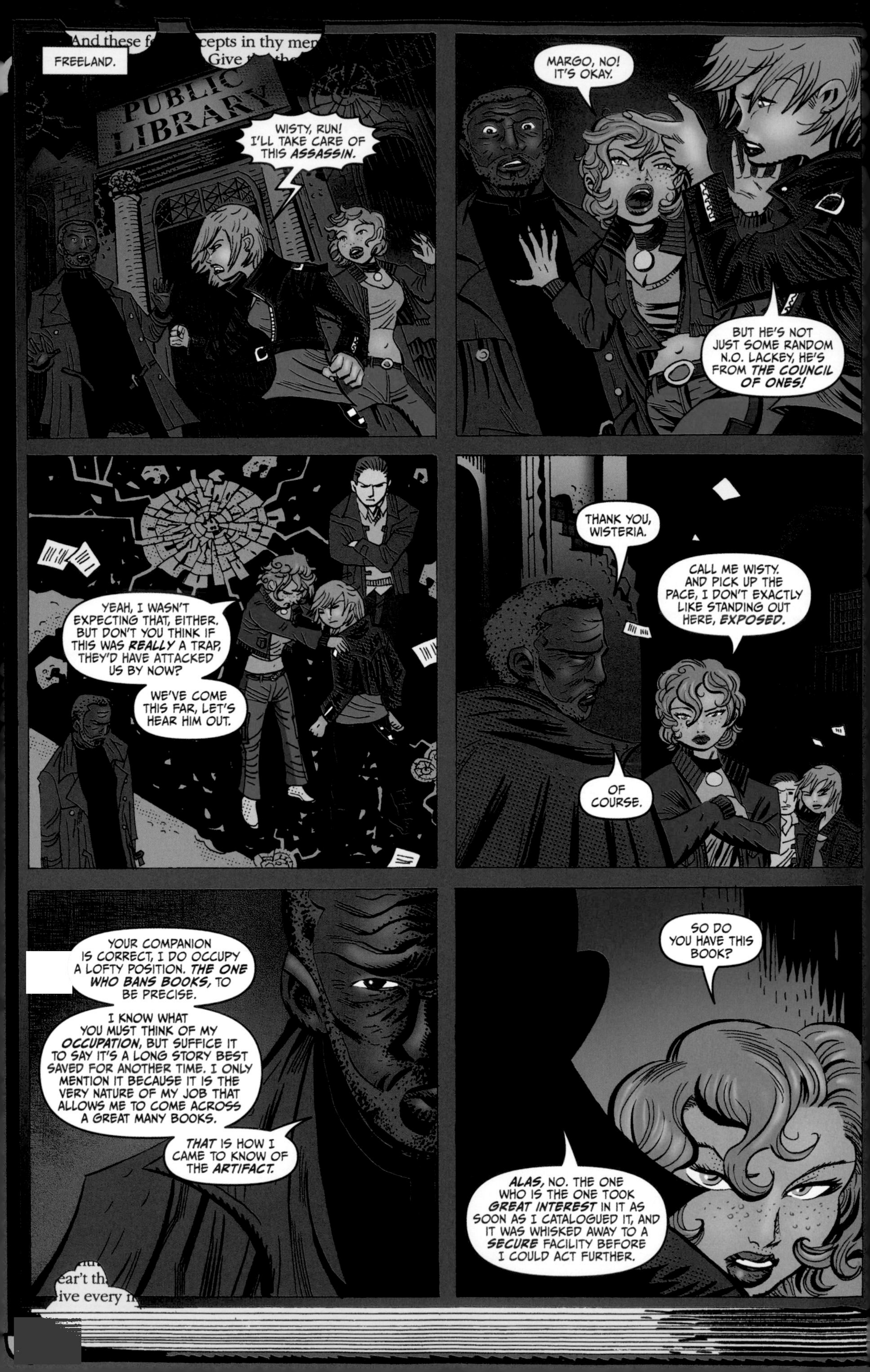
FREELAND.
WISTY, RUN! I'LL TAKE CARE OF THIS ASSASSIN.
MARGO, NO! IT'S OKAY.
BUT HE'S NOT JUST SOME RANDOM N.O. LACKEY, HE'S FROM THE COUNCIL OF ONES!
PUBLIC LIBRARY
YEAH, I WASN'T EXPECTING THAT, EITHER. BUT DON'T YOU THINK IF THIS WAS REALLY A TRAP, THEY'D HAVE ATTACKED US BY NOW?
WE'VE COME THIS FAR, LET'S HEAR HIM OUT.
THANK YOU, WISTERIA.
CALL ME WISTY. AND PICK UP THE PACE, I DON'T EXACTLY LIKE STANDING OUT HERE, EXPOSED.
OF COURSE.
YOUR COMPANION IS CORRECT, I DO OCCUPY A LOFTY POSITION. THE ONE WHO BANS BOOKS, TO BE PRECISE.
I KNOW WHAT YOU MUST THINK OF MY OCCUPATION, BUT SUFFICE IT TO SAY IT'S A LONG STORY BEST SAVED FOR ANOTHER TIME. I ONLY MENTION IT BECAUSE IT IS THE VERY NATURE OF MY JOB THAT ALLOWS ME TO COME ACROSS A GREAT MANY BOOKS.
THAT IS HOW I CAME TO KNOW OF THE ARTIFACT.
SO DO YOU HAVE THIS BOOK?
ALAS, NO. THE ONE WHO IS THE ONE TOOK GREAT INTEREST IN IT AS SOON AS I CATALOGUED IT, AND IT WAS WHISKED AWAY TO A SECURE FACILITY BEFORE I COULD ACT FURTHER.

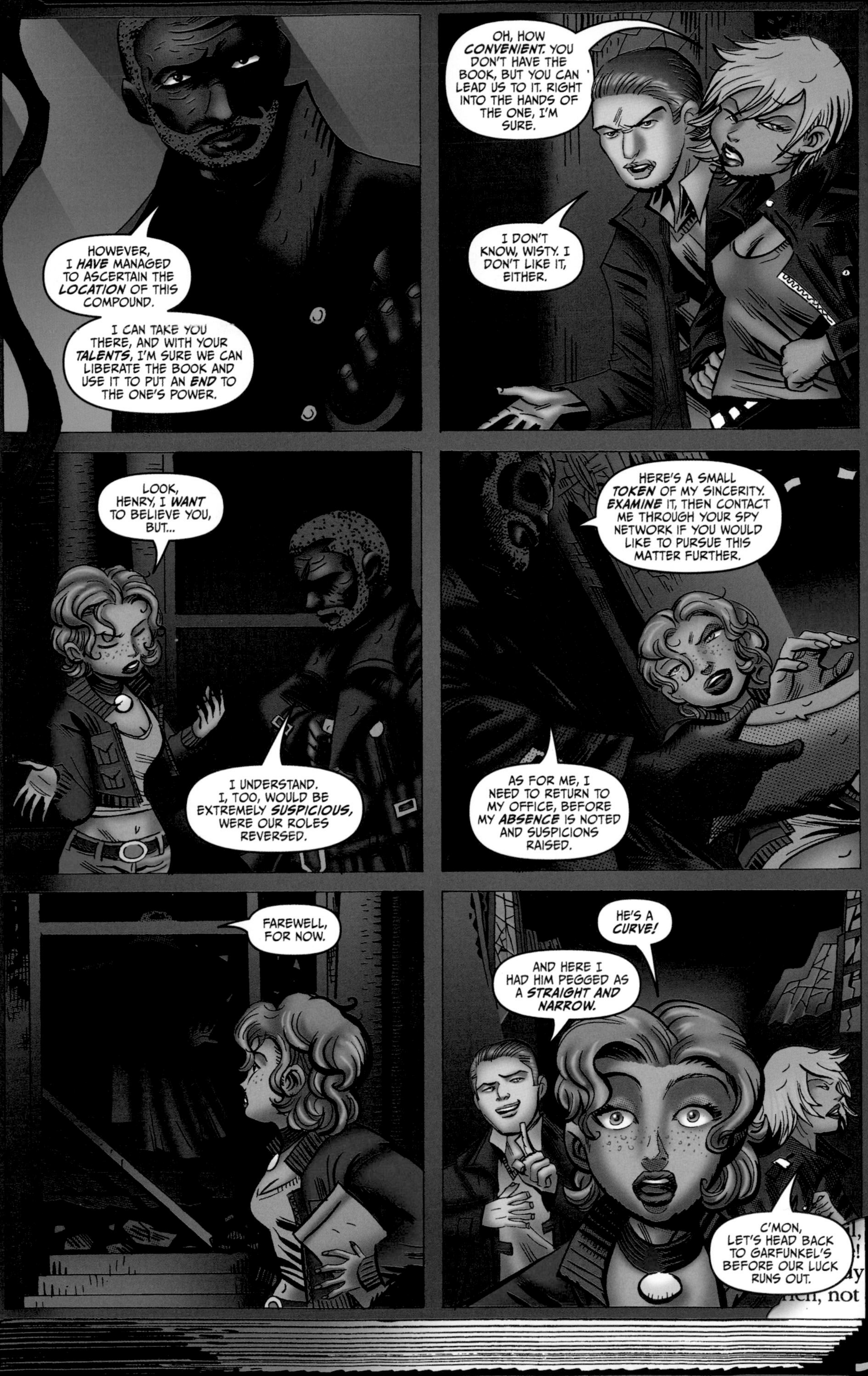
HOWEVER, I HAVE MANAGED TO ASCERTAIN THE LOCATION OF THIS COMPOUND.
I CAN TAKE YOU THERE, AND WITH YOUR TALENTS, I'M SURE WE CAN LIBERATE THE BOOK AND USE IT TO PUT AN END TO THE ONE'S POWER.
OH, HOW CONVENIENT. YOU DON'T HAVE THE BOOK, BUT YOU CAN LEAD US TO IT. RIGHT INTO THE HANDS OF THE ONE, I'M SURE.
I DON'T KNOW, WISTY. I DON'T LIKE IT, EITHER.
LOOK, HENRY, I WANT TO BELIEVE YOU, BUT...
I UNDERSTAND. I, TOO, WOULD BE EXTREMELY SUSPICIOUS, WERE OUR ROLES REVERSED.
HERE'S A SMALL TOKEN OF MY SINCERITY. EXAMINE IT, THEN CONTACT ME THROUGH YOUR SPY NETWORK IF YOU WOULD LIKE TO PURSUE THIS MATTER FURTHER.
AS FOR ME, I NEED TO RETURN TO MY OFFICE, BEFORE MY ABSENCE IS NOTED AND SUSPICIONS RAISED.
FAREWELL, FOR NOW.
HE'S A CURVE!
AND HERE I HAD HIM PEGGED AS A STRAIGHT AND NARROW.
C'MON, LET'S HEAD BACK TO GARFUNKEL'S BEFORE OUR LUCK RUNS OUT.

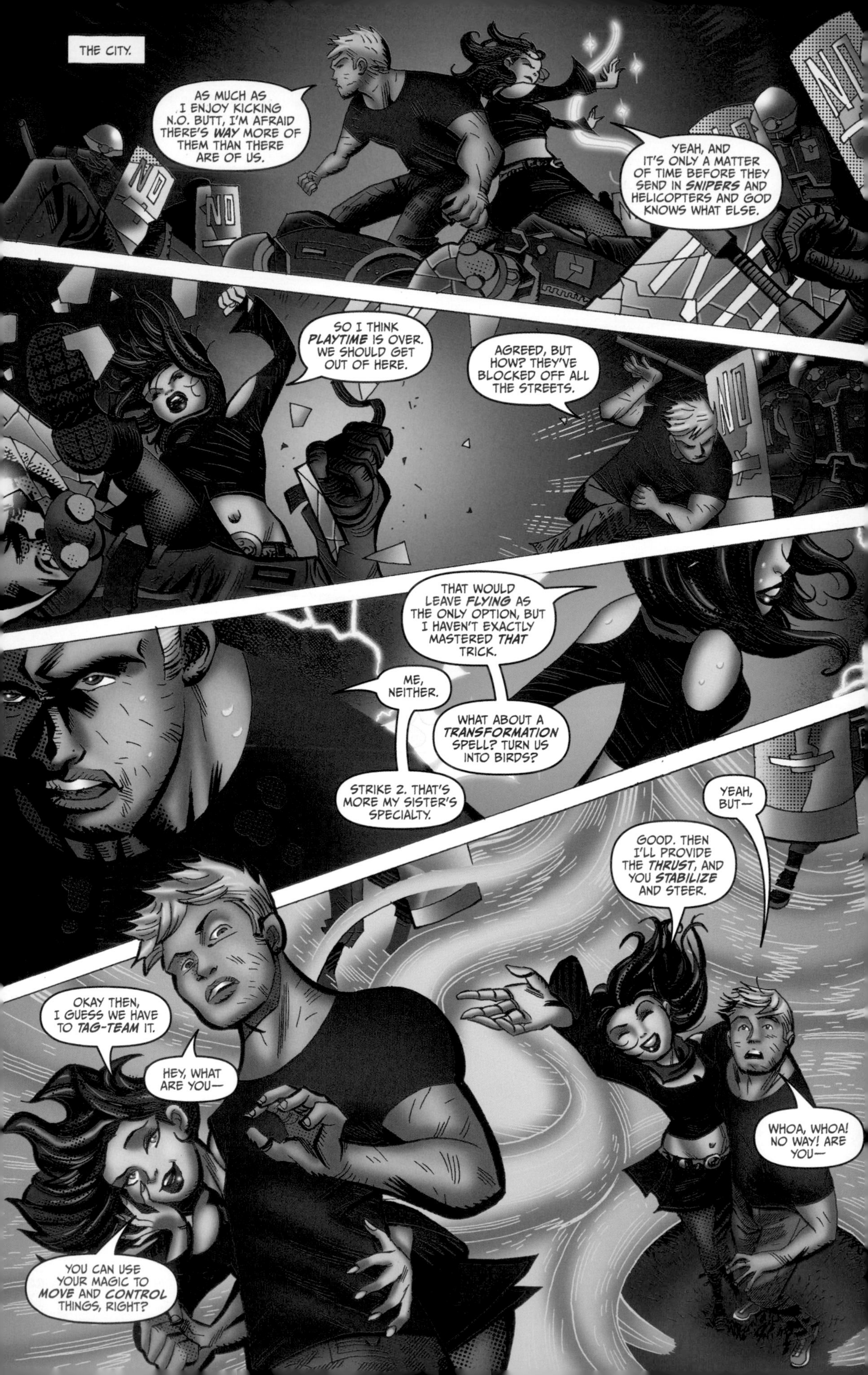
THE CITY.
AS MUCH AS I ENJOY KICKING N.O. BUTT, I'M AFRAID THERE'S WAY MORE OF THEM THAN THERE ARE OF US.
YEAH, AND IT'S ONLY A MATTER OF TIME BEFORE THEY SEND IN SNIPERS AND HELICOPTERS AND GOD KNOWS WHAT ELSE.
SO I THINK PLAYTIME IS OVER. WE SHOULD GET OUT OF HERE.
AGREED, BUT HOW? THEY'VE BLOCKED OFF ALL THE STREETS.
THAT WOULD LEAVE FLYING AS THE ONLY OPTION, BUT I HAVEN'T EXACTLY MASTERED THAT TRICK.
ME, NEITHER.
WHAT ABOUT A TRANSFORMATION SPELL? TURN US INTO BIRDS?
STRIKE 2. THAT'S MORE MY SISTER'S SPECIALTY.
OKAY THEN, I GUESS WE HAVE TO TAG-TEAM IT.
HEY, WHAT ARE YOU—
YOU CAN USE YOUR MAGIC TO MOVE AND CONTROL THINGS, RIGHT?
YEAH, BUT—
GOOD. THEN I'LL PROVIDE THE THRUST, AND YOU STABILIZE AND STEER.
WHOA, WHOA! NO WAY! ARE YOU—

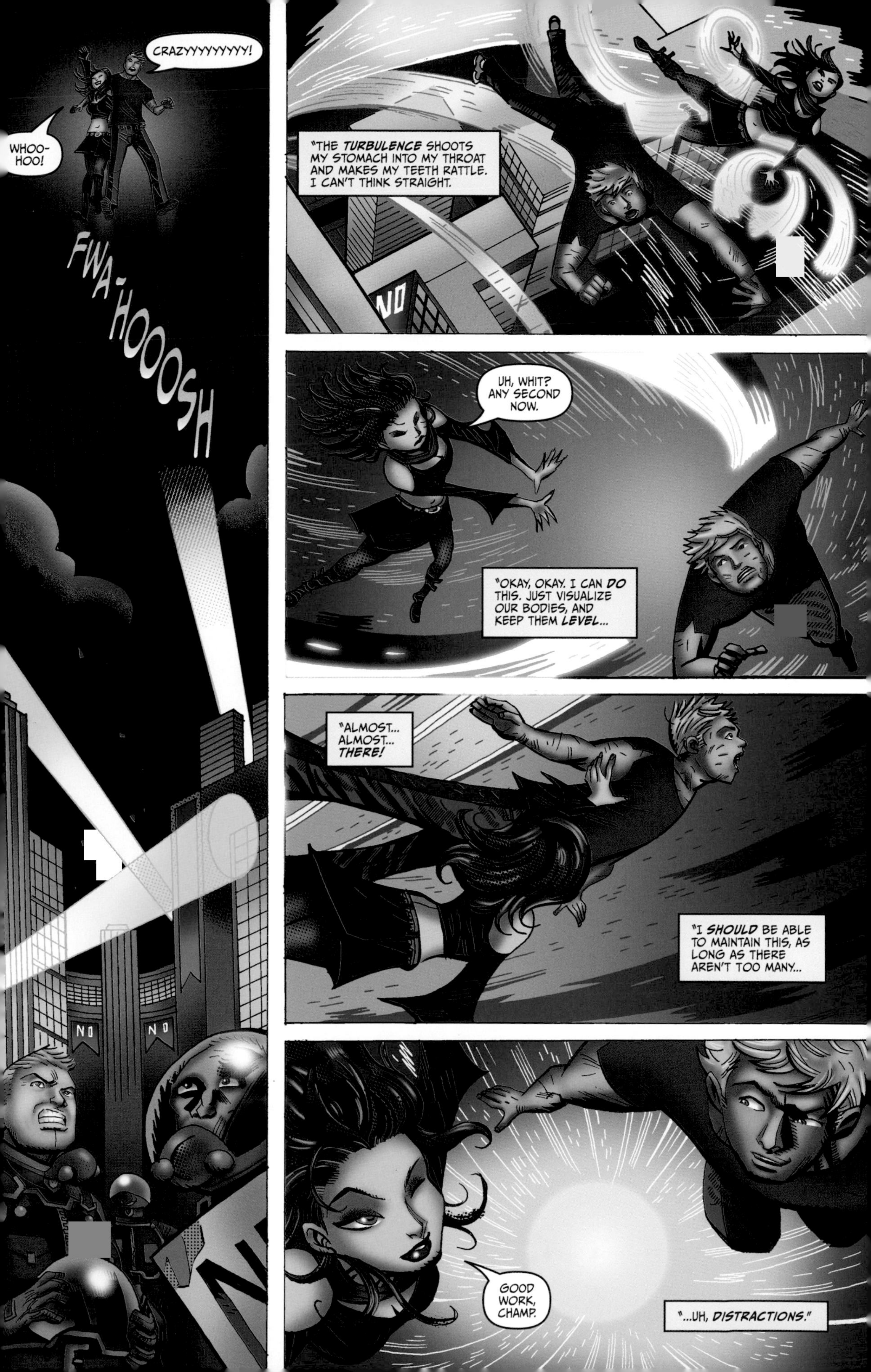
CRAZYYYYYYYYY!
WHOO-HOO!
FWA-HOOOSH
"THE TURBULENCE SHOOTS MY STOMACH INTO MY THROAT AND MAKES MY TEETH RATTLE. I CAN'T THINK STRAIGHT.
UH, WHIT? ANY SECOND NOW.
"OKAY, OKAY. I CAN DO THIS. JUST VISUALIZE OUR BODIES, AND KEEP THEM LEVEL...
"ALMOST... ALMOST... THERE!
"I SHOULD BE ABLE TO MAINTAIN THIS, AS LONG AS THERE AREN'T TOO MANY...
GOOD WORK, CHAMP.
"...UH, DISTRACTIONS."

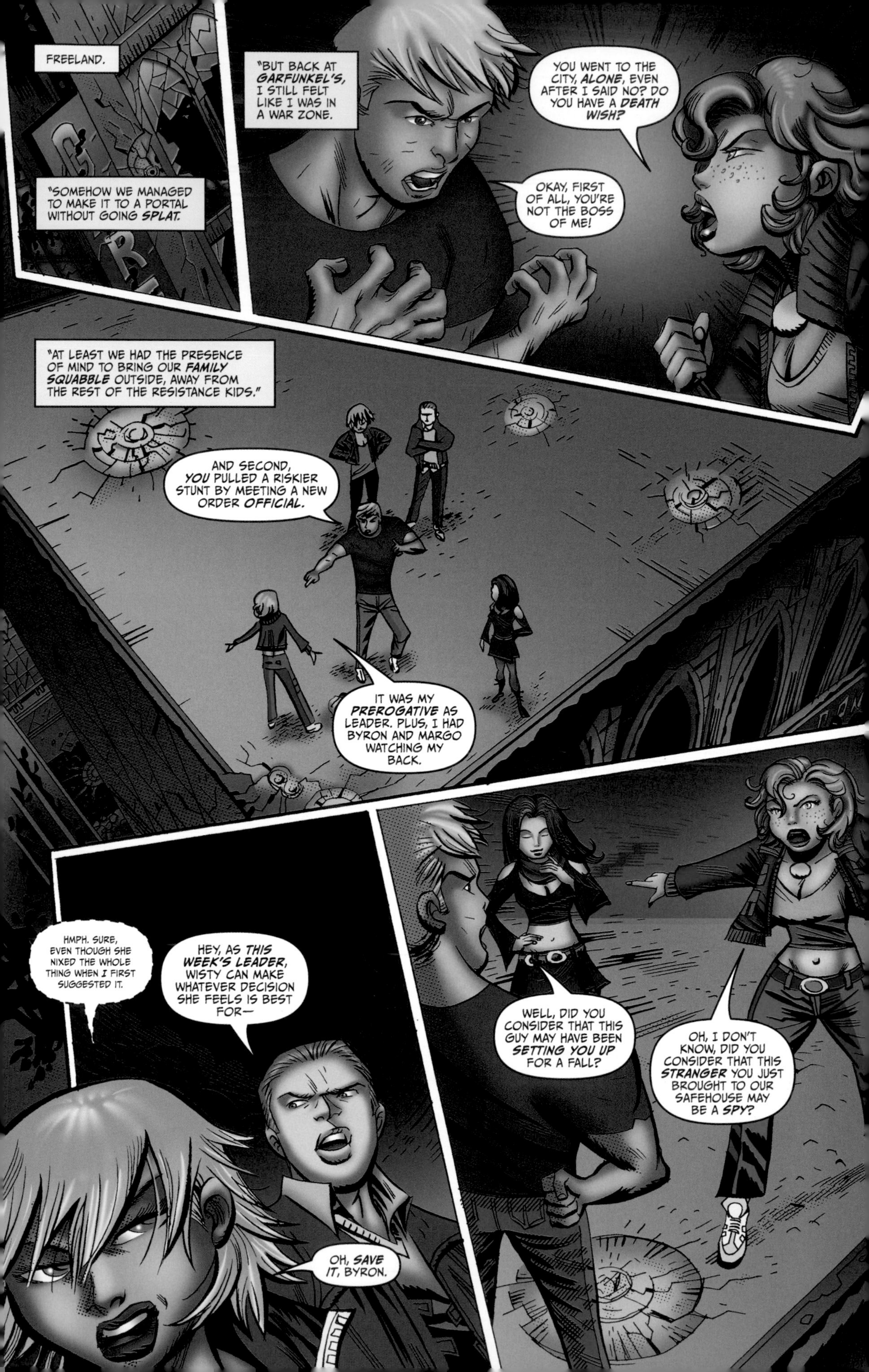
FREELAND.
"SOMEHOW WE MANAGED TO MAKE IT TO A PORTAL WITHOUT GOING SPLAT.
"BUT BACK AT GARFUNKEL'S, I STILL FELT LIKE I WAS IN A WAR ZONE.
YOU WENT TO THE CITY, ALONE, EVEN AFTER I SAID NO? DO YOU HAVE A DEATH WISH?
OKAY, FIRST OF ALL, YOU'RE NOT THE BOSS OF ME!
"AT LEAST WE HAD THE PRESENCE OF MIND TO BRING OUR FAMILY SQUABBLE OUTSIDE, AWAY FROM THE REST OF THE RESISTANCE KIDS."
AND SECOND, YOU PULLED A RISKIER STUNT BY MEETING A NEW ORDER OFFICIAL.
IT WAS MY PREROGATIVE AS LEADER. PLUS, I HAD BYRON AND MARGO WATCHING MY BACK.
HMPH. SURE, EVEN THOUGH SHE NIXED THE WHOLE THING WHEN I FIRST SUGGESTED IT.
HEY, AS THIS WEEK'S LEADER, WISTY CAN MAKE WHATEVER DECISION SHE FEELS IS BEST FOR—
OH, SAVE IT, BYRON.
WELL, DID YOU CONSIDER THAT THIS GUY MAY HAVE BEEN SETTING YOU UP FOR A FALL?
OH, I DON'T KNOW, DID YOU CONSIDER THAT THIS STRANGER YOU JUST BROUGHT TO OUR SAFEHOUSE MAY BE A SPY?

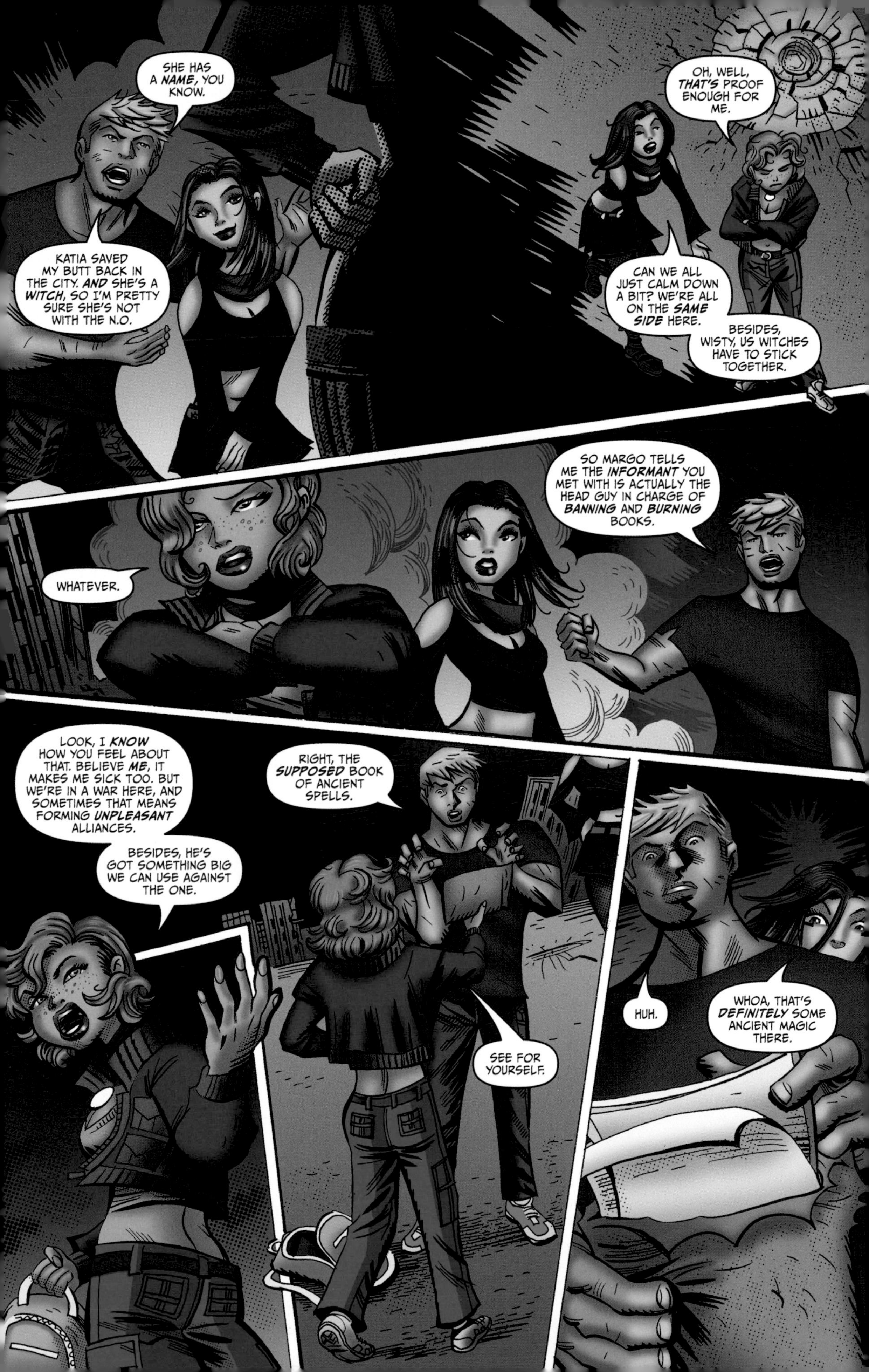
SHE HAS A NAME, YOU KNOW.
KATIA SAVED MY BUTT BACK IN THE CITY. AND SHE'S A WITCH, SO I'M PRETTY SURE SHE'S NOT WITH THE N.O.
OH, WELL, THAT'S PROOF ENOUGH FOR ME.
CAN WE ALL JUST CALM DOWN A BIT? WE'RE ALL ON THE SAME SIDE HERE.
BESIDES, WISTY, US WITCHES HAVE TO STICK TOGETHER.
SO MARGO TELLS ME THE INFORMANT YOU MET WITH IS ACTUALLY THE HEAD GUY IN CHARGE OF BANNING AND BURNING BOOKS.
WHATEVER.
LOOK, I KNOW HOW YOU FEEL ABOUT THAT. BELIEVE ME, IT MAKES ME SICK TOO. BUT WE'RE IN A WAR HERE, AND SOMETIMES THAT MEANS FORMING UNPLEASANT ALLIANCES.
BESIDES, HE'S GOT SOMETHING BIG WE CAN USE AGAINST THE ONE.
RIGHT, THE SUPPOSED BOOK OF ANCIENT SPELLS.
SEE FOR YOURSELF.
HUH.
WHOA, THAT'S DEFINITELY SOME ANCIENT MAGIC THERE.

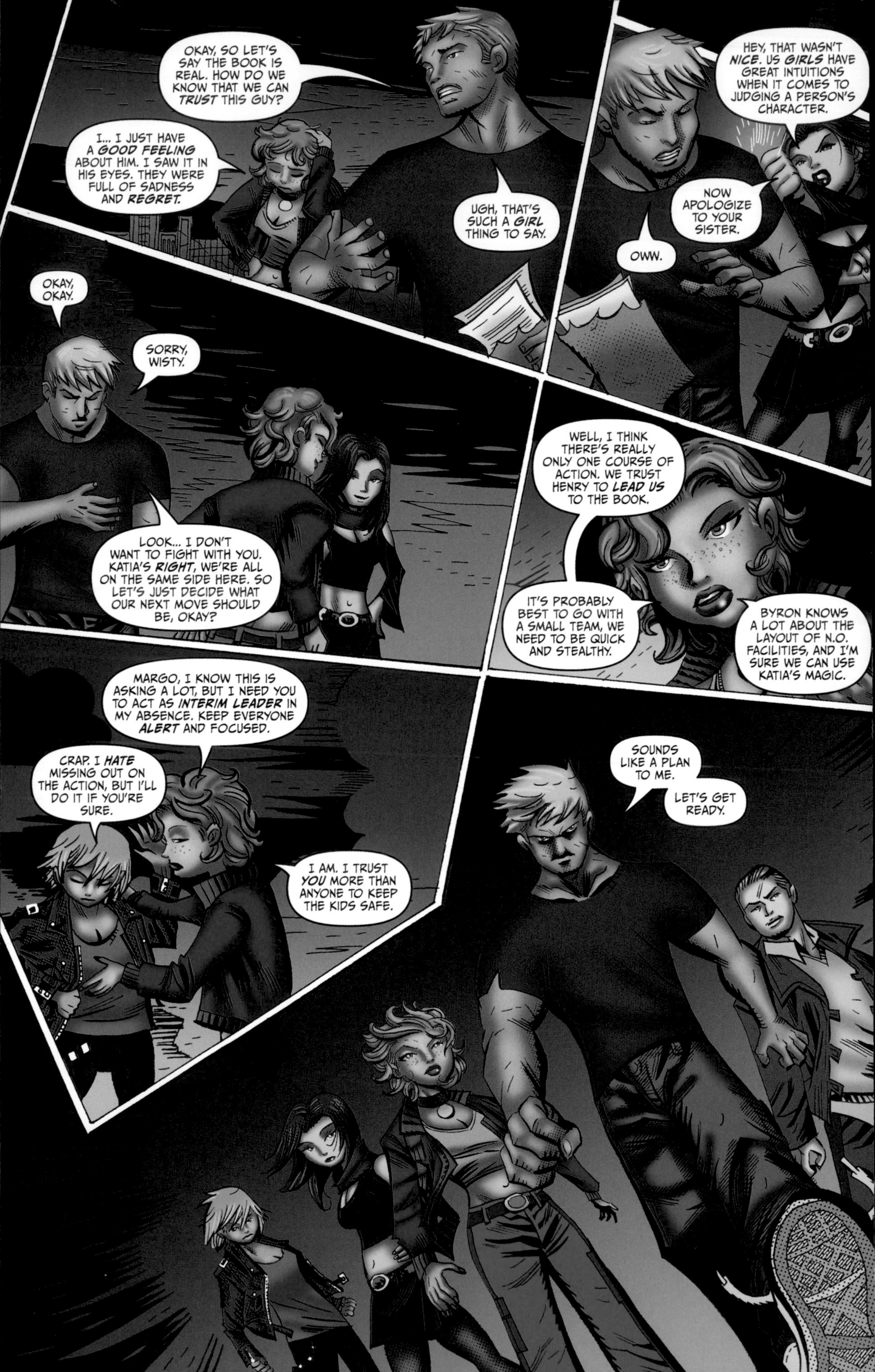

OKAY, SO LET'S SAY THE BOOK IS REAL. HOW DO WE KNOW THAT WE CAN TRUST THIS GUY?
I... I JUST HAVE A GOOD FEELING ABOUT HIM. I SAW IT IN HIS EYES. THEY WERE FULL OF SADNESS AND REGRET.
UGH, THAT'S SUCH A GIRL THING TO SAY.
HEY, THAT WASN'T NICE. US GIRLS HAVE GREAT INTUITIONS WHEN IT COMES TO JUDGING A PERSON'S CHARACTER.
NOW APOLOGIZE TO YOUR SISTER.
OWW.
OKAY, OKAY.
SORRY, WISTY.
LOOK... I DON'T WANT TO FIGHT WITH YOU. KATIA'S RIGHT, WE'RE ALL ON THE SAME SIDE HERE. SO LET'S JUST DECIDE WHAT OUR NEXT MOVE SHOULD BE, OKAY?
WELL, I THINK THERE'S REALLY ONLY ONE COURSE OF ACTION. WE TRUST HENRY TO LEAD US TO THE BOOK.
IT'S PROBABLY BEST TO GO WITH A SMALL TEAM, WE NEED TO BE QUICK AND STEALTHY.
BYRON KNOWS A LOT ABOUT THE LAYOUT OF N.O. FACILITIES, AND I'M SURE WE CAN USE KATIA'S MAGIC.
MARGO, I KNOW THIS IS ASKING A LOT, BUT I NEED YOU TO ACT AS INTERIM LEADER IN MY ABSENCE. KEEP EVERYONE ALERT AND FOCUSED.
CRAP. I HATE MISSING OUT ON THE ACTION, BUT I'LL DO IT IF YOU'RE SURE.
I AM. I TRUST YOU MORE THAN ANYONE TO KEEP THE KIDS SAFE.
SOUNDS LIKE A PLAN TO ME.
LET'S GET READY.

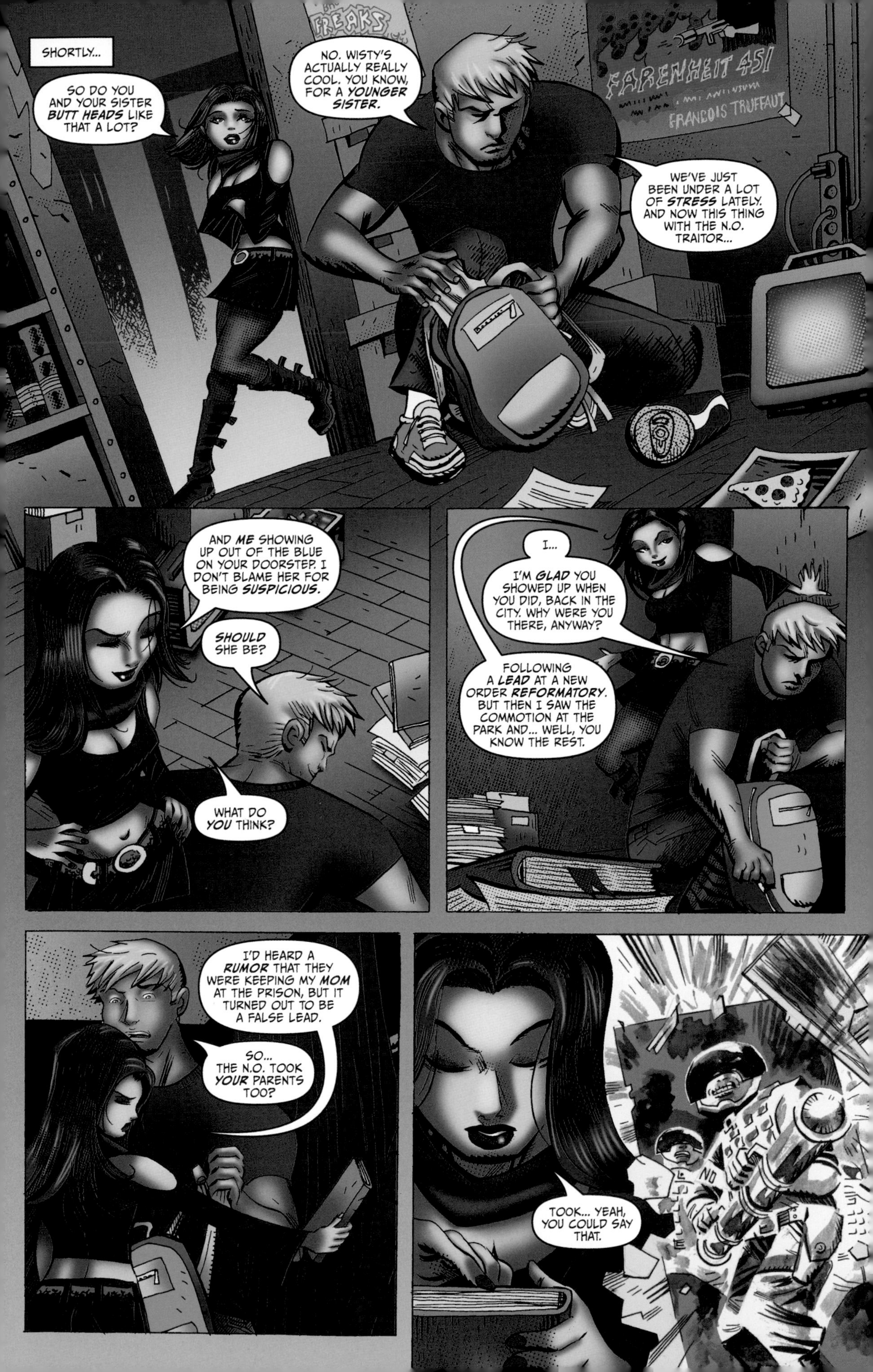
SHORTLY...
SO DO YOU AND YOUR SISTER BUTT HEADS LIKE THAT A LOT?
NO. WISTY'S ACTUALLY REALLY COOL. YOU KNOW, FOR A YOUNGER SISTER.
FREAKS
FARENHEIT 451
FRANCOIS TRUFFAUT
WE'VE JUST BEEN UNDER A LOT OF STRESS LATELY. AND NOW THIS THING WITH THE N.O. TRAITOR...
AND ME SHOWING UP OUT OF THE BLUE ON YOUR DOORSTEP. I DON'T BLAME HER FOR BEING SUSPICIOUS.
SHOULD SHE BE?
WHAT DO YOU THINK?
I...
I'M GLAD YOU SHOWED UP WHEN YOU DID, BACK IN THE CITY. WHY WERE YOU THERE, ANYWAY?
FOLLOWING A LEAD AT A NEW ORDER REFORMATORY. BUT THEN I SAW THE COMMOTION AT THE PARK AND... WELL, YOU KNOW THE REST.
I'D HEARD A RUMOR THAT THEY WERE KEEPING MY MOM AT THE PRISON, BUT IT TURNED OUT TO BE A FALSE LEAD.
SO... THE N.O. TOOK YOUR PARENTS TOO?
TOOK... YEAH, YOU COULD SAY THAT.

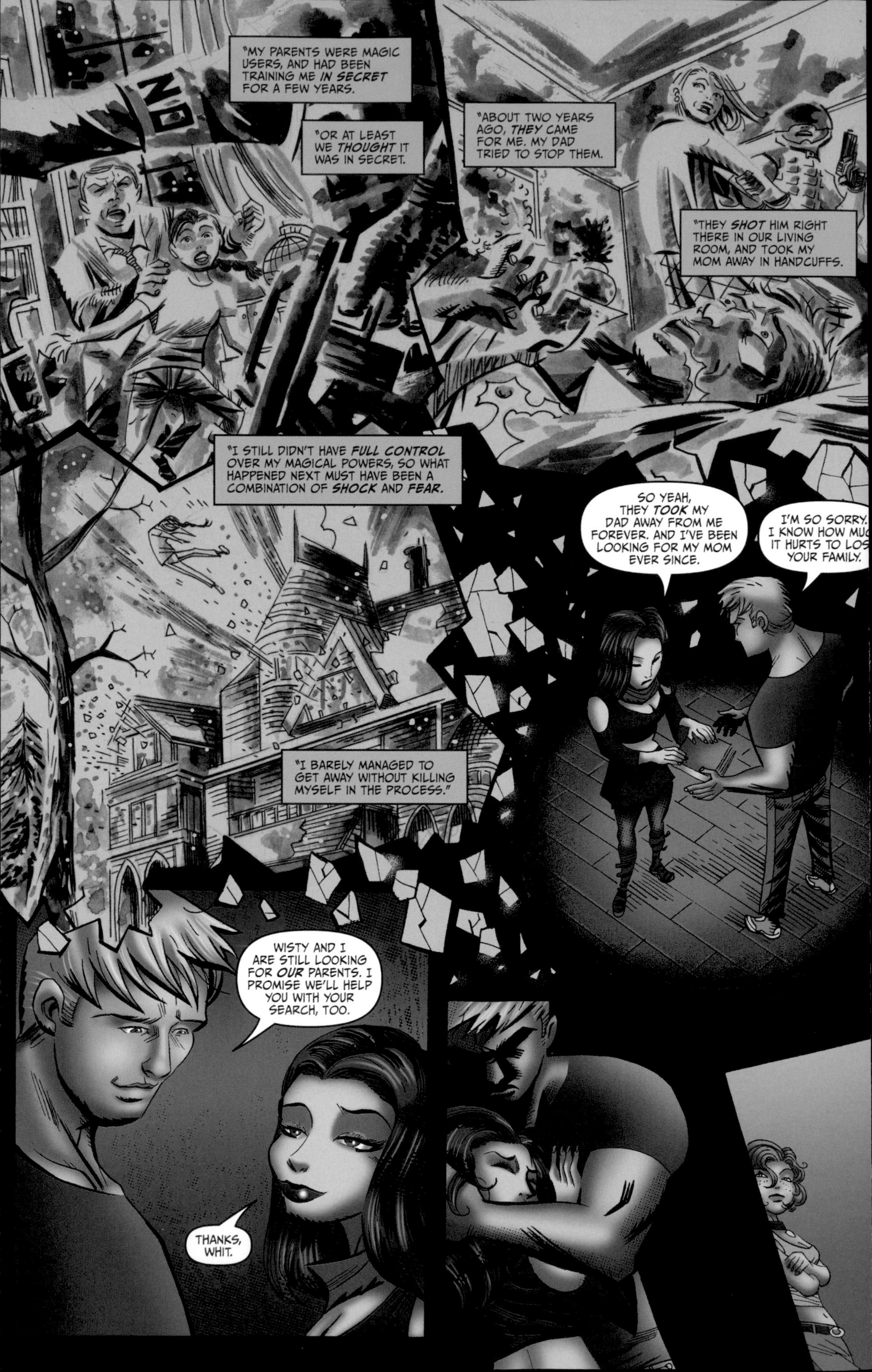

"MY PARENTS WERE MAGIC USERS, AND HAD BEEN TRAINING ME *IN SECRET* FOR A FEW YEARS.
"OR AT LEAST WE *THOUGHT* IT WAS IN SECRET.
"ABOUT TWO YEARS AGO, *THEY* CAME FOR ME. MY DAD TRIED TO STOP THEM.
"THEY *SHOT* HIM RIGHT THERE IN OUR LIVING ROOM, AND TOOK MY MOM AWAY IN HANDCUFFS.
"I STILL DIDN'T HAVE *FULL CONTROL* OVER MY MAGICAL POWERS, SO WHAT HAPPENED NEXT MUST HAVE BEEN A COMBINATION OF *SHOCK* AND *FEAR*.
"I BARELY MANAGED TO GET AWAY WITHOUT KILLING MYSELF IN THE PROCESS."
SO YEAH, THEY *TOOK* MY DAD AWAY FROM ME FOREVER. AND I'VE BEEN LOOKING FOR MY MOM EVER SINCE.
I'M SO SORRY. I KNOW HOW MUC IT HURTS TO LOS YOUR FAMILY.
WISTY AND I ARE STILL LOOKING FOR *OUR* PARENTS. I PROMISE WE'LL HELP YOU WITH YOUR SEARCH, TOO.
THANKS, WHIT.

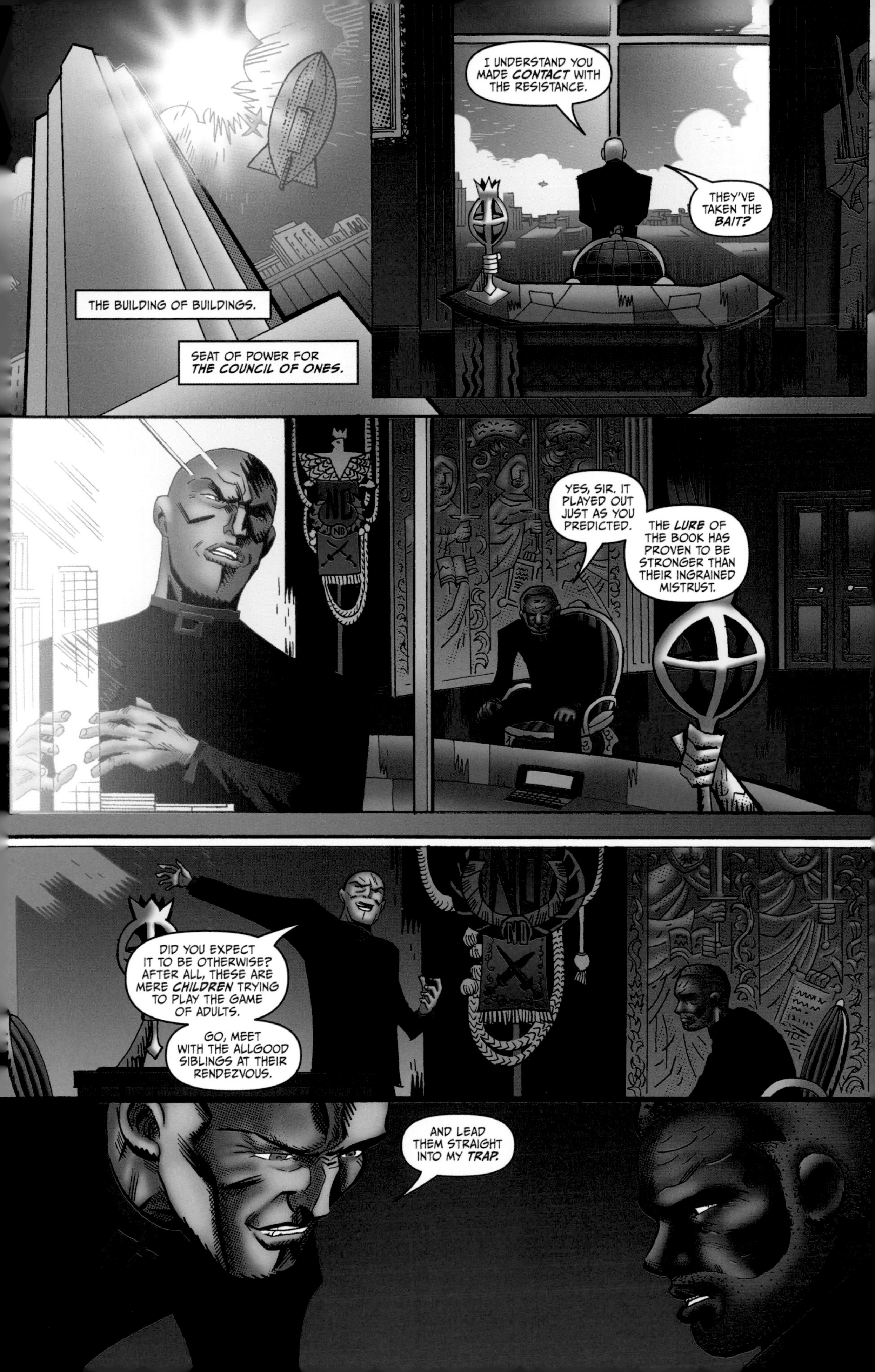

THE BUILDING OF BUILDINGS.
SEAT OF POWER FOR THE COUNCIL OF ONES.
I UNDERSTAND YOU MADE CONTACT WITH THE RESISTANCE.
THEY'VE TAKEN THE BAIT?
YES, SIR. IT PLAYED OUT JUST AS YOU PREDICTED.
THE LURE OF THE BOOK HAS PROVEN TO BE STRONGER THAN THEIR INGRAINED MISTRUST.
DID YOU EXPECT IT TO BE OTHERWISE? AFTER ALL, THESE ARE MERE CHILDREN TRYING TO PLAY THE GAME OF ADULTS.
GO, MEET WITH THE ALLGOOD SIBLINGS AT THEIR RENDEZVOUS.
AND LEAD THEM STRAIGHT INTO MY TRAP.

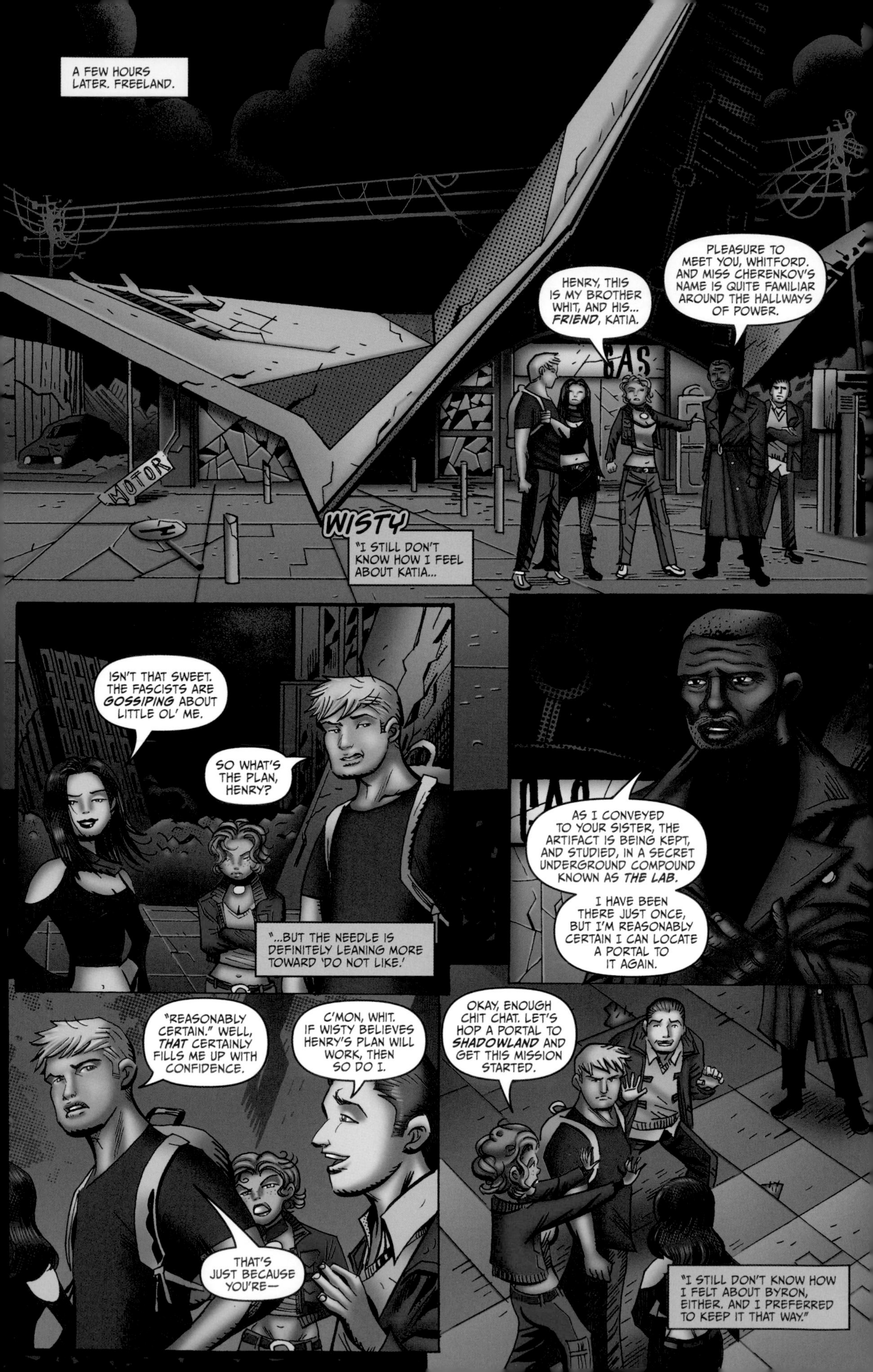
A FEW HOURS LATER. FREELAND.
HENRY, THIS IS MY BROTHER WHIT, AND HIS... FRIEND, KATIA.
PLEASURE TO MEET YOU, WHITFORD. AND MISS CHERENKOV'S NAME IS QUITE FAMILIAR AROUND THE HALLWAYS OF POWER.
GAS
MOTOR
WISTY
"I STILL DON'T KNOW HOW I FEEL ABOUT KATIA...
ISN'T THAT SWEET. THE FASCISTS ARE GOSSIPING ABOUT LITTLE OL' ME.
SO WHAT'S THE PLAN, HENRY?
"...BUT THE NEEDLE IS DEFINITELY LEANING MORE TOWARD 'DO NOT LIKE.'
AS I CONVEYED TO YOUR SISTER, THE ARTIFACT IS BEING KEPT, AND STUDIED, IN A SECRET UNDERGROUND COMPOUND KNOWN AS THE LAB.
I HAVE BEEN THERE JUST ONCE, BUT I'M REASONABLY CERTAIN I CAN LOCATE A PORTAL TO IT AGAIN.
"REASONABLY CERTAIN." WELL, THAT CERTAINLY FILLS ME UP WITH CONFIDENCE.
C'MON, WHIT. IF WISTY BELIEVES HENRY'S PLAN WILL WORK, THEN SO DO I.
THAT'S JUST BECAUSE YOU'RE—
OKAY, ENOUGH CHIT CHAT. LET'S HOP A PORTAL TO SHADOWLAND AND GET THIS MISSION STARTED.
"I STILL DON'T KNOW HOW I FELT ABOUT BYRON, EITHER. AND I PREFERRED TO KEEP IT THAT WAY."

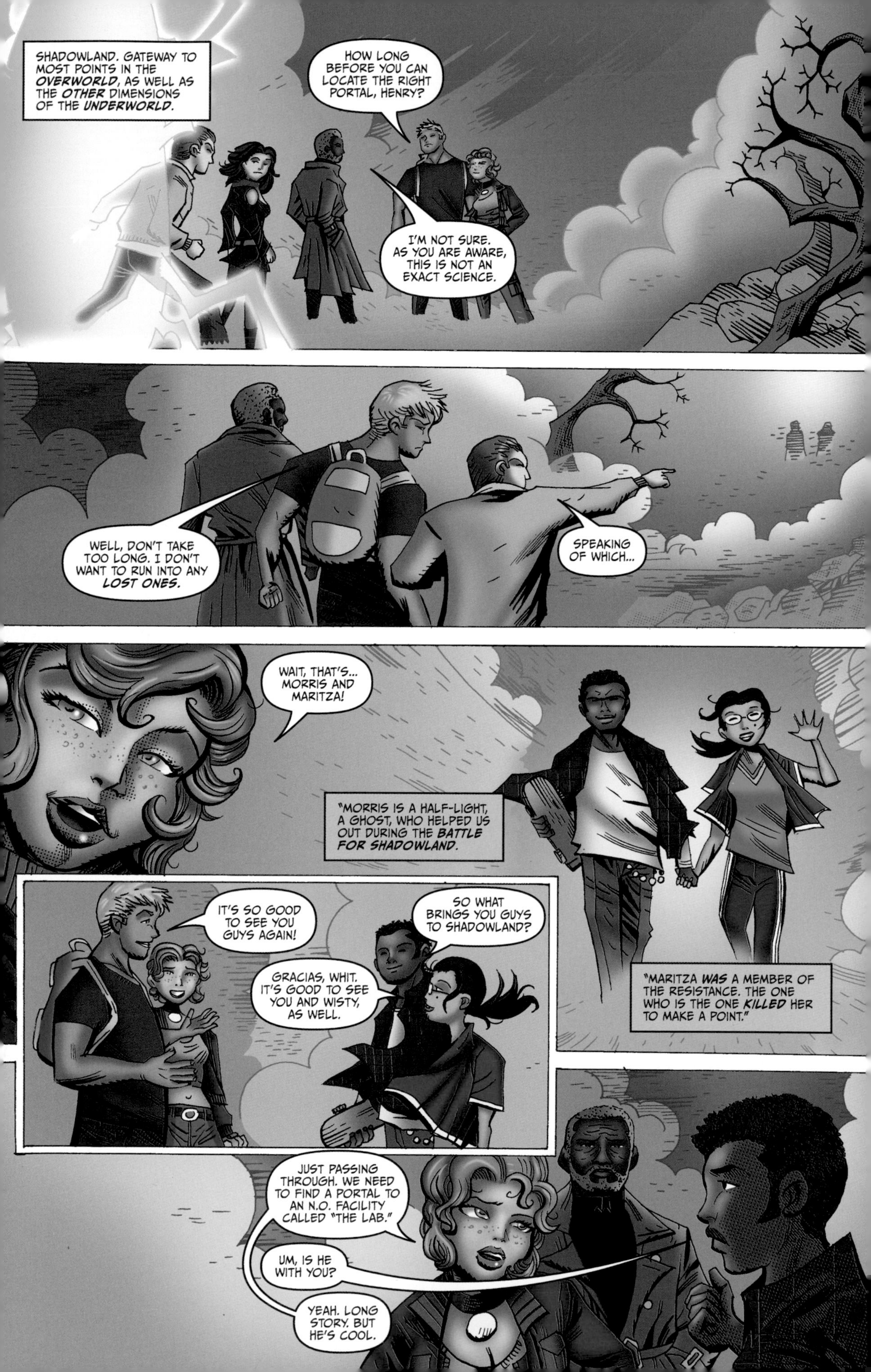
SHADOWLAND. GATEWAY TO MOST POINTS IN THE *OVERWORLD*, AS WELL AS THE *OTHER* DIMENSIONS OF THE *UNDERWORLD*.
HOW LONG BEFORE YOU CAN LOCATE THE RIGHT PORTAL, HENRY?
I'M NOT SURE. AS YOU ARE AWARE, THIS IS NOT AN EXACT SCIENCE.
WELL, DON'T TAKE TOO LONG. I DON'T WANT TO RUN INTO ANY *LOST ONES.*
SPEAKING OF WHICH...
WAIT, THAT'S... MORRIS AND MARITZA!
"MORRIS IS A HALF-LIGHT, A GHOST, WHO HELPED US OUT DURING THE *BATTLE FOR SHADOWLAND*.
"MARITZA *WAS* A MEMBER OF THE RESISTANCE. THE ONE WHO IS THE ONE *KILLED* HER TO MAKE A POINT."
IT'S SO GOOD TO SEE YOU GUYS AGAIN!
SO WHAT BRINGS YOU GUYS TO SHADOWLAND?
GRACIAS, WHIT. IT'S GOOD TO SEE YOU AND WISTY, AS WELL.
JUST PASSING THROUGH. WE NEED TO FIND A PORTAL TO AN N.O. FACILITY CALLED "THE LAB."
UM, IS HE WITH YOU?
YEAH. LONG STORY. BUT HE'S COOL.

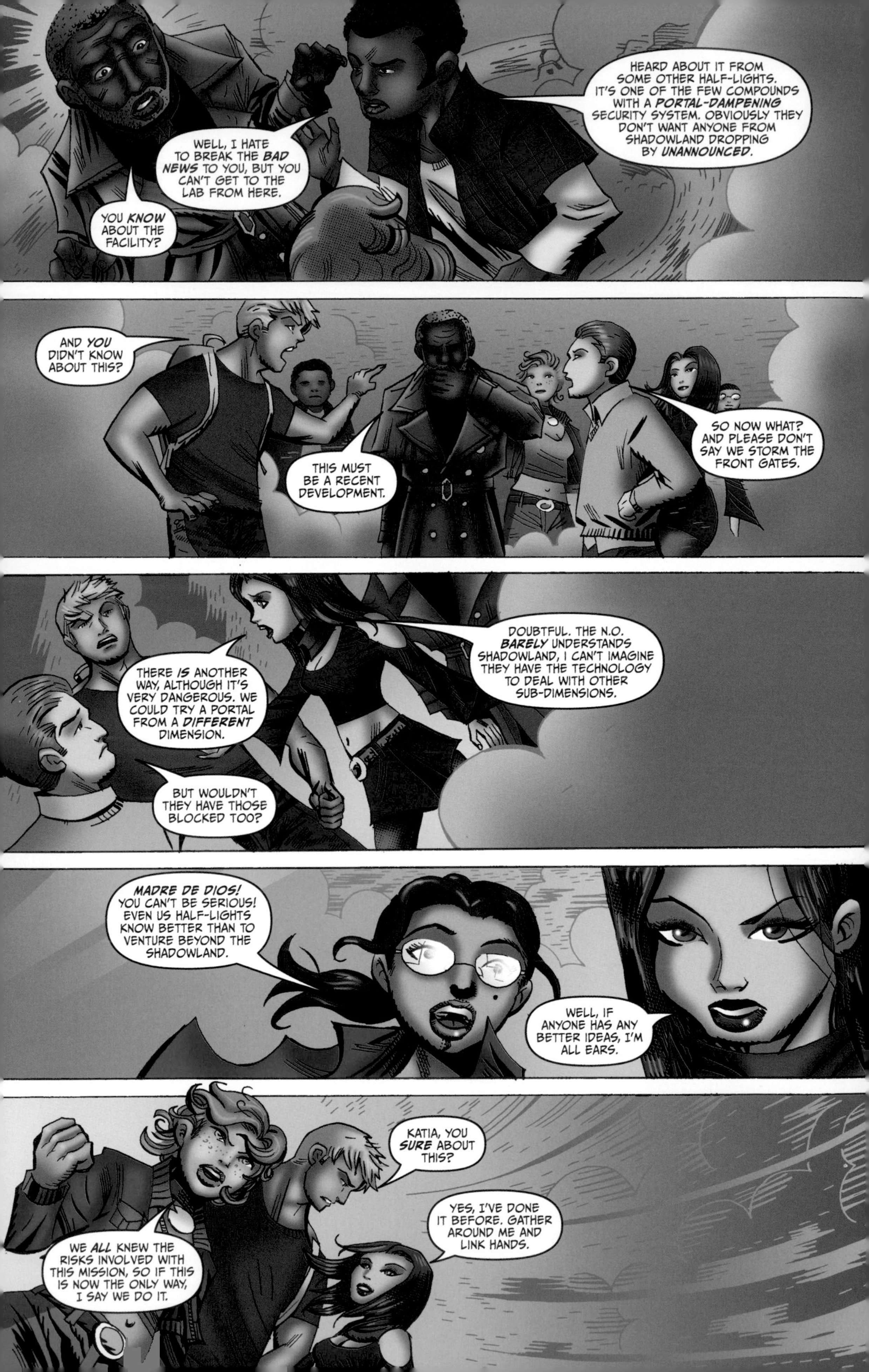
YOU KNOW ABOUT THE FACILITY?
WELL, I HATE TO BREAK THE BAD NEWS TO YOU, BUT YOU CAN'T GET TO THE LAB FROM HERE.
HEARD ABOUT IT FROM SOME OTHER HALF-LIGHTS. IT'S ONE OF THE FEW COMPOUNDS WITH A PORTAL-DAMPENING SECURITY SYSTEM. OBVIOUSLY THEY DON'T WANT ANYONE FROM SHADOWLAND DROPPING BY UNANNOUNCED.
AND YOU DIDN'T KNOW ABOUT THIS?
THIS MUST BE A RECENT DEVELOPMENT.
SO NOW WHAT? AND PLEASE DON'T SAY WE STORM THE FRONT GATES.
THERE IS ANOTHER WAY, ALTHOUGH IT'S VERY DANGEROUS. WE COULD TRY A PORTAL FROM A DIFFERENT DIMENSION.
BUT WOULDN'T THEY HAVE THOSE BLOCKED TOO?
DOUBTFUL. THE N.O. BARELY UNDERSTANDS SHADOWLAND, I CAN'T IMAGINE THEY HAVE THE TECHNOLOGY TO DEAL WITH OTHER SUB-DIMENSIONS.
MADRE DE DIOS! YOU CAN'T BE SERIOUS! EVEN US HALF-LIGHTS KNOW BETTER THAN TO VENTURE BEYOND THE SHADOWLAND.
WELL, IF ANYONE HAS ANY BETTER IDEAS, I'M ALL EARS.
KATIA, YOU SURE ABOUT THIS?
WE ALL KNEW THE RISKS INVOLVED WITH THIS MISSION, SO IF THIS IS NOW THE ONLY WAY, I SAY WE DO IT.
YES, I'VE DONE IT BEFORE. GATHER AROUND ME AND LINK HANDS.

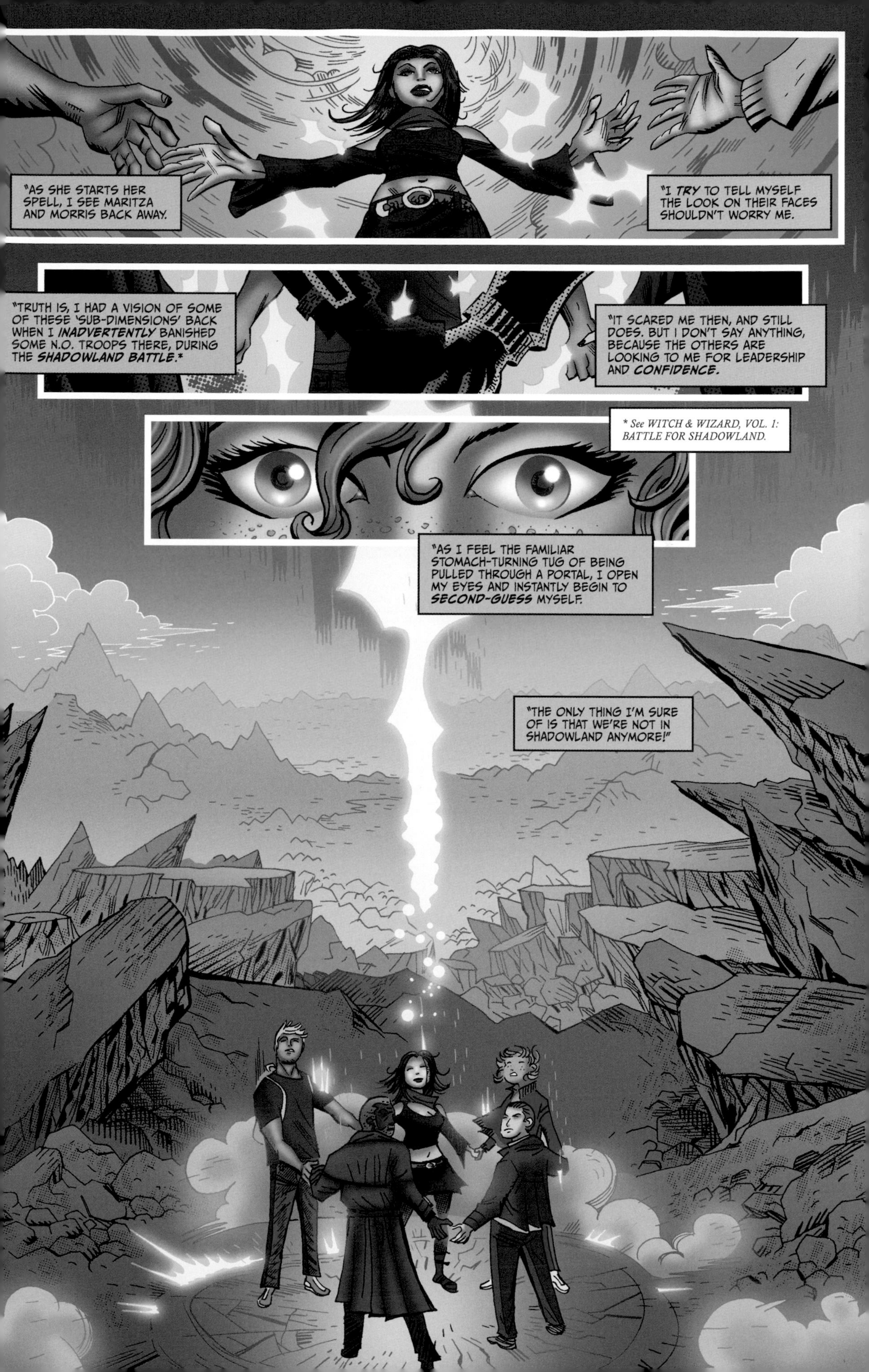

"AS SHE STARTS HER SPELL, I SEE MARITZA AND MORRIS BACK AWAY.
"I TRY TO TELL MYSELF THE LOOK ON THEIR FACES SHOULDN'T WORRY ME.
"TRUTH IS, I HAD A VISION OF SOME OF THESE 'SUB-DIMENSIONS' BACK WHEN I INADVERTENTLY BANISHED SOME N.O. TROOPS THERE, DURING THE SHADOWLAND BATTLE.*
"IT SCARED ME THEN, AND STILL DOES. BUT I DON'T SAY ANYTHING, BECAUSE THE OTHERS ARE LOOKING TO ME FOR LEADERSHIP AND CONFIDENCE.
* See WITCH & WIZARD, VOL. 1: BATTLE FOR SHADOWLAND.
"AS I FEEL THE FAMILIAR STOMACH-TURNING TUG OF BEING PULLED THROUGH A PORTAL, I OPEN MY EYES AND INSTANTLY BEGIN TO SECOND-GUESS MYSELF.
"THE ONLY THING I'M SURE OF IS THAT WE'RE NOT IN SHADOWLAND ANYMORE!"

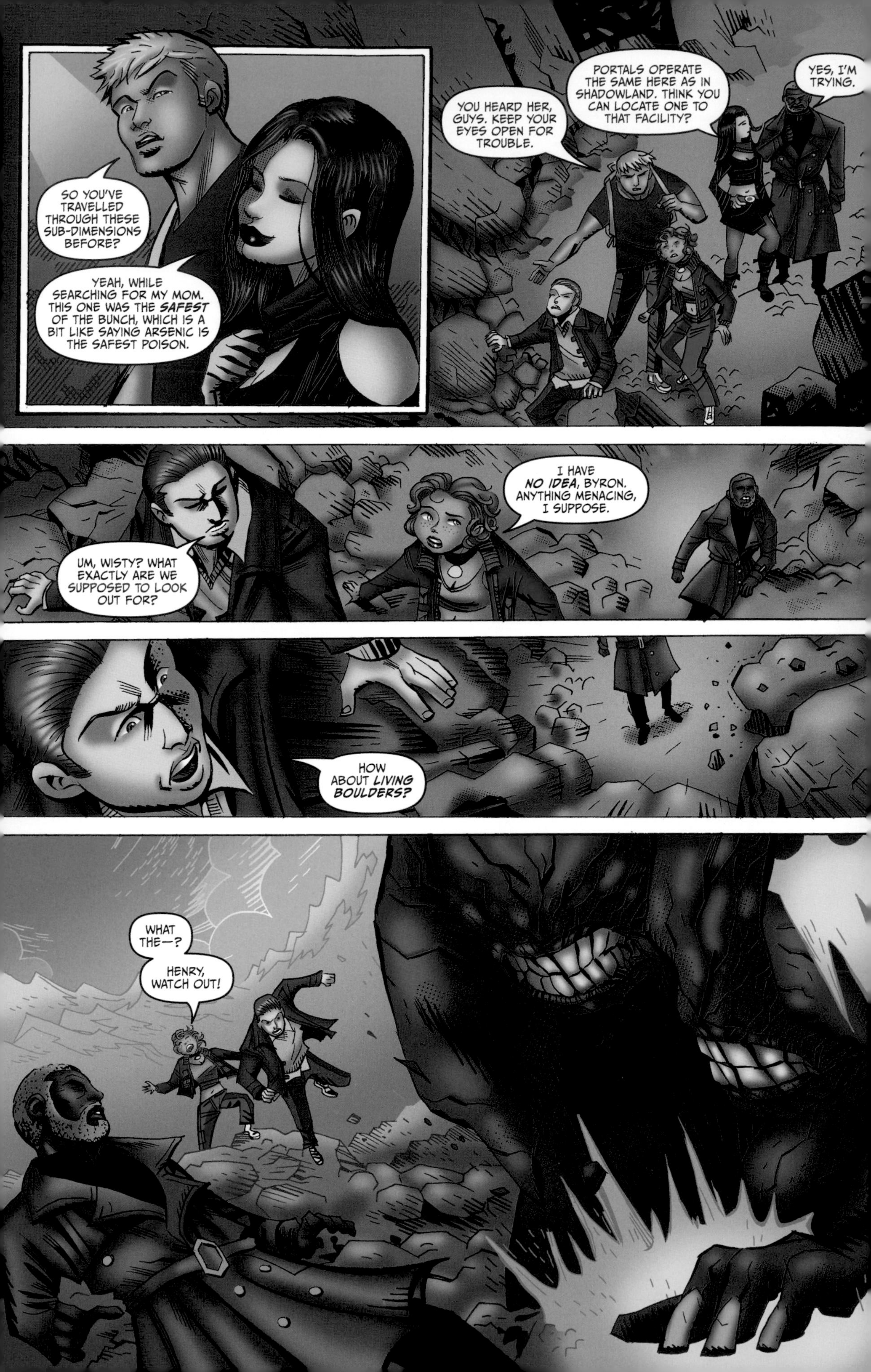
SO YOU'VE TRAVELLED THROUGH THESE SUB-DIMENSIONS BEFORE?
YEAH, WHILE SEARCHING FOR MY MOM. THIS ONE WAS THE SAFEST OF THE BUNCH, WHICH IS A BIT LIKE SAYING ARSENIC IS THE SAFEST POISON.
YOU HEARD HER, GUYS. KEEP YOUR EYES OPEN FOR TROUBLE.
PORTALS OPERATE THE SAME HERE AS IN SHADOWLAND. THINK YOU CAN LOCATE ONE TO THAT FACILITY?
YES, I'M TRYING.
UM, WISTY? WHAT EXACTLY ARE WE SUPPOSED TO LOOK OUT FOR?
I HAVE NO IDEA, BYRON. ANYTHING MENACING, I SUPPOSE.
HOW ABOUT LIVING BOULDERS?
WHAT THE—?
HENRY, WATCH OUT!

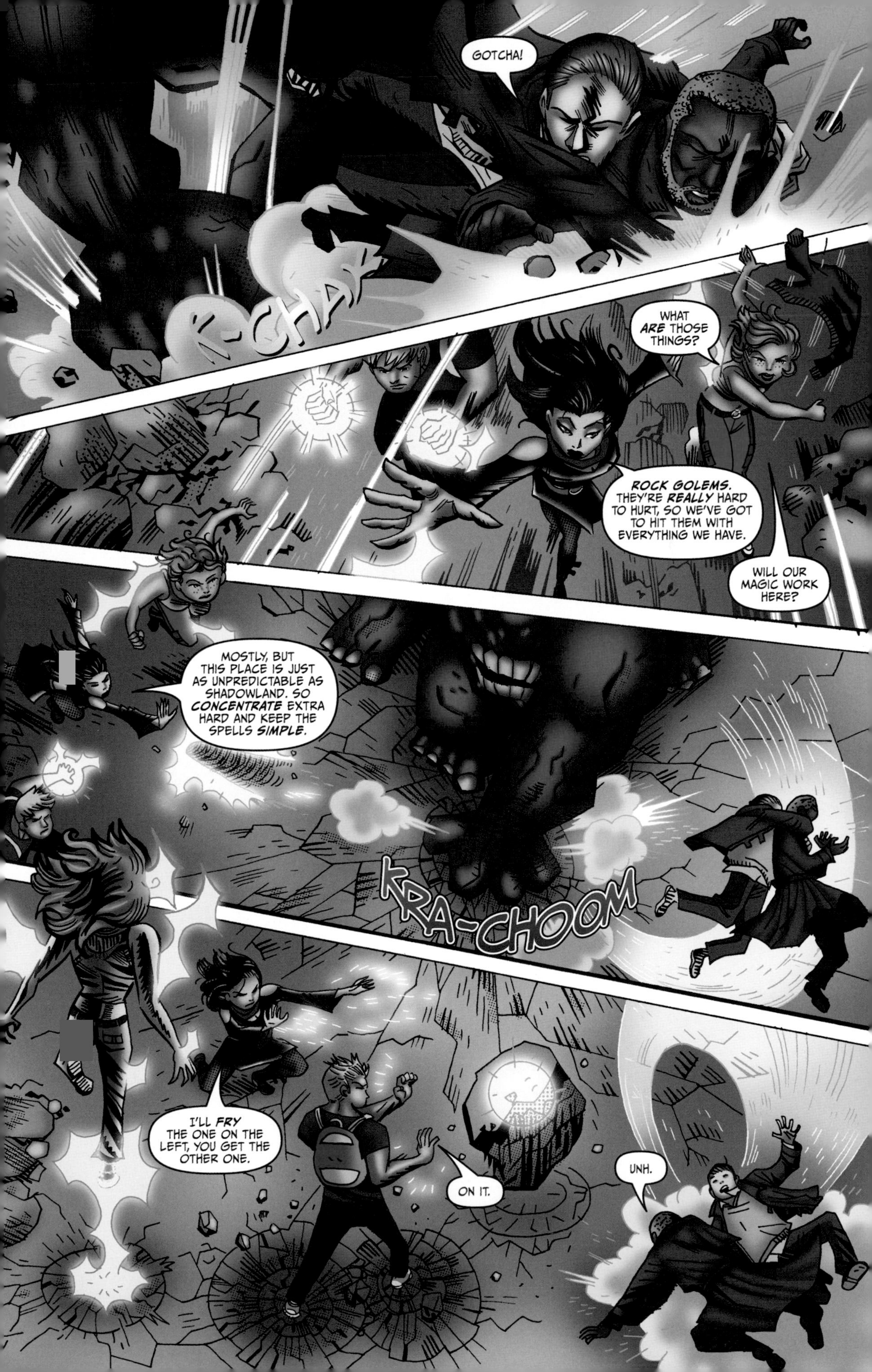
GOTCHA!
K-CHAK
WHAT ARE THOSE THINGS?
ROCK GOLEMS. THEY'RE REALLY HARD TO HURT, SO WE'VE GOT TO HIT THEM WITH EVERYTHING WE HAVE.
WILL OUR MAGIC WORK HERE?
MOSTLY, BUT THIS PLACE IS JUST AS UNPREDICTABLE AS SHADOWLAND. SO CONCENTRATE EXTRA HARD AND KEEP THE SPELLS SIMPLE.
KRA-CHOOM
I'LL FRY THE ONE ON THE LEFT, YOU GET THE OTHER ONE.
ON IT.
UNH.

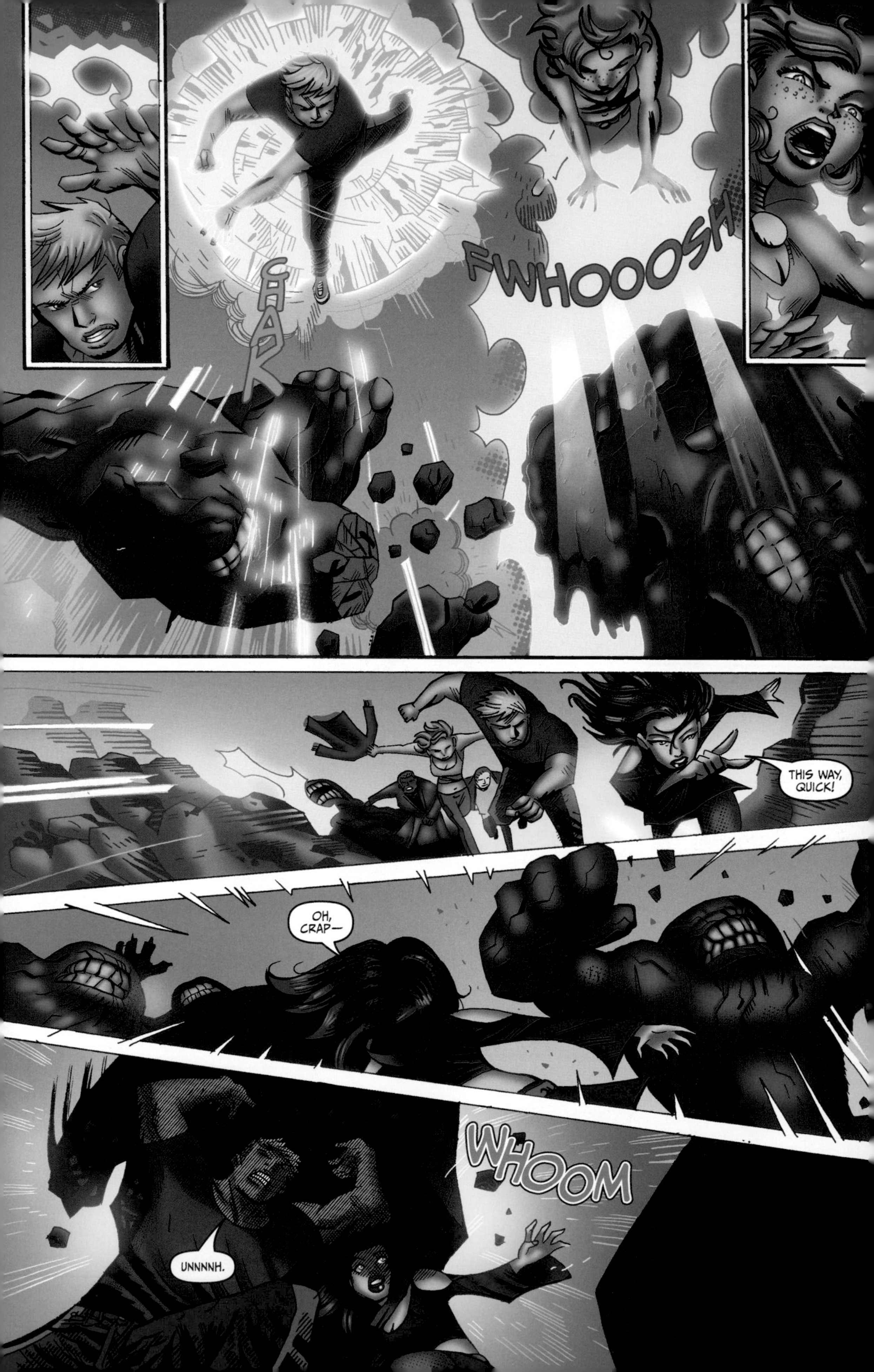

HAK
FWHOOOSH
THIS WAY, QUICK!
OH, CRAP—
WHOOM
UNNNNH.

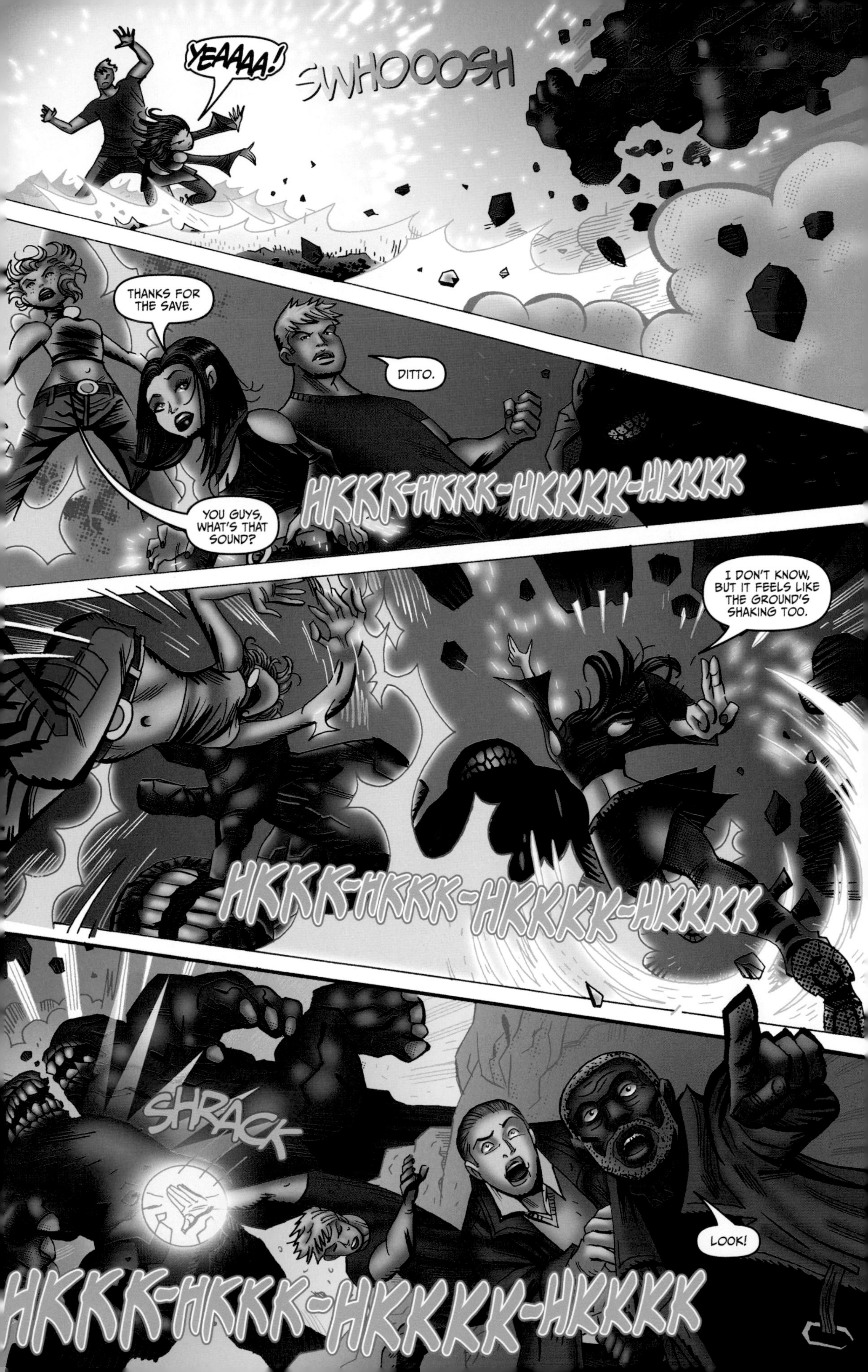
YEAAAA!
SWHOOOOSH
THANKS FOR THE SAVE.
DITTO.
HKKK-HKKK-HKKKK-HKKKK
YOU GUYS, WHAT'S THAT SOUND?
I DON'T KNOW, BUT IT FEELS LIKE THE GROUND'S SHAKING TOO.
HKKK-HKKK-HKKKK-HKKKK
SHRACK
LOOK!
HKKK-HKKK-HKKKK-HKKKK

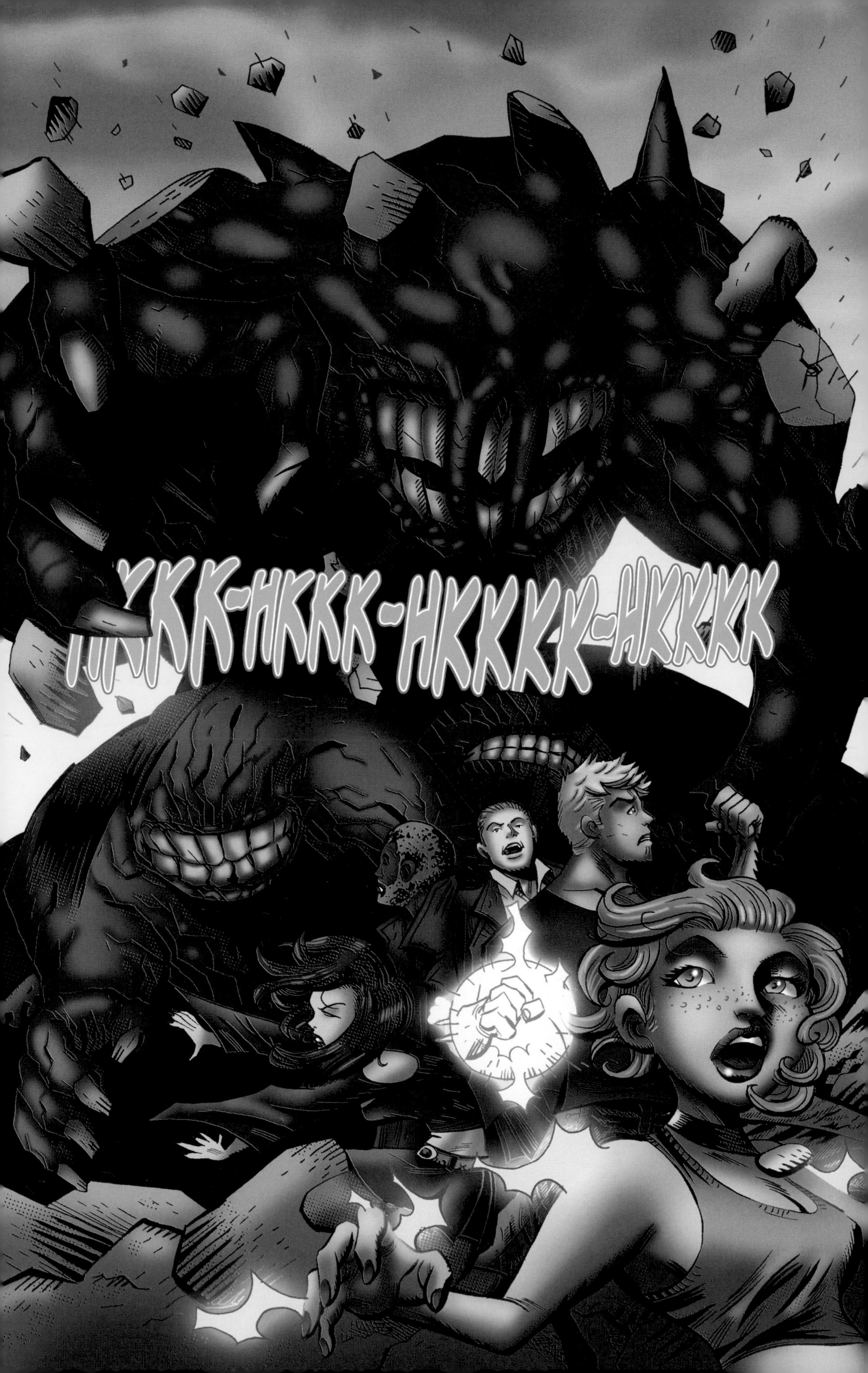
HKKK-HKKKK-HKKKK-HKKKK

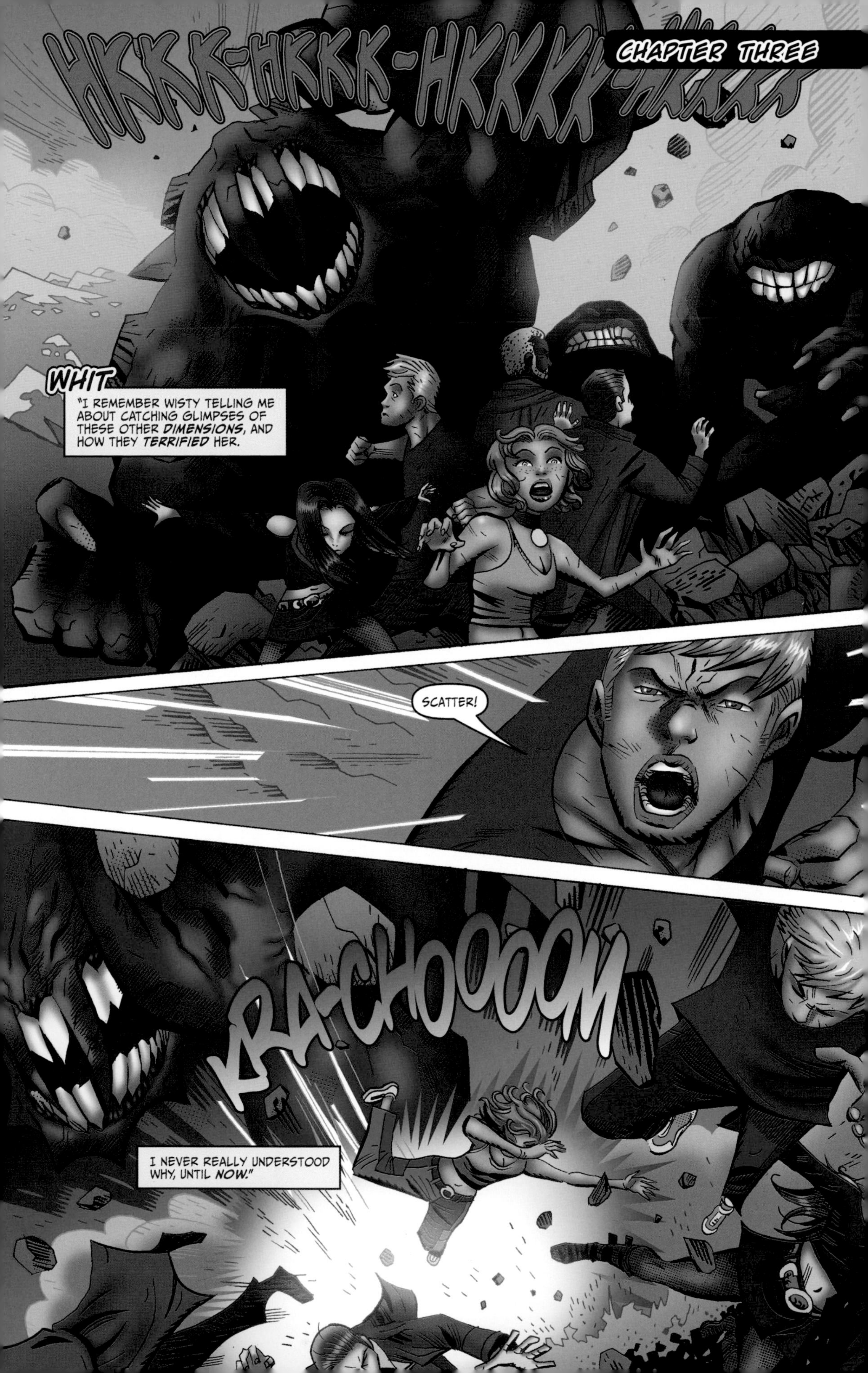
CHAPTER THREE
HKKK-HKKK-HKKKK-HKKKK
WHIT
"I REMEMBER WISTY TELLING ME ABOUT CATCHING GLIMPSES OF THESE OTHER DIMENSIONS, AND HOW THEY TERRIFIED HER.
SCATTER!
KRA-CHOOOOM
I NEVER REALLY UNDERSTOOD WHY, UNTIL NOW."

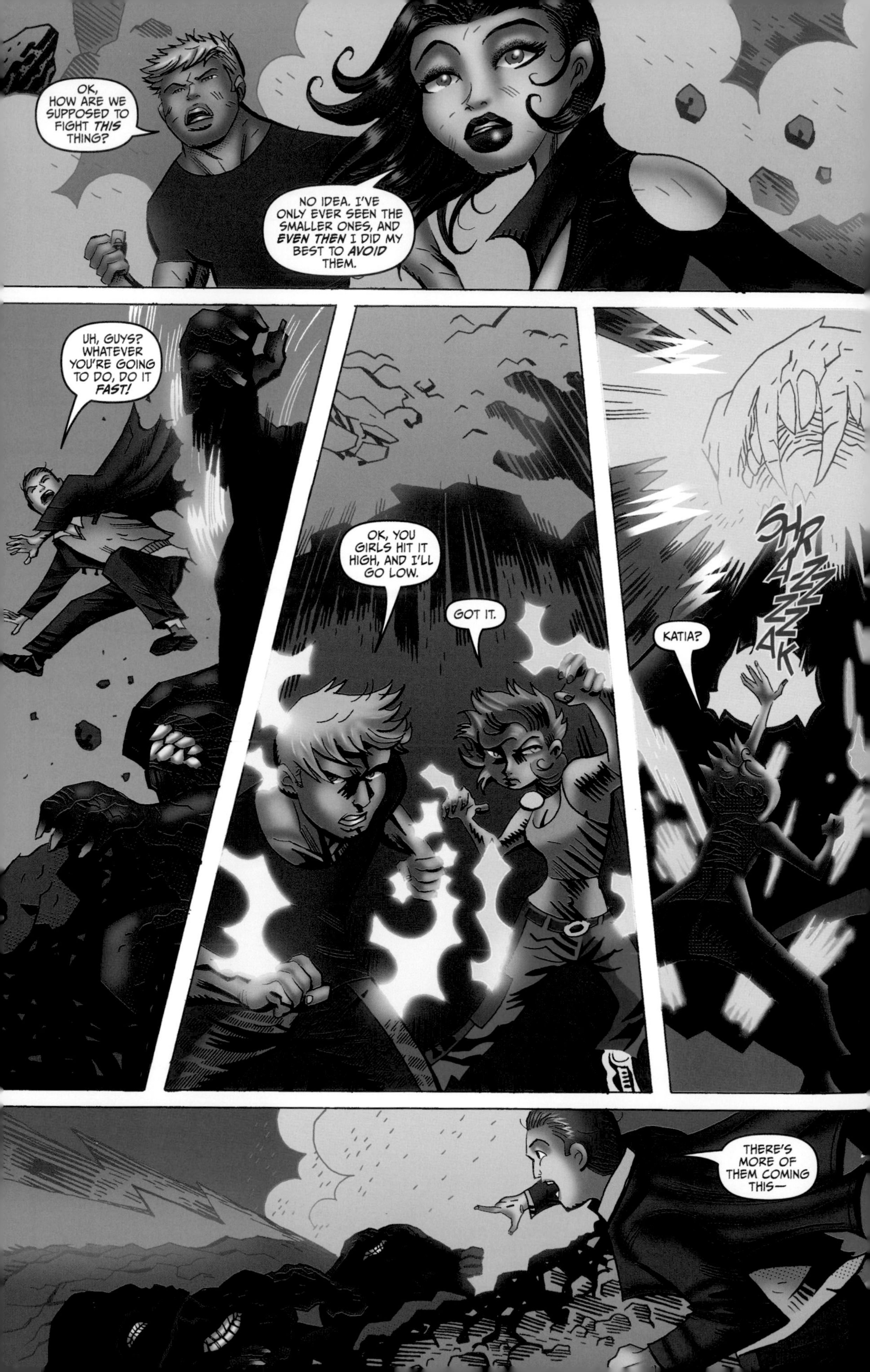
OK, HOW ARE WE SUPPOSED TO FIGHT THIS THING?
NO IDEA. I'VE ONLY EVER SEEN THE SMALLER ONES, AND EVEN THEN I DID MY BEST TO AVOID THEM.
UH, GUYS? WHATEVER YOU'RE GOING TO DO, DO IT FAST!
OK, YOU GIRLS HIT IT HIGH, AND I'LL GO LOW.
GOT IT.
SHRAZZZAK
KATIA?
THERE'S MORE OF THEM COMING THIS—

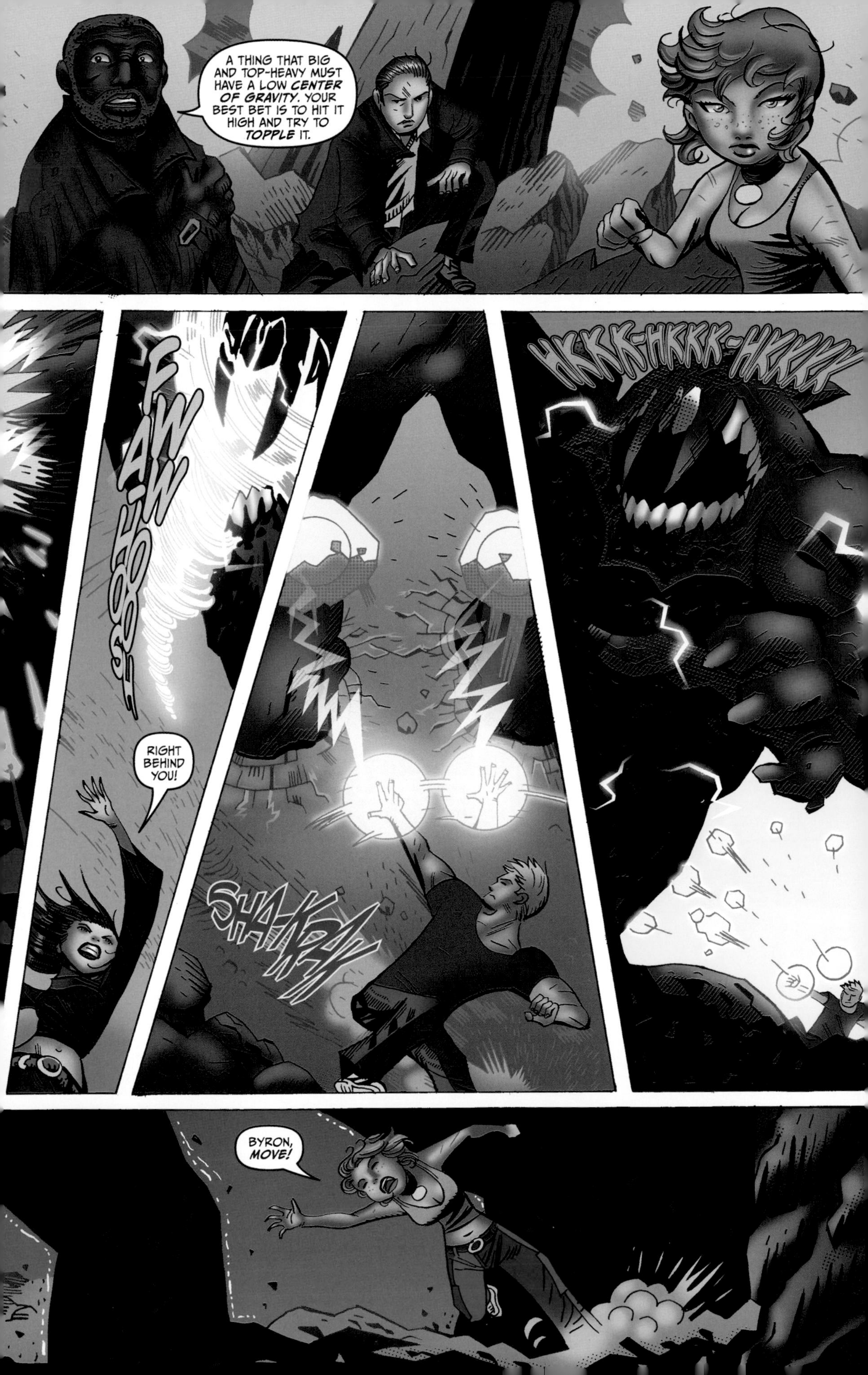
A THING THAT BIG AND TOP-HEAVY MUST HAVE A LOW CENTER OF GRAVITY. YOUR BEST BET IS TO HIT IT HIGH AND TRY TO TOPPLE IT.
FWAW-HOOOSH
RIGHT BEHIND YOU!
SHA-KRA
HKKK-HKKK-HKKK
BYRON, MOVE!

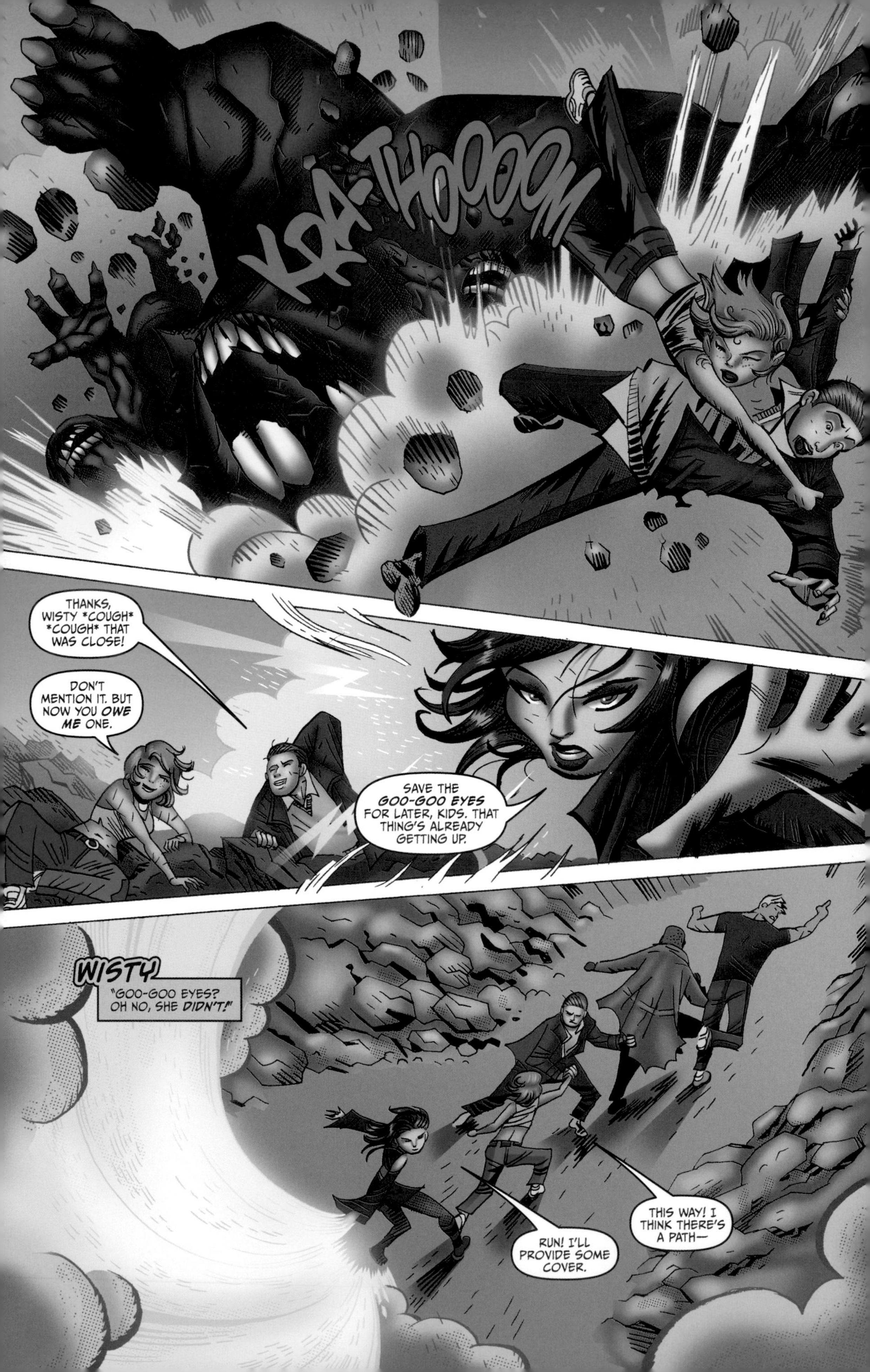
KA-THOOOOM
THANKS, WISTY *COUGH* *COUGH* THAT WAS CLOSE!
DON'T MENTION IT. BUT NOW YOU *OWE ME* ONE.
SAVE THE **GOO-GOO EYES** FOR LATER, KIDS. THAT THING'S ALREADY GETTING UP.
WISTY
"GOO-GOO EYES? OH NO, SHE *DIDN'T!*"
THIS WAY! I THINK THERE'S A PATH—
RUN! I'LL PROVIDE SOME COVER.

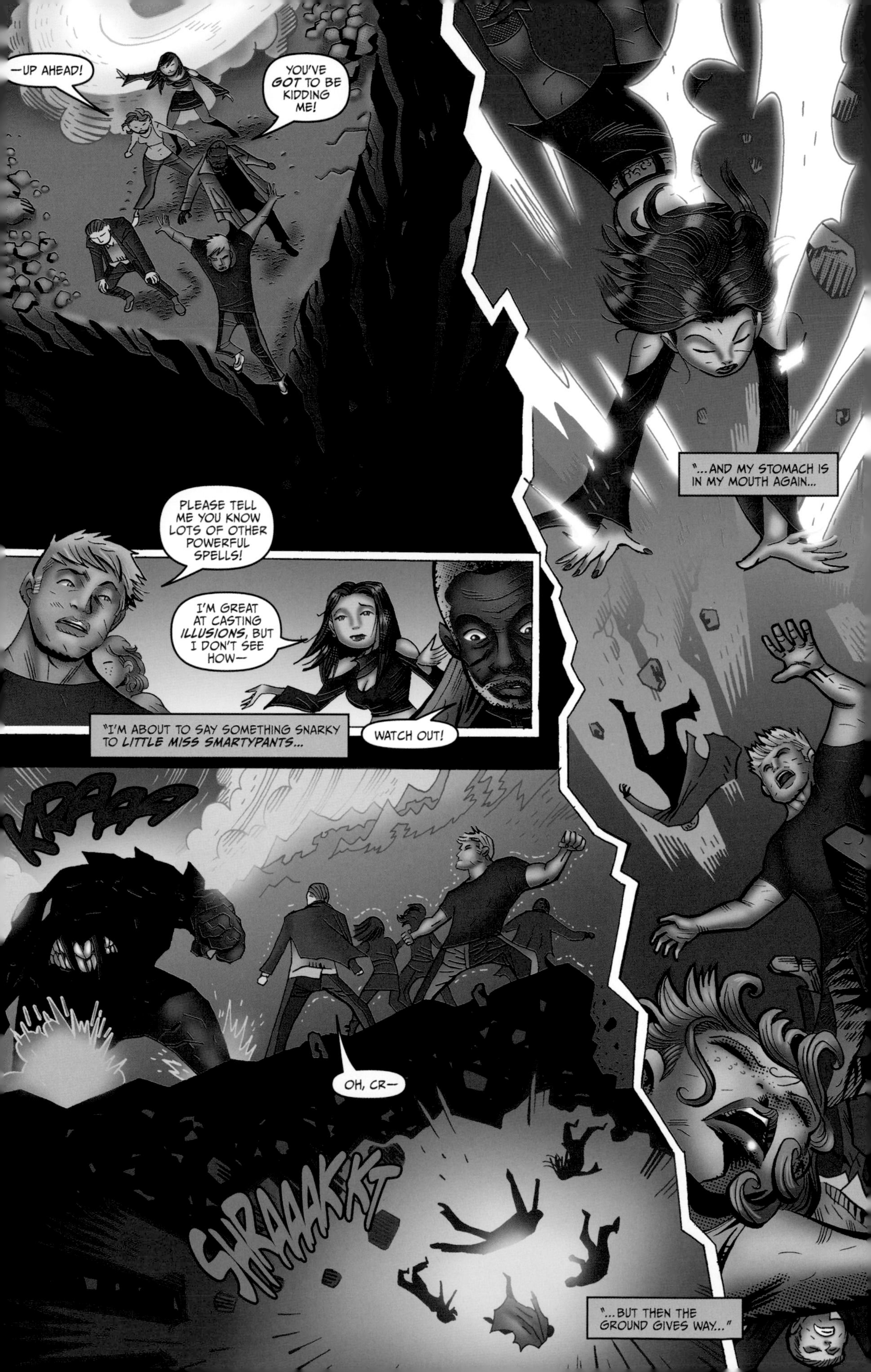

—UP AHEAD!
YOU'VE GOT TO BE KIDDING ME!
"...AND MY STOMACH IS IN MY MOUTH AGAIN...
PLEASE TELL ME YOU KNOW LOTS OF OTHER POWERFUL SPELLS!
I'M GREAT AT CASTING ILLUSIONS, BUT I DON'T SEE HOW—
"I'M ABOUT TO SAY SOMETHING SNARKY TO LITTLE MISS SMARTYPANTS...
WATCH OUT!
KRAAA
OH, CR—
SHRAAAKKT
"...BUT THEN THE GROUND GIVES WAY..."

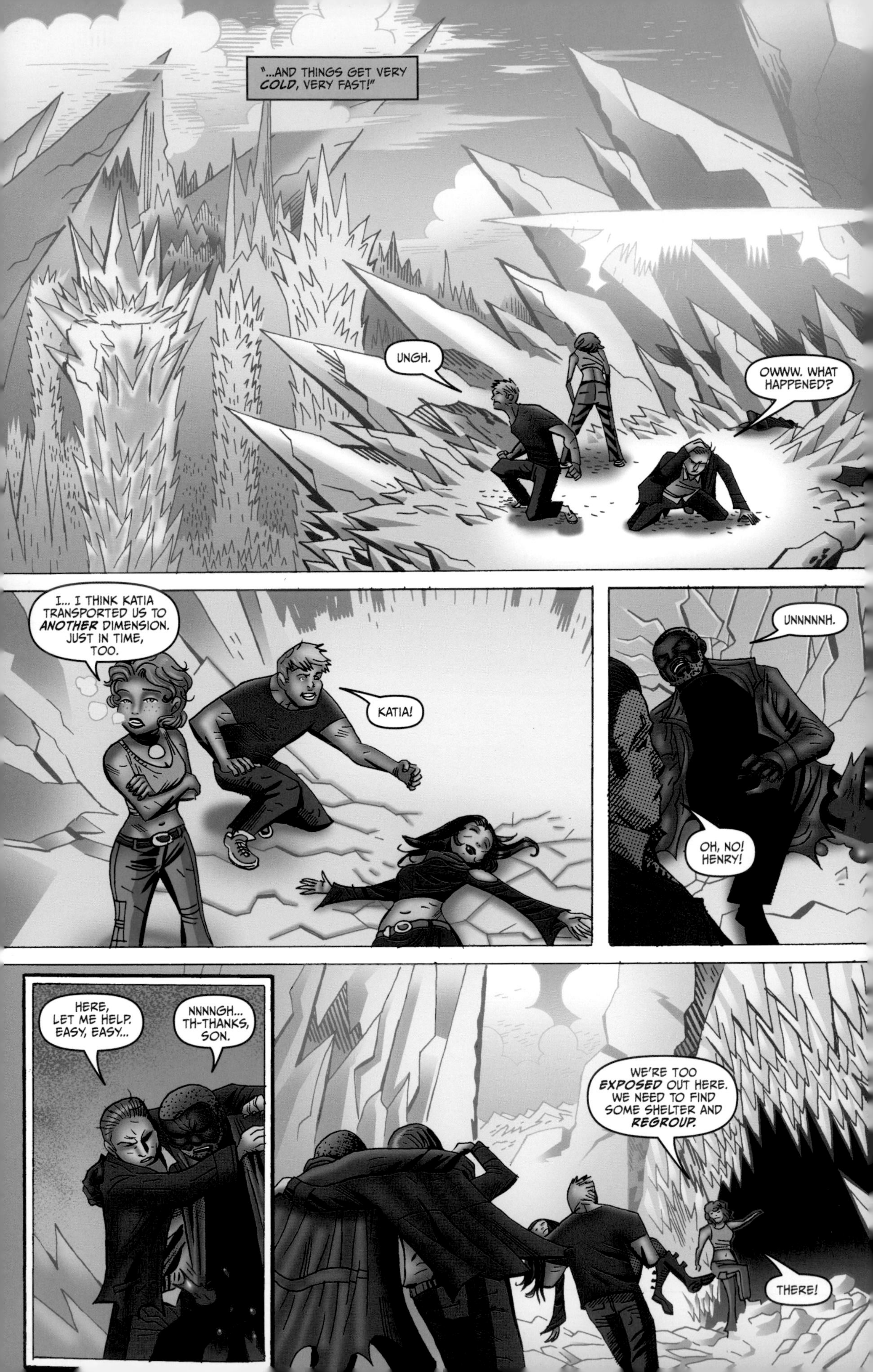
"...AND THINGS GET VERY COLD, VERY FAST!"
UNGH.
OWWW. WHAT HAPPENED?
I... I THINK KATIA TRANSPORTED US TO ANOTHER DIMENSION. JUST IN TIME, TOO.
KATIA!
UNNNNNH.
OH, NO! HENRY!
HERE, LET ME HELP. EASY, EASY...
NNNNGH... TH-THANKS, SON.
WE'RE TOO EXPOSED OUT HERE. WE NEED TO FIND SOME SHELTER AND REGROUP.
THERE!

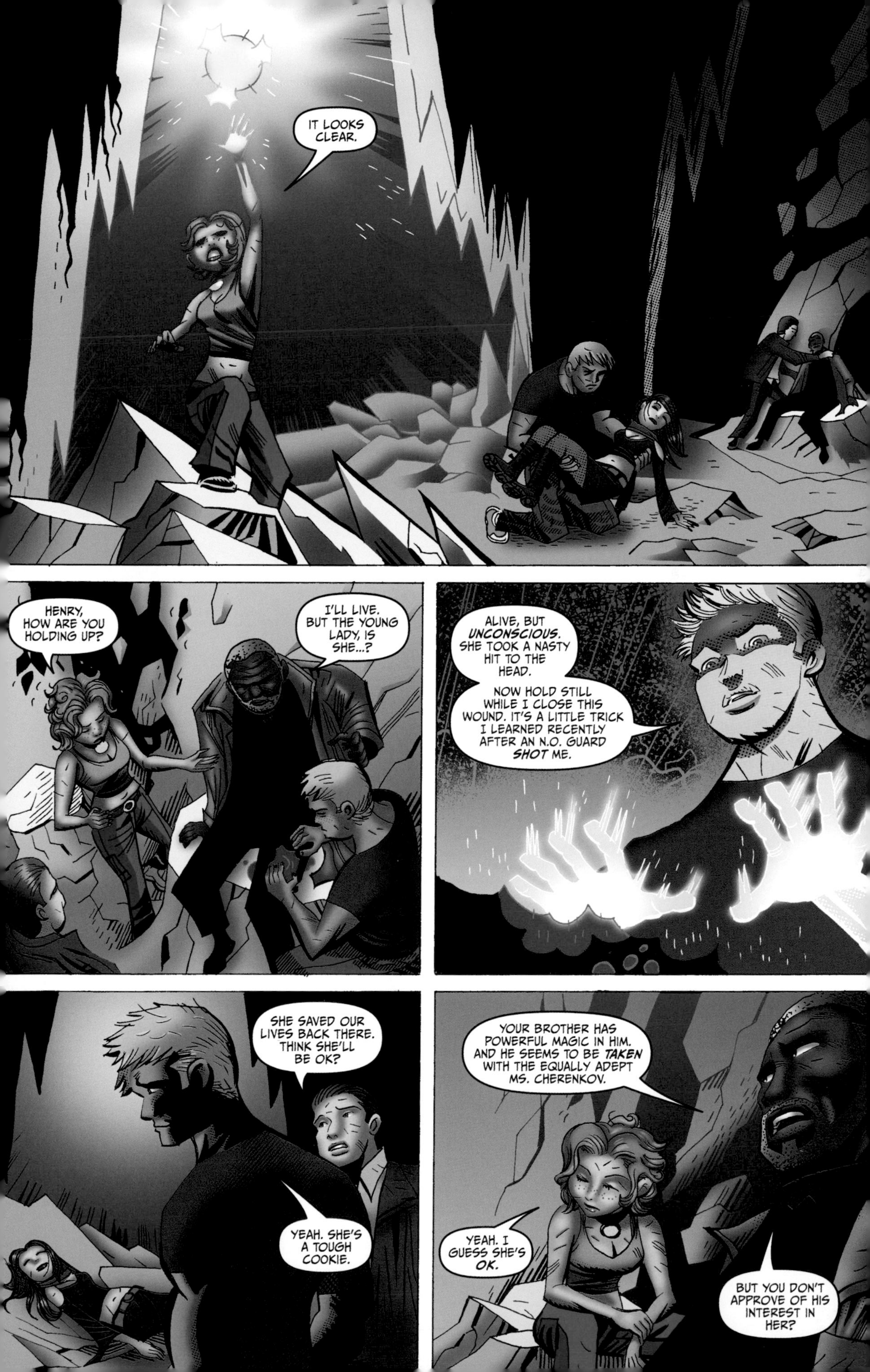
IT LOOKS CLEAR.
HENRY, HOW ARE YOU HOLDING UP?
I'LL LIVE. BUT THE YOUNG LADY, IS SHE...?
ALIVE, BUT UNCONSCIOUS. SHE TOOK A NASTY HIT TO THE HEAD.
NOW HOLD STILL WHILE I CLOSE THIS WOUND. IT'S A LITTLE TRICK I LEARNED RECENTLY AFTER AN N.O. GUARD SHOT ME.
SHE SAVED OUR LIVES BACK THERE. THINK SHE'LL BE OK?
YEAH. SHE'S A TOUGH COOKIE.
YOUR BROTHER HAS POWERFUL MAGIC IN HIM. AND HE SEEMS TO BE TAKEN WITH THE EQUALLY ADEPT MS. CHERENKOV.
YEAH. I GUESS SHE'S OK.
BUT YOU DON'T APPROVE OF HIS INTEREST IN HER?

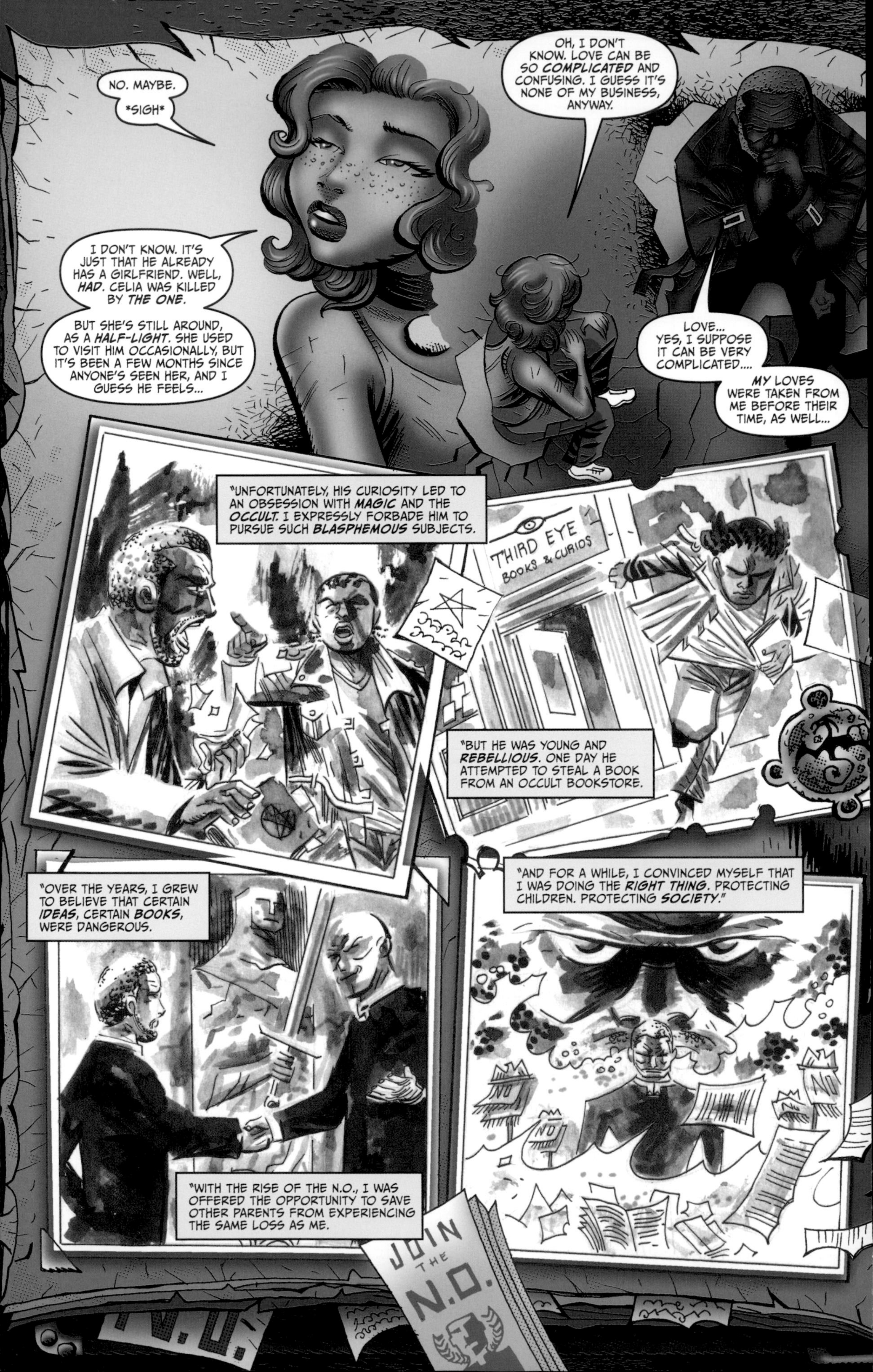
NO. MAYBE.
SIGH
OH, I DON'T KNOW. LOVE CAN BE SO COMPLICATED AND CONFUSING. I GUESS IT'S NONE OF MY BUSINESS, ANYWAY.
I DON'T KNOW. IT'S JUST THAT HE ALREADY HAS A GIRLFRIEND. WELL, HAD. CELIA WAS KILLED BY THE ONE.
BUT SHE'S STILL AROUND, AS A HALF-LIGHT. SHE USED TO VISIT HIM OCCASIONALLY, BUT IT'S BEEN A FEW MONTHS SINCE ANYONE'S SEEN HER, AND I GUESS HE FEELS...
LOVE... YES, I SUPPOSE IT CAN BE VERY COMPLICATED....
MY LOVES WERE TAKEN FROM ME BEFORE THEIR TIME, AS WELL...
"UNFORTUNATELY, HIS CURIOSITY LED TO AN OBSESSION WITH MAGIC AND THE OCCULT. I EXPRESSLY FORBADE HIM TO PURSUE SUCH BLASPHEMOUS SUBJECTS.
THIRD EYE
BOOKS & CURIOS
"BUT HE WAS YOUNG AND REBELLIOUS. ONE DAY HE ATTEMPTED TO STEAL A BOOK FROM AN OCCULT BOOKSTORE.
"OVER THE YEARS, I GREW TO BELIEVE THAT CERTAIN IDEAS, CERTAIN BOOKS, WERE DANGEROUS.
"WITH THE RISE OF THE N.O., I WAS OFFERED THE OPPORTUNITY TO SAVE OTHER PARENTS FROM EXPERIENCING THE SAME LOSS AS ME.
"AND FOR A WHILE, I CONVINCED MYSELF THAT I WAS DOING THE RIGHT THING. PROTECTING CHILDREN. PROTECTING SOCIETY."
NO
NO
NO
JOIN THE N.O.
N.O.

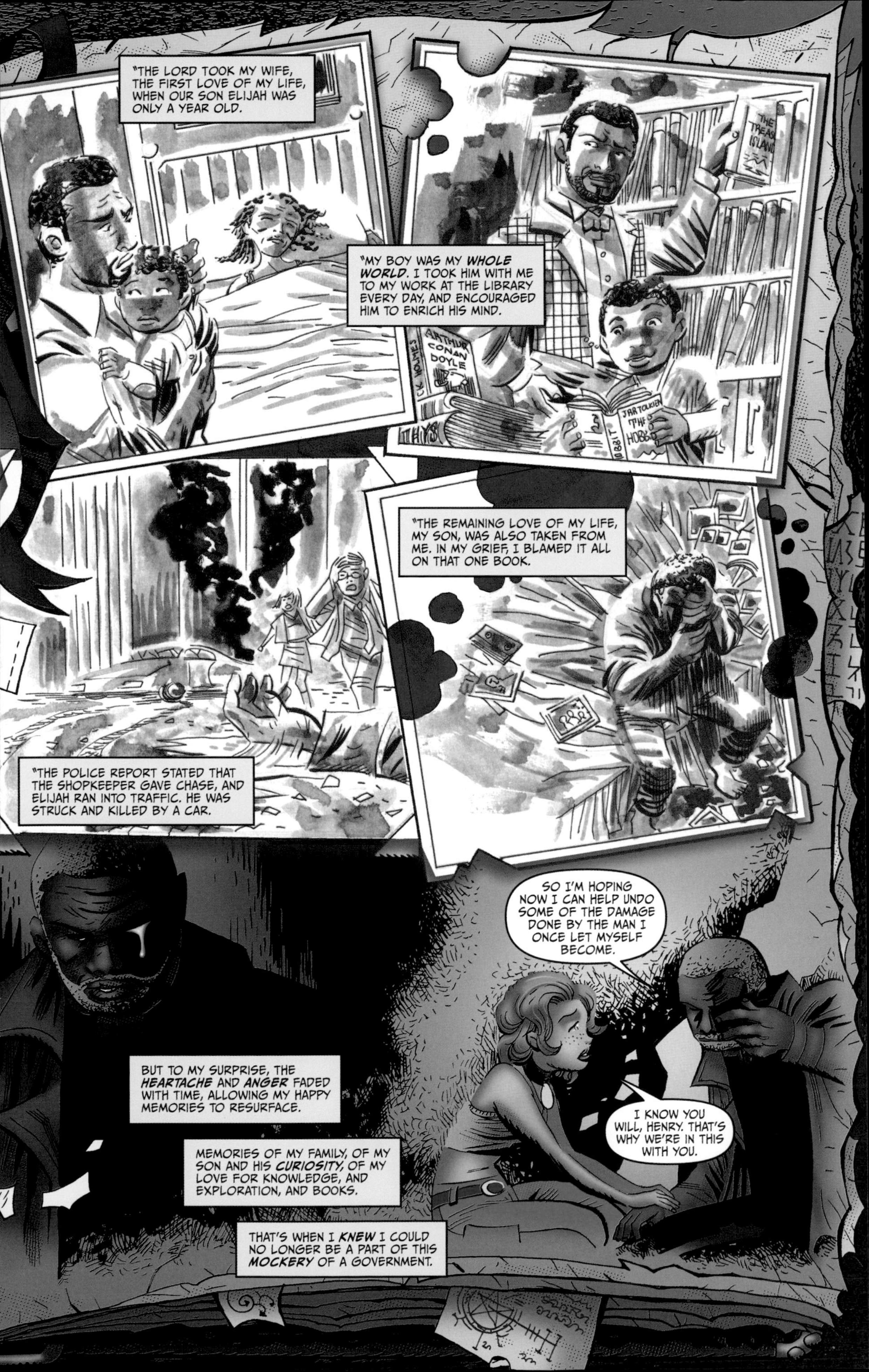
"THE LORD TOOK MY WIFE, THE FIRST LOVE OF MY LIFE, WHEN OUR SON ELIJAH WAS ONLY A YEAR OLD.
"MY BOY WAS MY WHOLE WORLD. I TOOK HIM WITH ME TO MY WORK AT THE LIBRARY EVERY DAY, AND ENCOURAGED HIM TO ENRICH HIS MIND.
TREASURE ISLAND
ARTHUR CONAN DOYLE
JRR TOLKIEN THE HOBBIT
"THE POLICE REPORT STATED THAT THE SHOPKEEPER GAVE CHASE, AND ELIJAH RAN INTO TRAFFIC. HE WAS STRUCK AND KILLED BY A CAR.
"THE REMAINING LOVE OF MY LIFE, MY SON, WAS ALSO TAKEN FROM ME. IN MY GRIEF, I BLAMED IT ALL ON THAT ONE BOOK.
BUT TO MY SURPRISE, THE HEARTACHE AND ANGER FADED WITH TIME, ALLOWING MY HAPPY MEMORIES TO RESURFACE.
MEMORIES OF MY FAMILY, OF MY SON AND HIS CURIOSITY, OF MY LOVE FOR KNOWLEDGE, AND EXPLORATION, AND BOOKS.
THAT'S WHEN I KNEW I COULD NO LONGER BE A PART OF THIS MOCKERY OF A GOVERNMENT.
SO I'M HOPING NOW I CAN HELP UNDO SOME OF THE DAMAGE DONE BY THE MAN I ONCE LET MYSELF BECOME.
I KNOW YOU WILL, HENRY. THAT'S WHY WE'RE IN THIS WITH YOU.

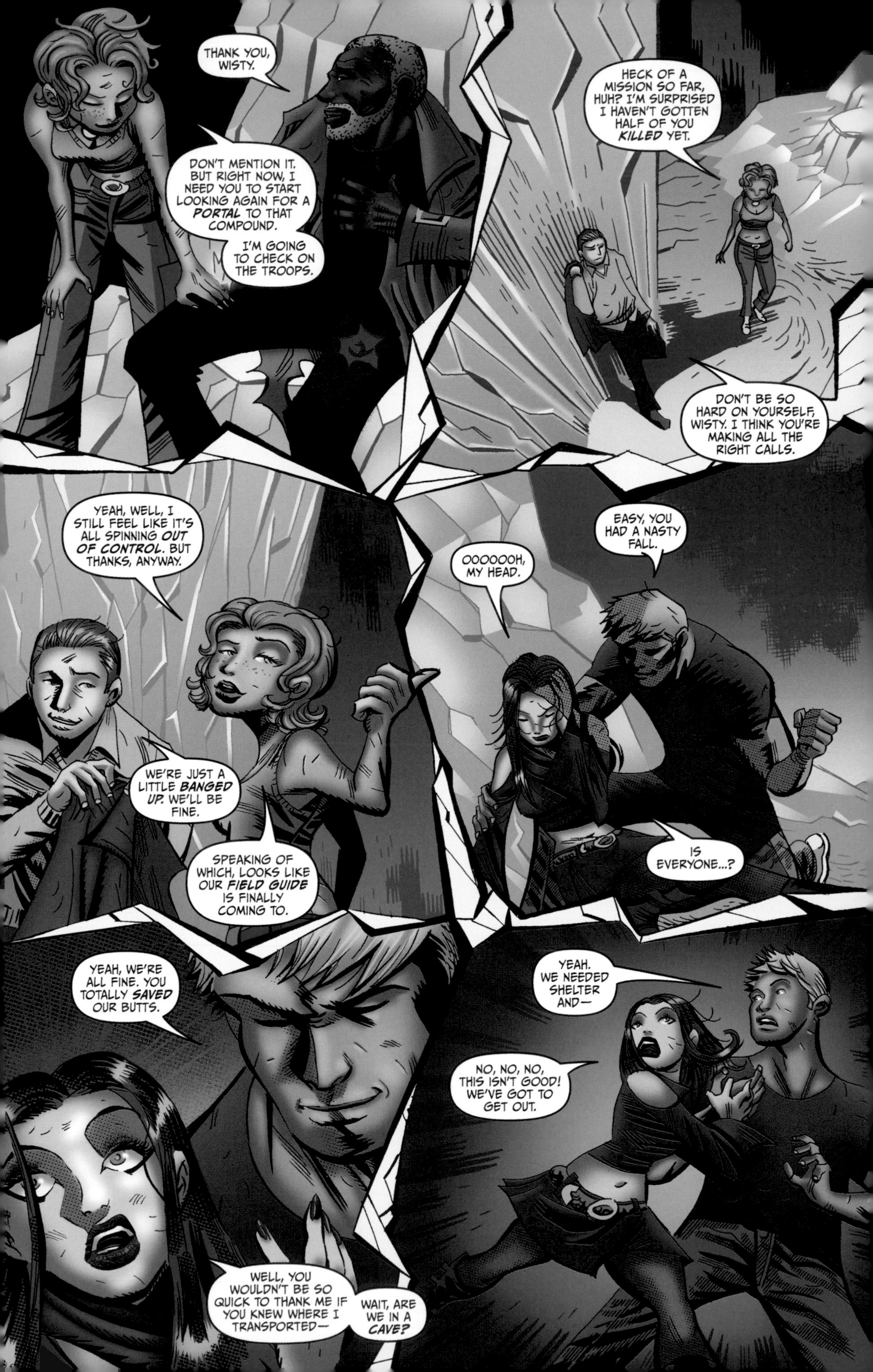
THANK YOU, WISTY.
DON'T MENTION IT. BUT RIGHT NOW, I NEED YOU TO START LOOKING AGAIN FOR A PORTAL TO THAT COMPOUND.
I'M GOING TO CHECK ON THE TROOPS.
HECK OF A MISSION SO FAR, HUH? I'M SURPRISED I HAVEN'T GOTTEN HALF OF YOU KILLED YET.
DON'T BE SO HARD ON YOURSELF, WISTY. I THINK YOU'RE MAKING ALL THE RIGHT CALLS.
YEAH, WELL, I STILL FEEL LIKE IT'S ALL SPINNING OUT OF CONTROL. BUT THANKS, ANYWAY.
WE'RE JUST A LITTLE BANGED UP. WE'LL BE FINE.
SPEAKING OF WHICH, LOOKS LIKE OUR FIELD GUIDE IS FINALLY COMING TO.
OOOOOOH, MY HEAD.
EASY, YOU HAD A NASTY FALL.
IS EVERYONE...?
YEAH, WE'RE ALL FINE. YOU TOTALLY SAVED OUR BUTTS.
WELL, YOU WOULDN'T BE SO QUICK TO THANK ME IF YOU KNEW WHERE I TRANSPORTED—
WAIT, ARE WE IN A CAVE?
YEAH. WE NEEDED SHELTER AND—
NO, NO, NO, THIS ISN'T GOOD! WE'VE GOT TO GET OUT.

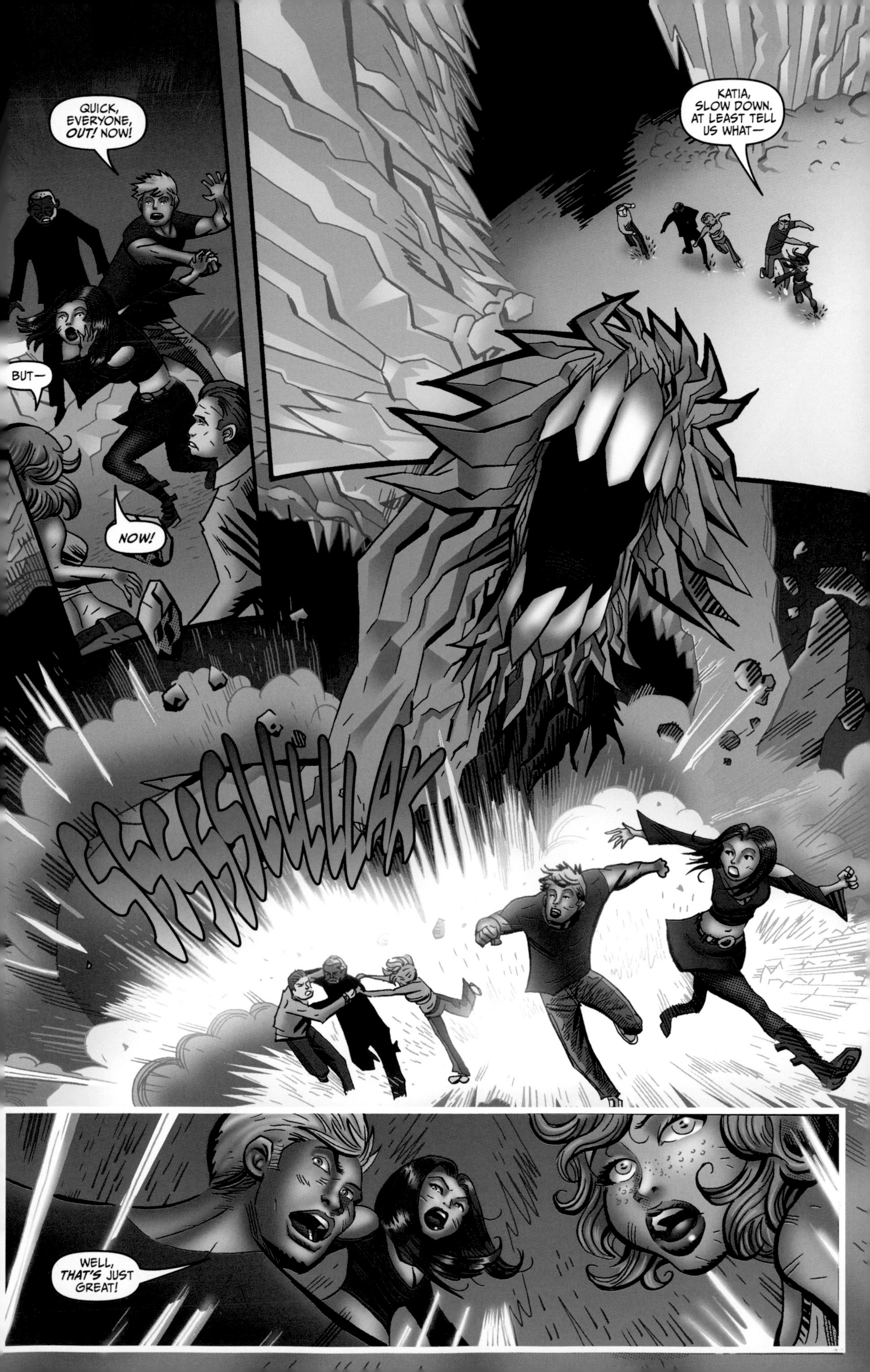
QUICK, EVERYONE, OUT! NOW!
BUT—
NOW!
KATIA, SLOW DOWN. AT LEAST TELL US WHAT—
SKKSHLLLAK
WELL, THAT'S JUST GREAT!

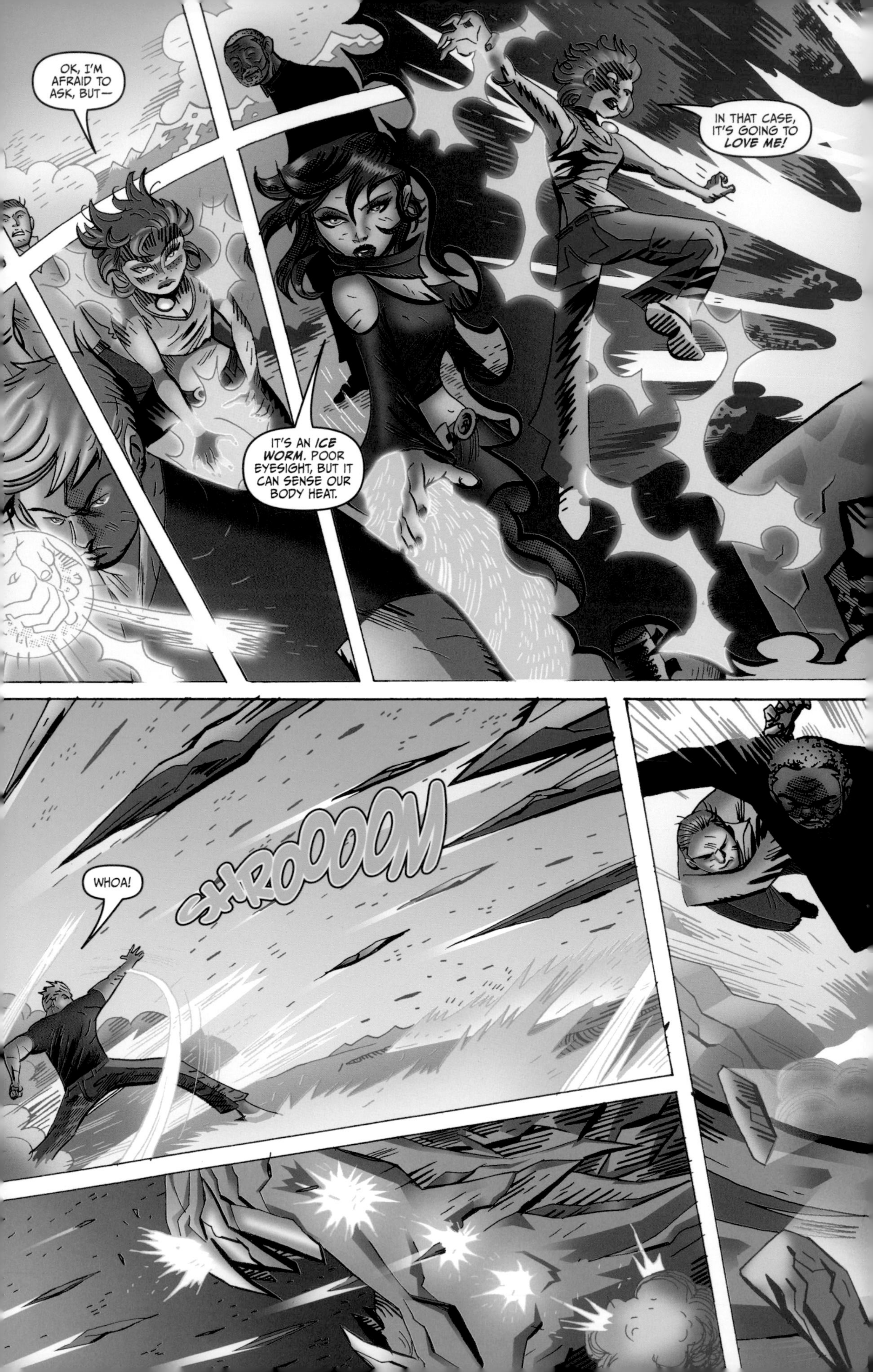
OK, I'M AFRAID TO ASK, BUT—
IT'S AN ICE WORM. POOR EYESIGHT, BUT IT CAN SENSE OUR BODY HEAT.
IN THAT CASE, IT'S GOING TO LOVE ME!
SHROOOOM
WHOA!

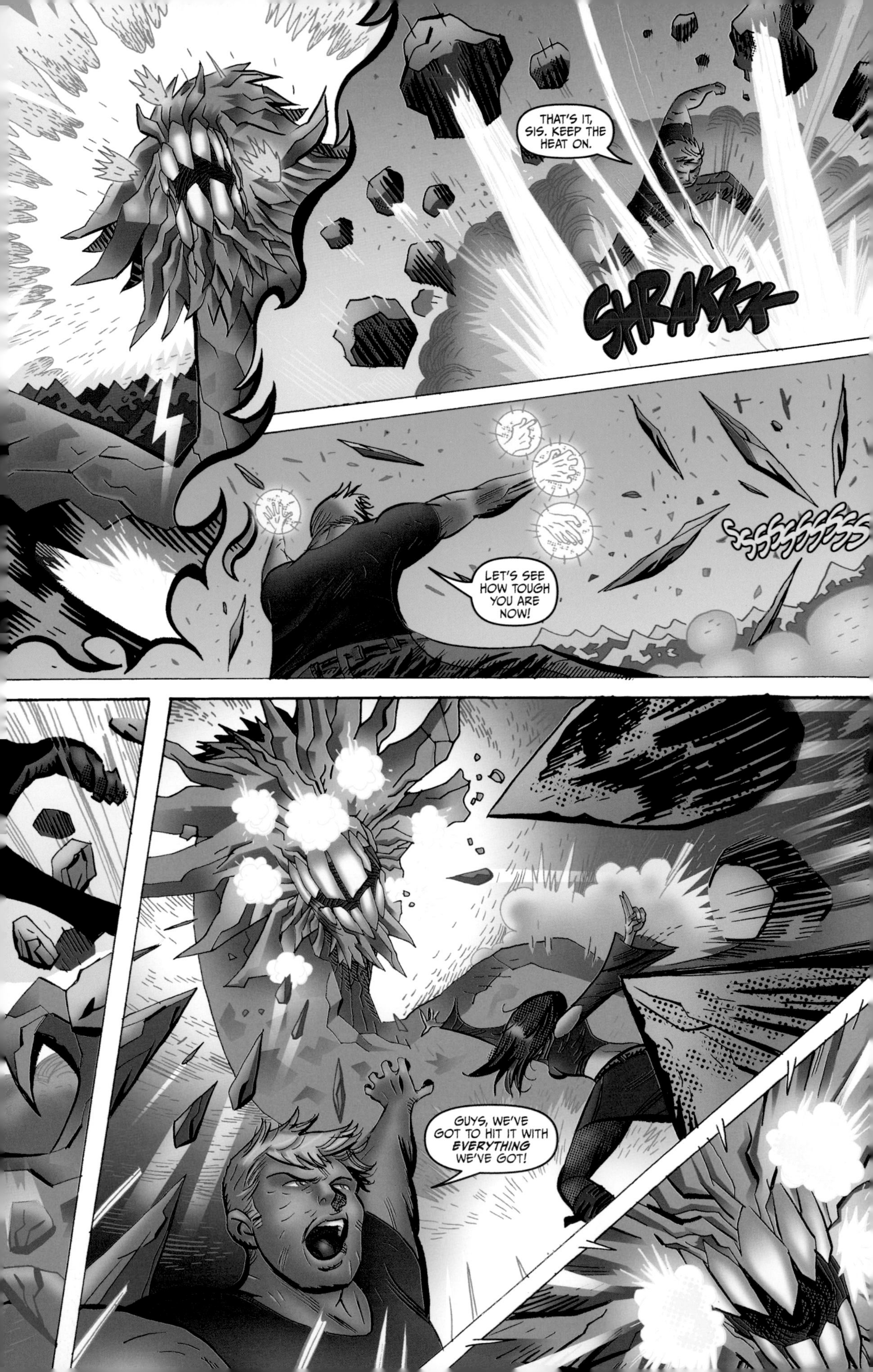
THAT'S IT, SIS. KEEP THE HEAT ON.
SHRAKKK
SSSSSSSSSSSS
LET'S SEE HOW TOUGH YOU ARE NOW!
GUYS, WE'VE GOT TO HIT IT WITH *EVERYTHING* WE'VE GOT!

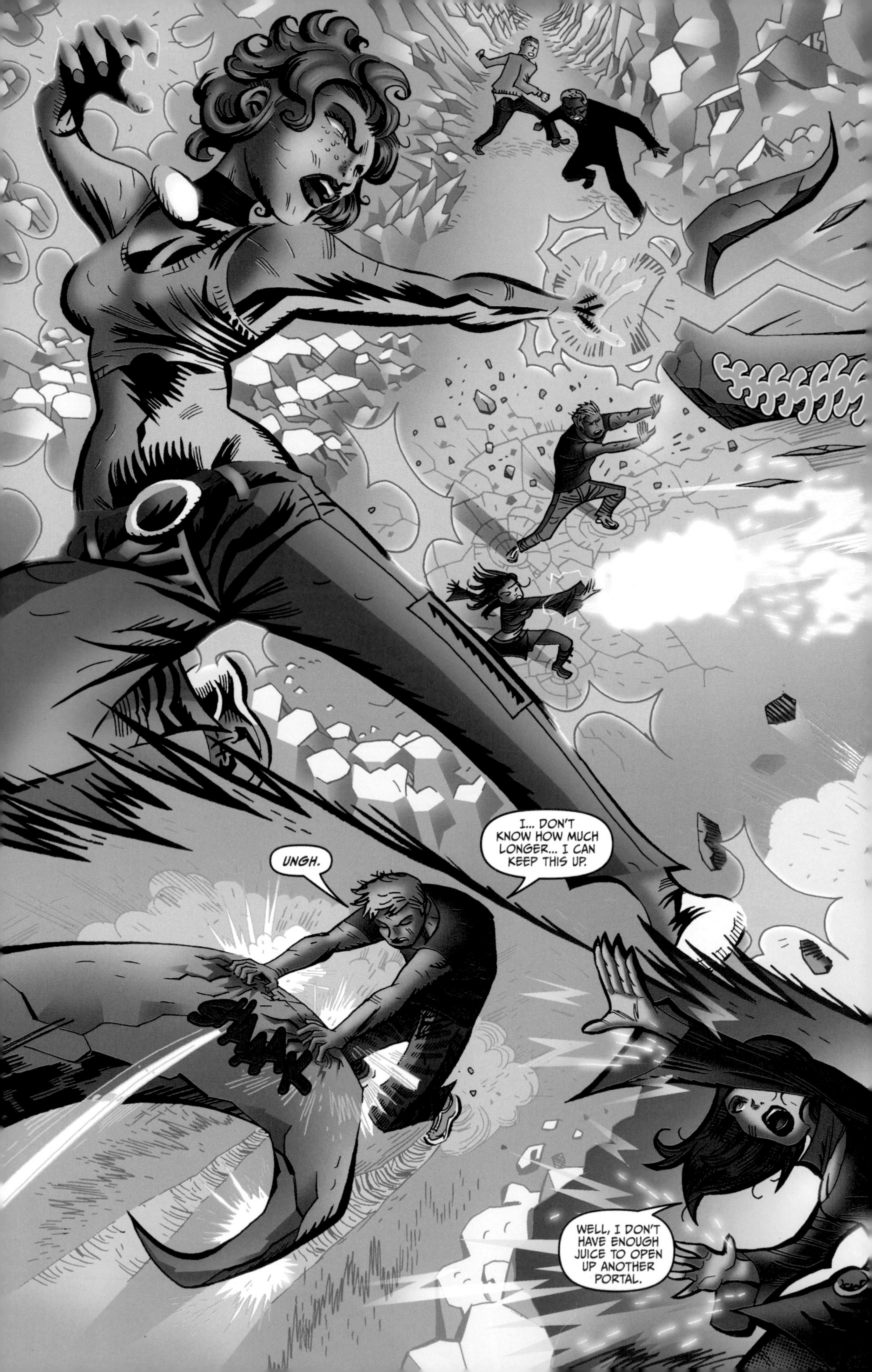
SSSSSSSS
UNGH.
I... DON'T KNOW HOW MUCH LONGER... I CAN KEEP THIS UP.
SHAAK
WELL, I DON'T HAVE ENOUGH JUICE TO OPEN UP ANOTHER PORTAL.

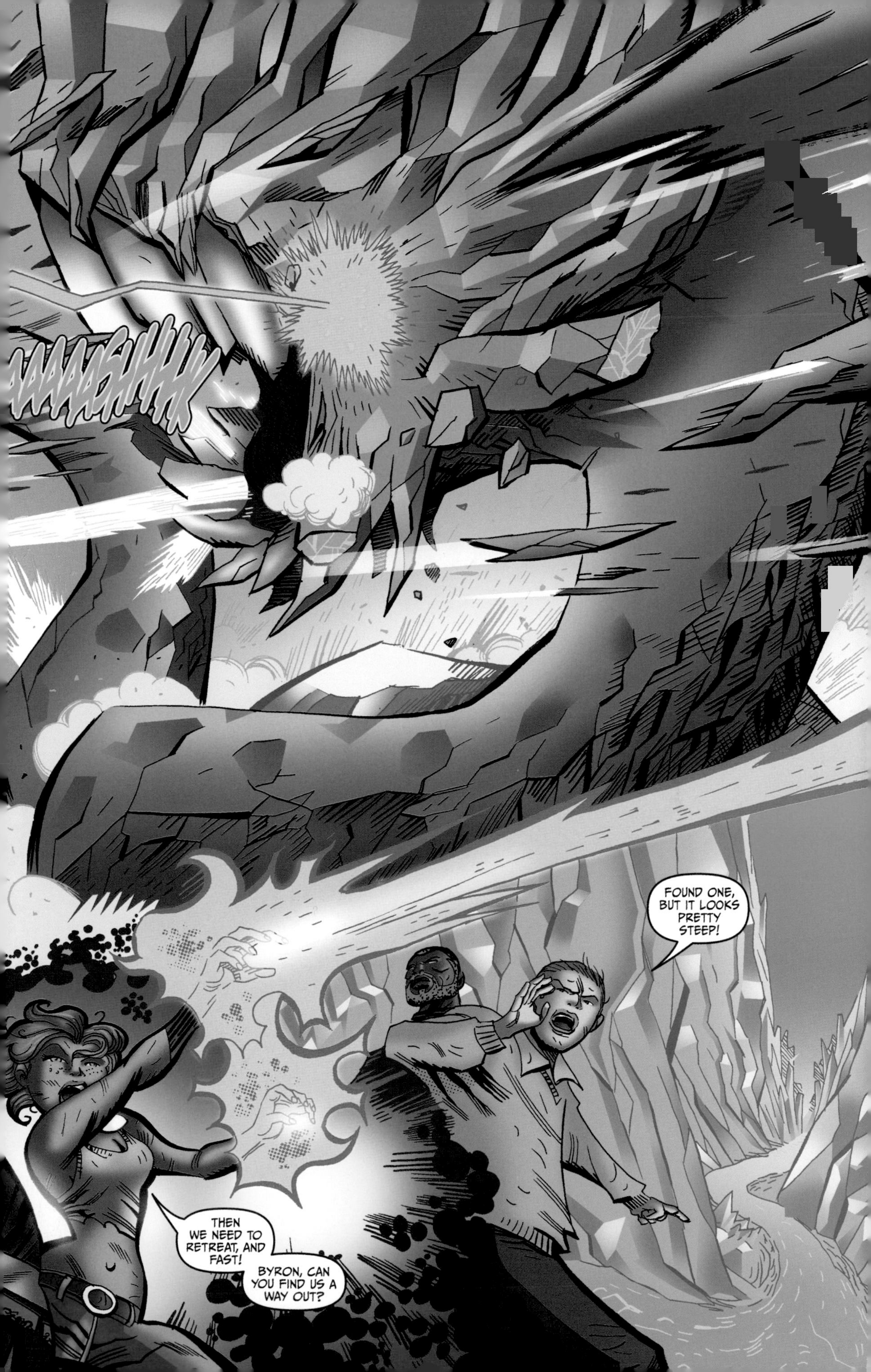
AAAAAGHHHK
FOUND ONE, BUT IT LOOKS PRETTY STEEP!
THEN WE NEED TO RETREAT, AND FAST!
BYRON, CAN YOU FIND US A WAY OUT?

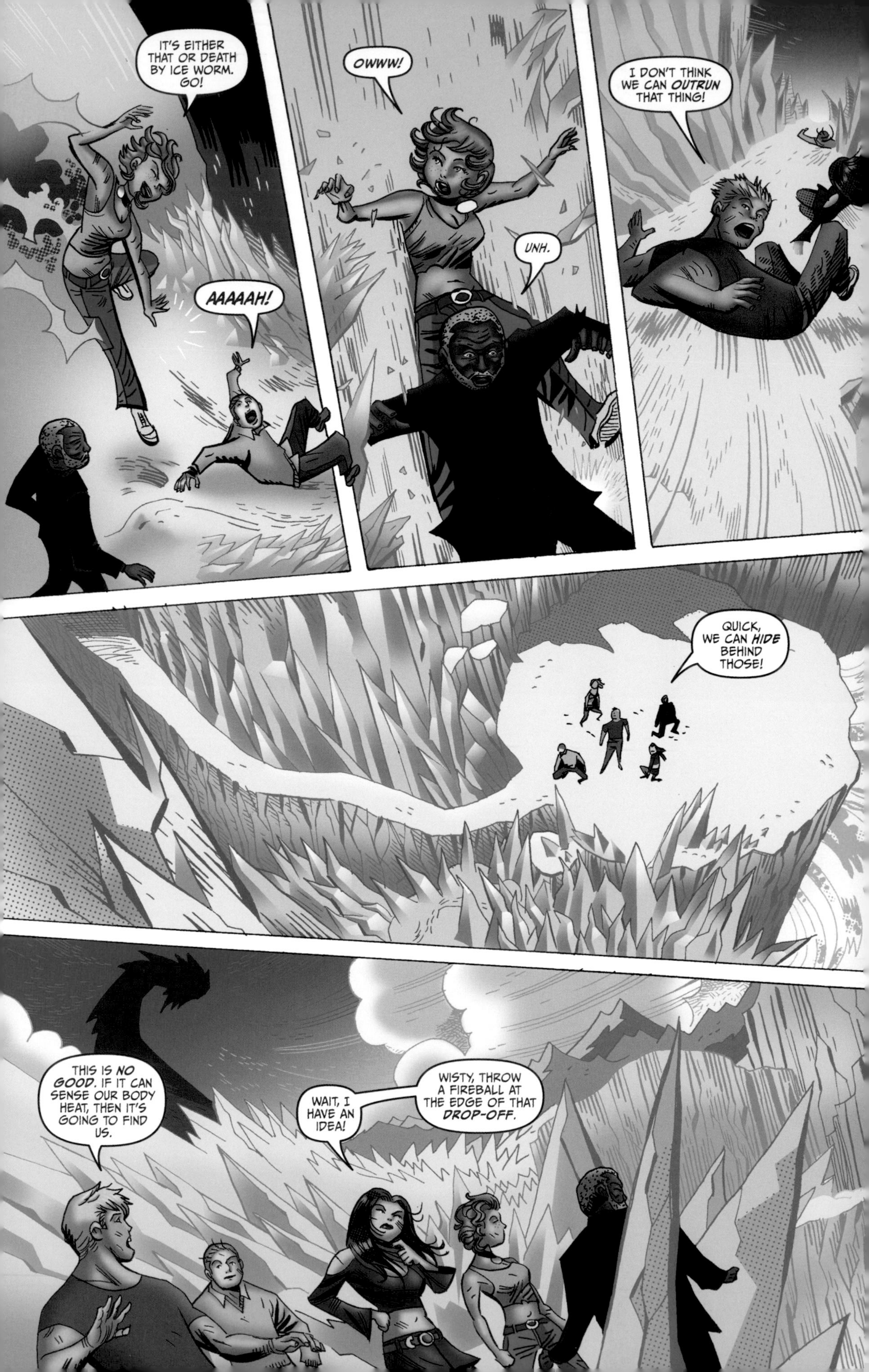
IT'S EITHER THAT OR DEATH BY ICE WORM. GO!
AAAAAH!
OWWW!
UNH.
I DON'T THINK WE CAN OUTRUN THAT THING!
QUICK, WE CAN HIDE BEHIND THOSE!
THIS IS NO GOOD. IF IT CAN SENSE OUR BODY HEAT, THEN IT'S GOING TO FIND US.
WAIT, I HAVE AN IDEA!
WISTY, THROW A FIREBALL AT THE EDGE OF THAT DROP-OFF.

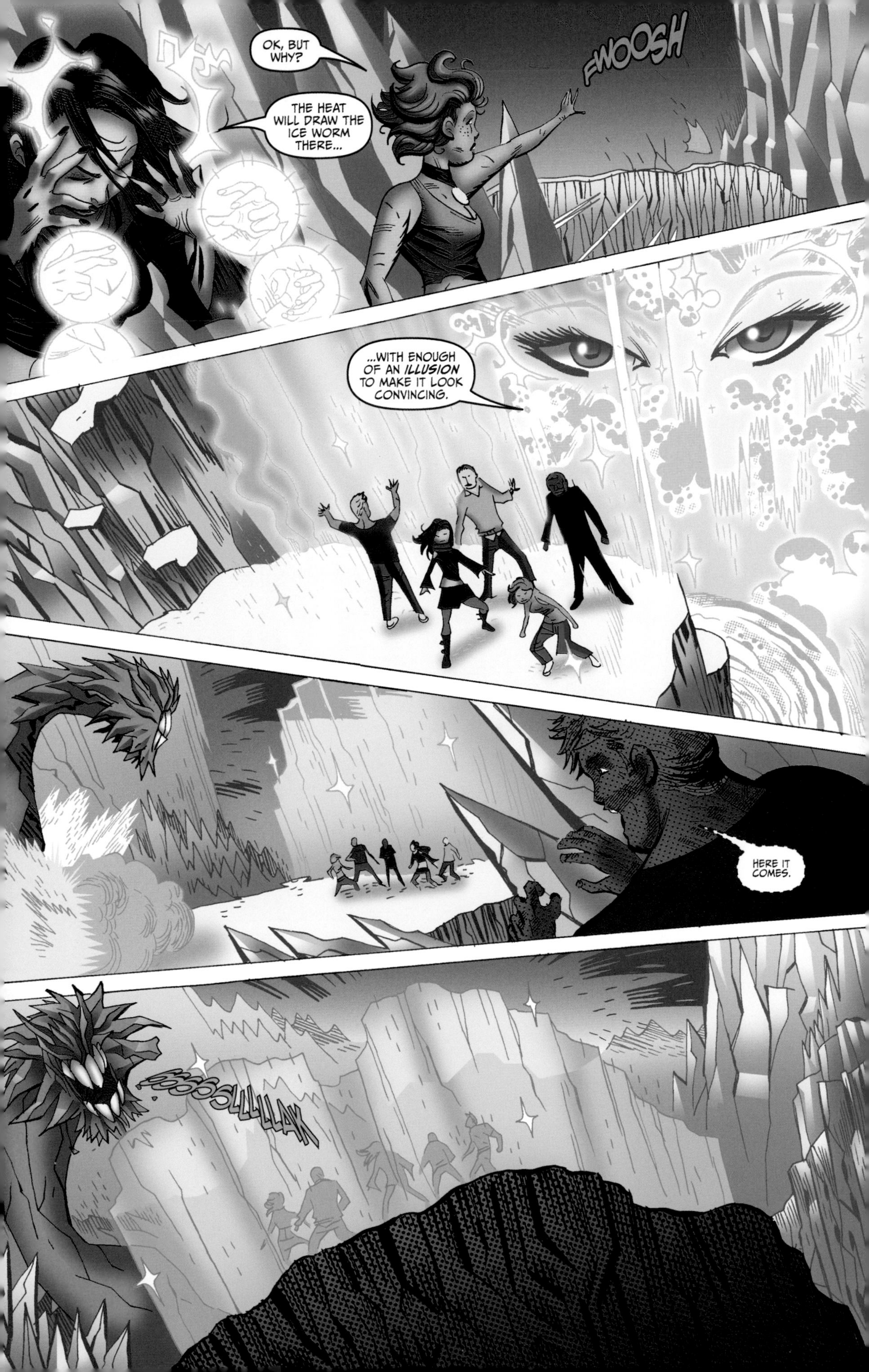
OK, BUT WHY?
FWOOSH
THE HEAT WILL DRAW THE ICE WORM THERE...
...WITH ENOUGH OF AN ILLUSION TO MAKE IT LOOK CONVINCING.
HERE IT COMES.
SSSSSLLLLLLAK

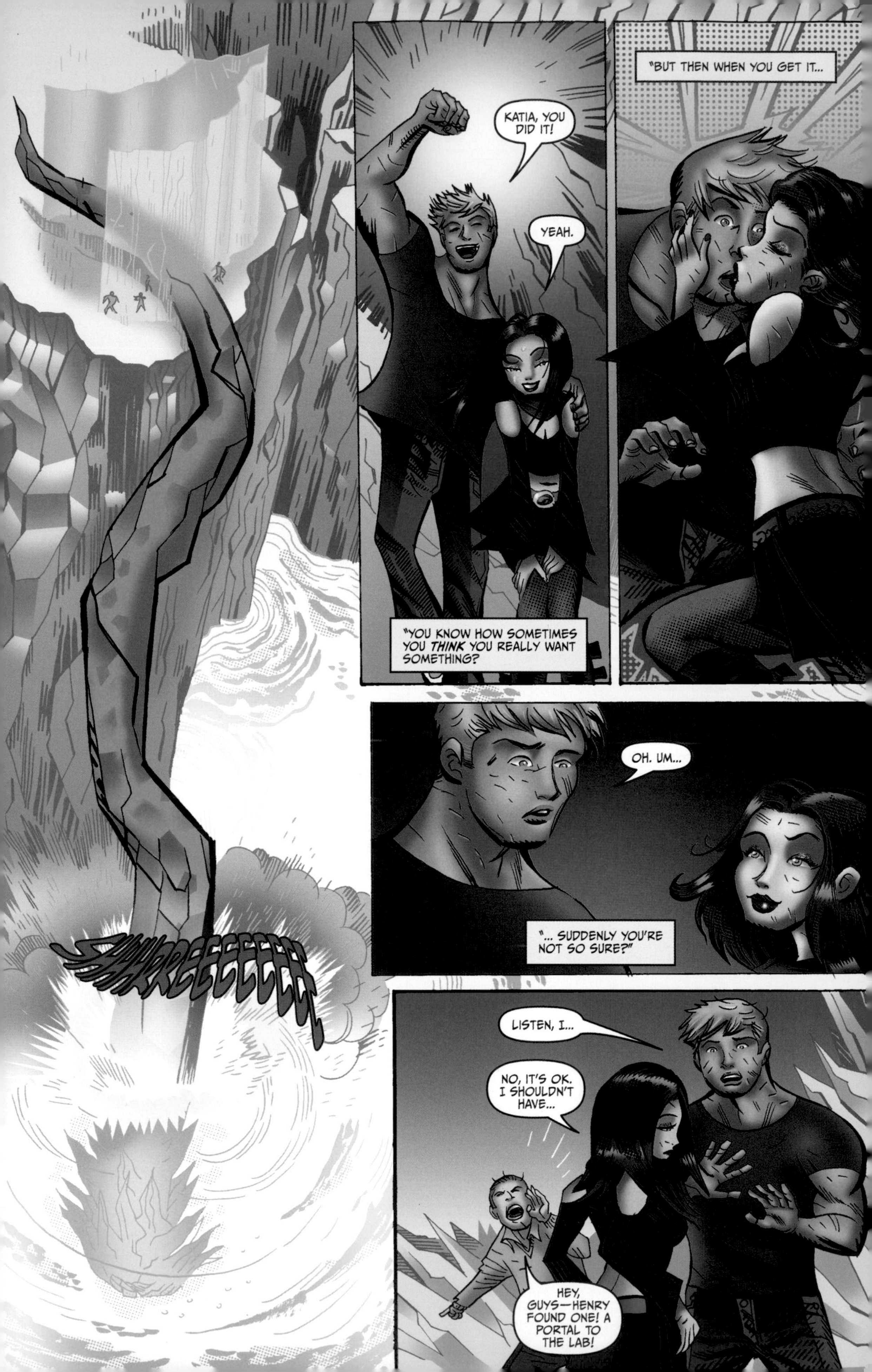
SHHREEEEEEEE!
KATIA, YOU DID IT!
YEAH.
"YOU KNOW HOW SOMETIMES YOU THINK YOU REALLY WANT SOMETHING?
"BUT THEN WHEN YOU GET IT...
OH. UM...
"... SUDDENLY YOU'RE NOT SO SURE?"
LISTEN, I...
NO, IT'S OK. I SHOULDN'T HAVE...
HEY, GUYS—HENRY FOUND ONE! A PORTAL TO THE LAB!

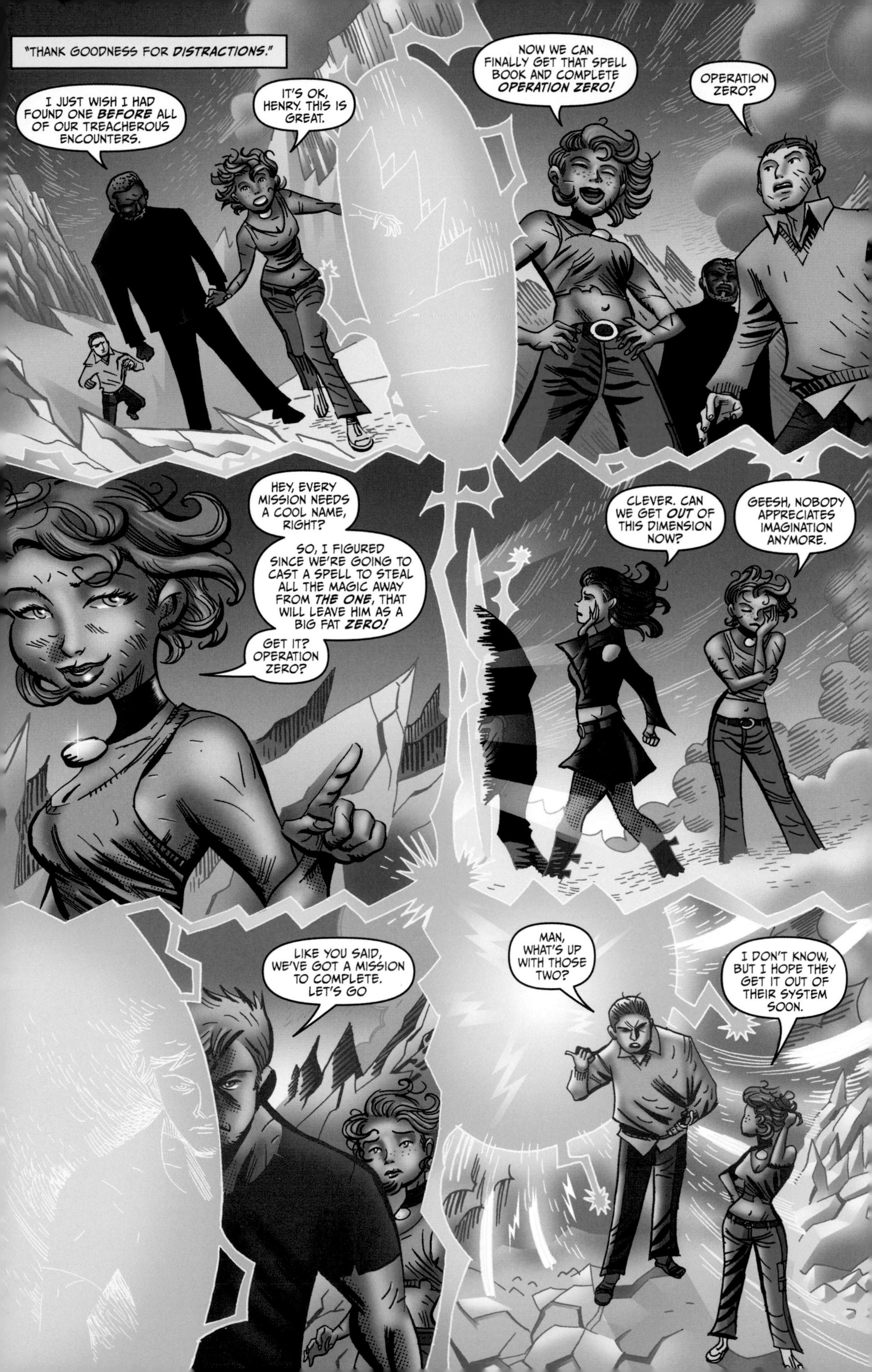
"THANK GOODNESS FOR *DISTRACTIONS*."
I JUST WISH I HAD FOUND ONE *BEFORE* ALL OF OUR TREACHEROUS ENCOUNTERS.
IT'S OK, HENRY. THIS IS GREAT.
NOW WE CAN FINALLY GET THAT SPELL BOOK AND COMPLETE *OPERATION ZERO!*
OPERATION ZERO?
HEY, EVERY MISSION NEEDS A COOL NAME, RIGHT?
SO, I FIGURED SINCE WE'RE GOING TO CAST A SPELL TO STEAL ALL THE MAGIC AWAY FROM *THE ONE*, THAT WILL LEAVE HIM AS A BIG FAT *ZERO!*
GET IT? OPERATION ZERO?
CLEVER. CAN WE GET *OUT* OF THIS DIMENSION NOW?
GEESH, NOBODY APPRECIATES IMAGINATION ANYMORE.
LIKE YOU SAID, WE'VE GOT A MISSION TO COMPLETE. LET'S GO
MAN, WHAT'S UP WITH THOSE TWO?
I DON'T KNOW, BUT I HOPE THEY GET IT OUT OF THEIR SYSTEM SOON.

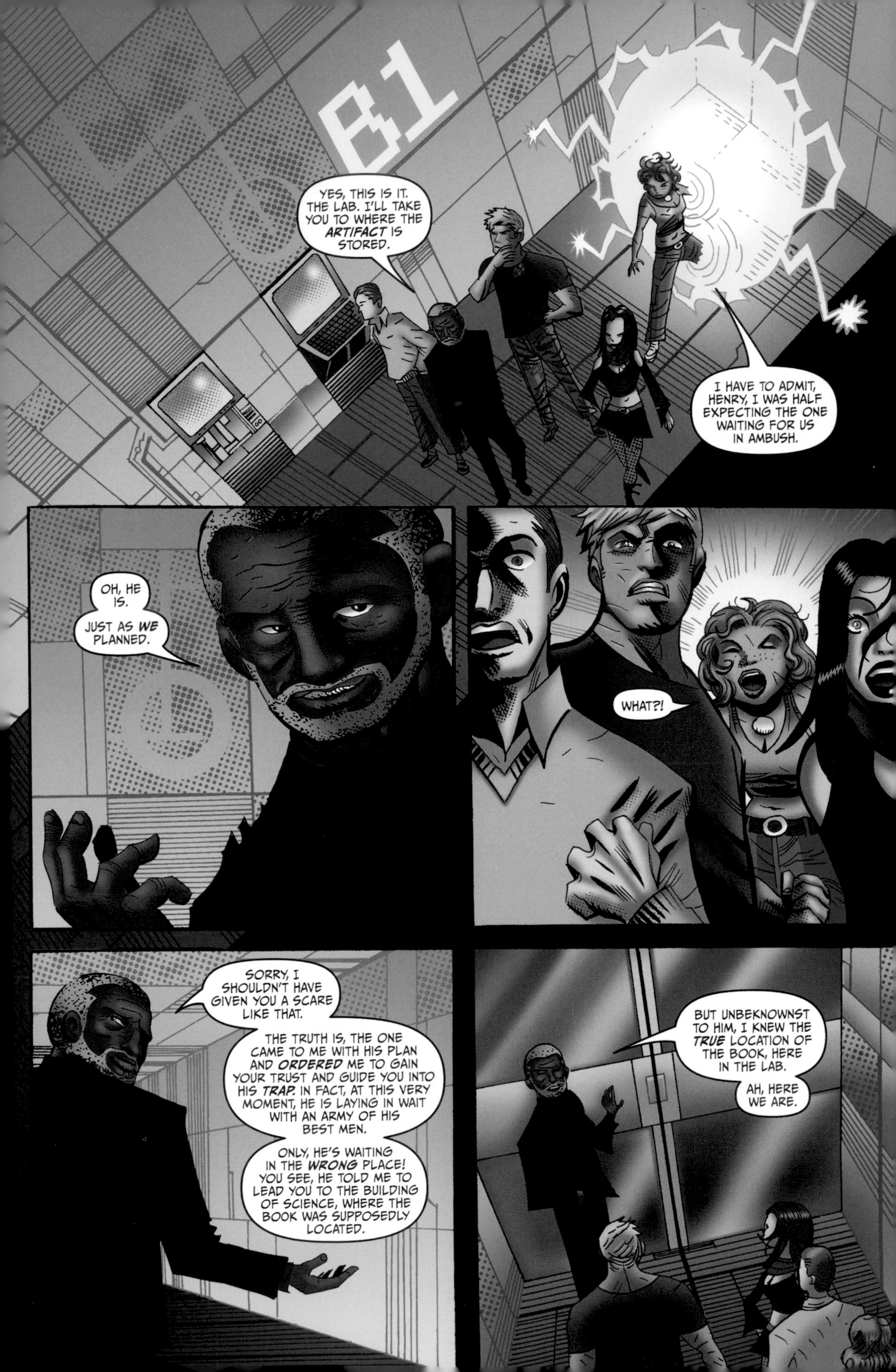
81
YES, THIS IS IT. THE LAB. I'LL TAKE YOU TO WHERE THE ARTIFACT IS STORED.
I HAVE TO ADMIT, HENRY, I WAS HALF EXPECTING THE ONE WAITING FOR US IN AMBUSH.
OH, HE IS.
JUST AS WE PLANNED.
WHAT?!
SORRY, I SHOULDN'T HAVE GIVEN YOU A SCARE LIKE THAT.
THE TRUTH IS, THE ONE CAME TO ME WITH HIS PLAN AND ORDERED ME TO GAIN YOUR TRUST AND GUIDE YOU INTO HIS TRAP. IN FACT, AT THIS VERY MOMENT, HE IS LAYING IN WAIT WITH AN ARMY OF HIS BEST MEN.
ONLY, HE'S WAITING IN THE WRONG PLACE! YOU SEE, HE TOLD ME TO LEAD YOU TO THE BUILDING OF SCIENCE, WHERE THE BOOK WAS SUPPOSEDLY LOCATED.
BUT UNBEKNOWNST TO HIM, I KNEW THE TRUE LOCATION OF THE BOOK, HERE IN THE LAB.
AH, HERE WE ARE.

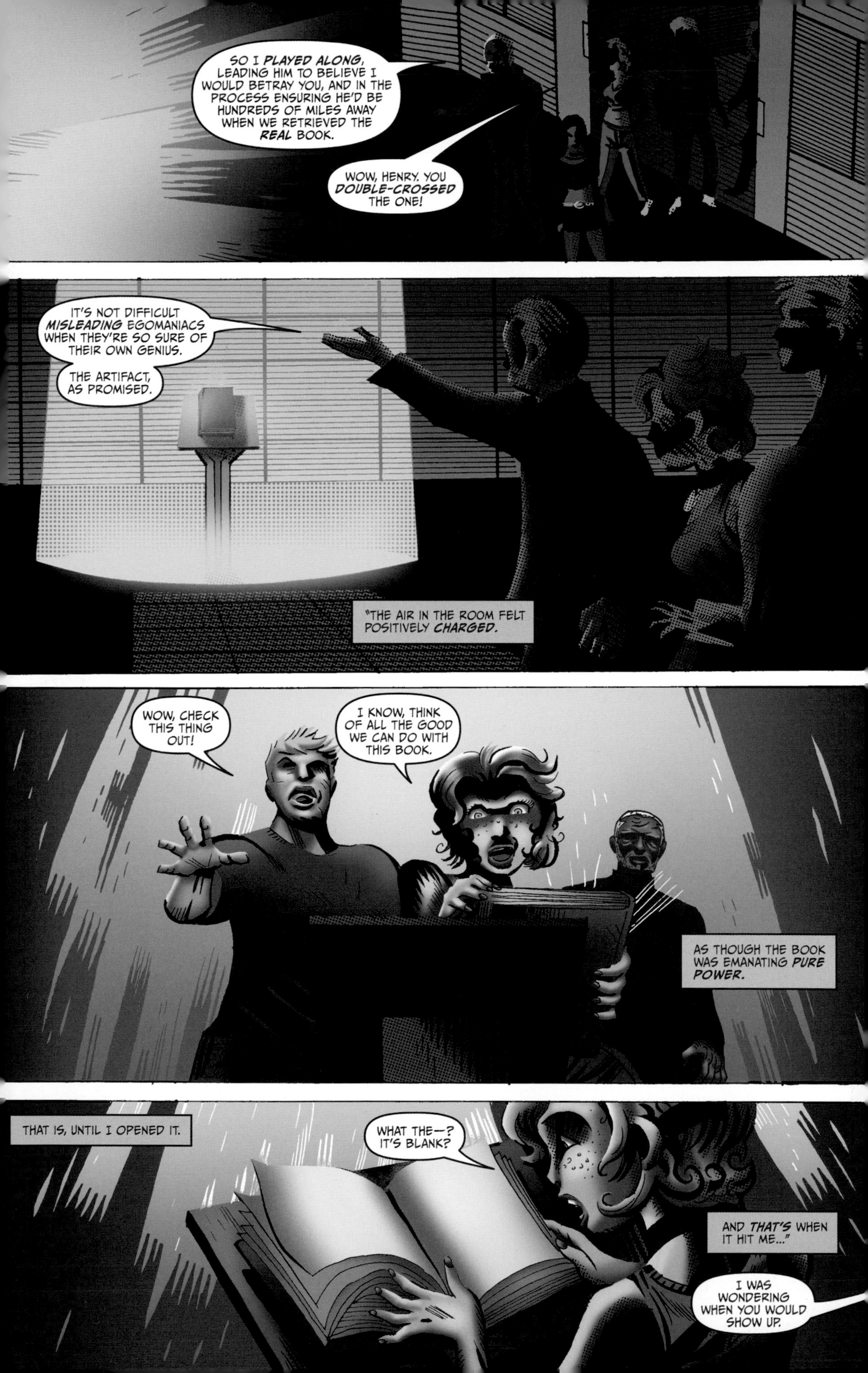
SO I PLAYED ALONG, LEADING HIM TO BELIEVE I WOULD BETRAY YOU, AND IN THE PROCESS ENSURING HE'D BE HUNDREDS OF MILES AWAY WHEN WE RETRIEVED THE REAL BOOK.
WOW, HENRY. YOU DOUBLE-CROSSED THE ONE!
IT'S NOT DIFFICULT MISLEADING EGOMANIACS WHEN THEY'RE SO SURE OF THEIR OWN GENIUS.
THE ARTIFACT, AS PROMISED.
"THE AIR IN THE ROOM FELT POSITIVELY CHARGED.
WOW, CHECK THIS THING OUT!
I KNOW, THINK OF ALL THE GOOD WE CAN DO WITH THIS BOOK.
AS THOUGH THE BOOK WAS EMANATING PURE POWER.
THAT IS, UNTIL I OPENED IT.
WHAT THE—? IT'S BLANK?
AND THAT'S WHEN IT HIT ME..."
I WAS WONDERING WHEN YOU WOULD SHOW UP.

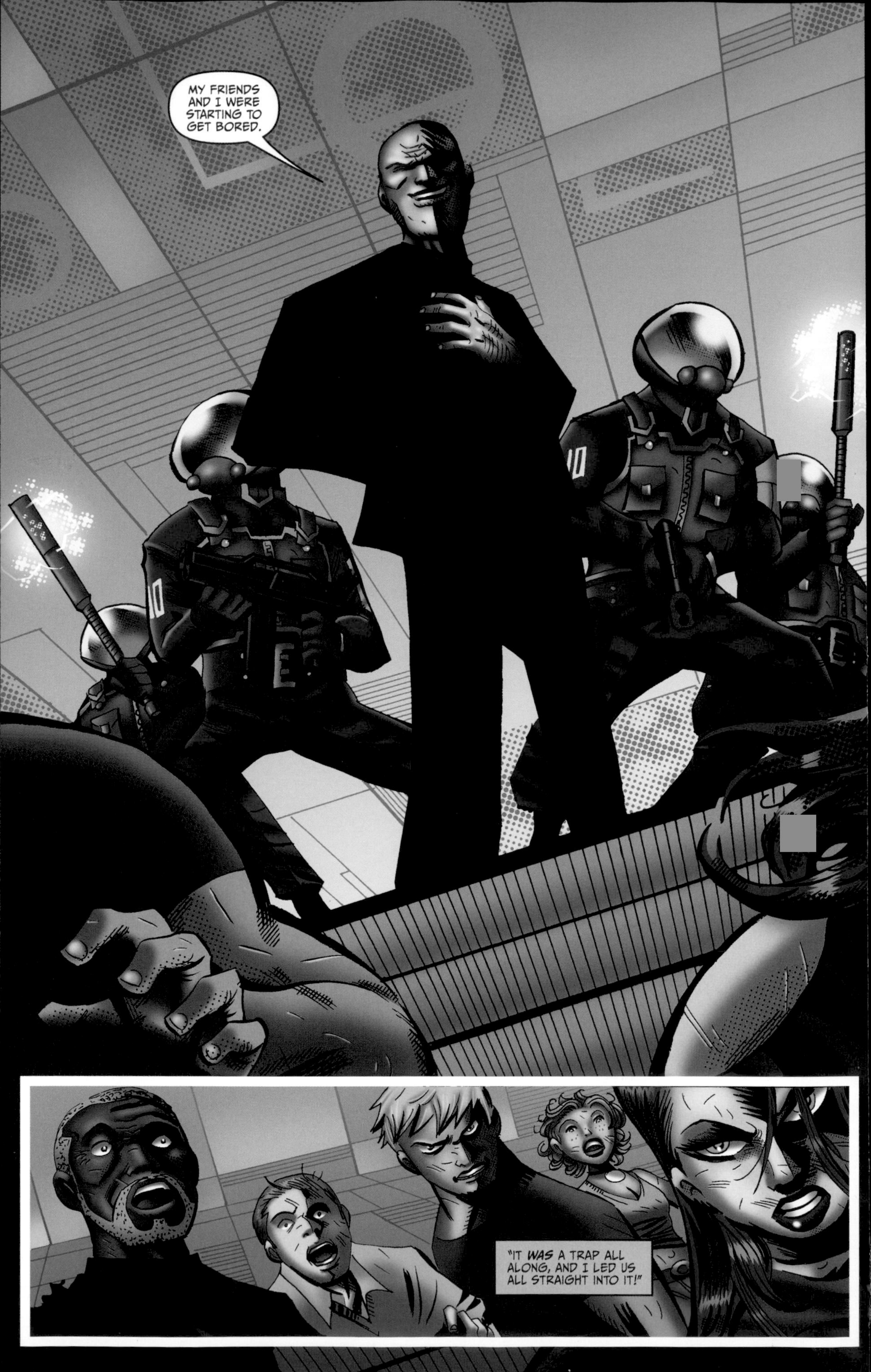
MY FRIENDS AND I WERE STARTING TO GET BORED.
"IT WAS A TRAP ALL ALONG, AND I LED US ALL STRAIGHT INTO IT!"

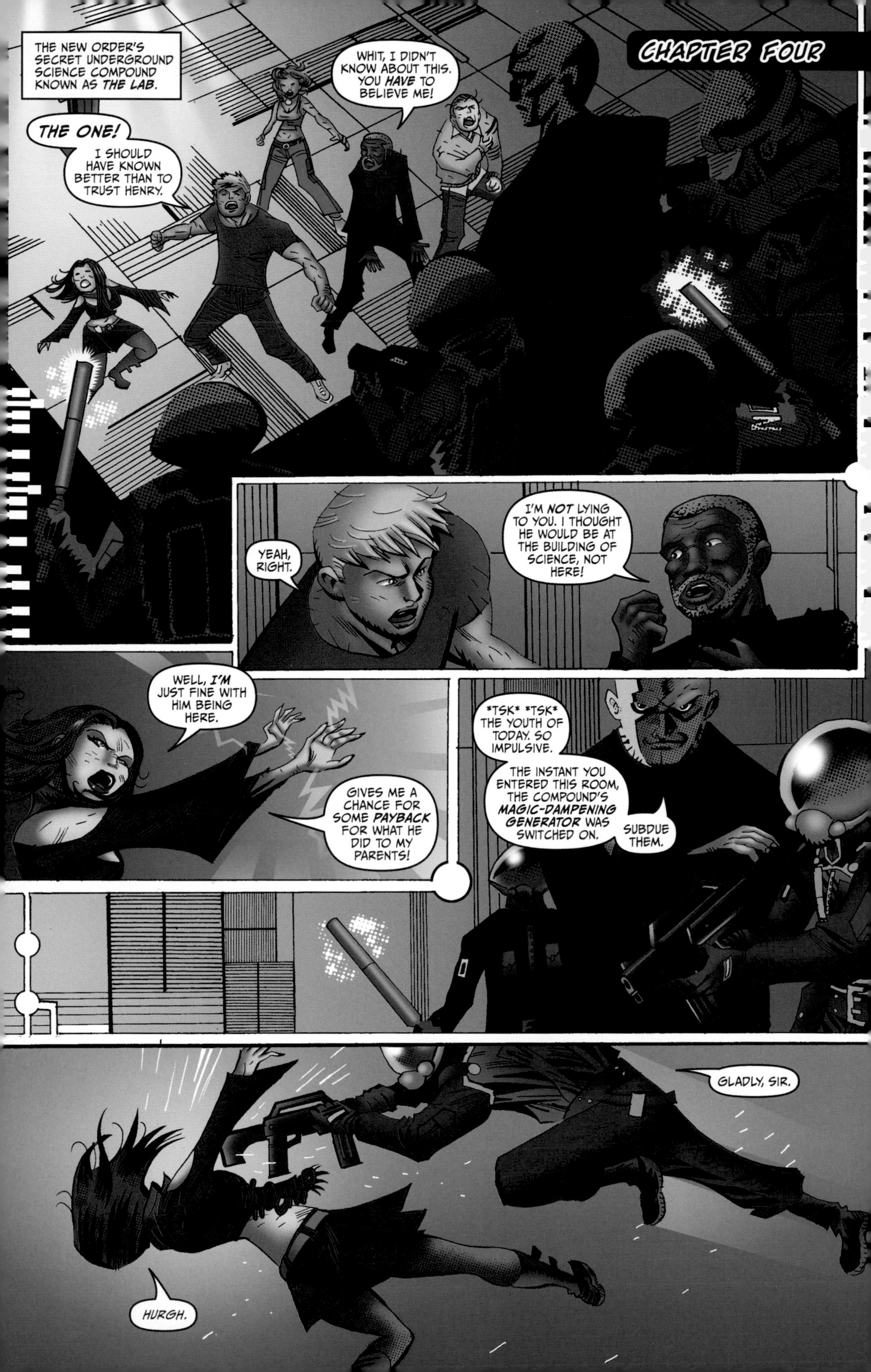
CHAPTER FOUR
THE NEW ORDER'S SECRET UNDERGROUND SCIENCE COMPOUND KNOWN AS THE LAB.
WHIT, I DIDN'T KNOW ABOUT THIS. YOU HAVE TO BELIEVE ME!
THE ONE!
I SHOULD HAVE KNOWN BETTER THAN TO TRUST HENRY.
YEAH, RIGHT.
I'M NOT LYING TO YOU. I THOUGHT HE WOULD BE AT THE BUILDING OF SCIENCE, NOT HERE!
WELL, I'M JUST FINE WITH HIM BEING HERE.
GIVES ME A CHANCE FOR SOME PAYBACK FOR WHAT HE DID TO MY PARENTS!
TSK *TSK* THE YOUTH OF TODAY. SO IMPULSIVE.
THE INSTANT YOU ENTERED THIS ROOM, THE COMPOUND'S MAGIC-DAMPENING GENERATOR WAS SWITCHED ON.
SUBDUE THEM.
GLADLY, SIR.
HURGH.

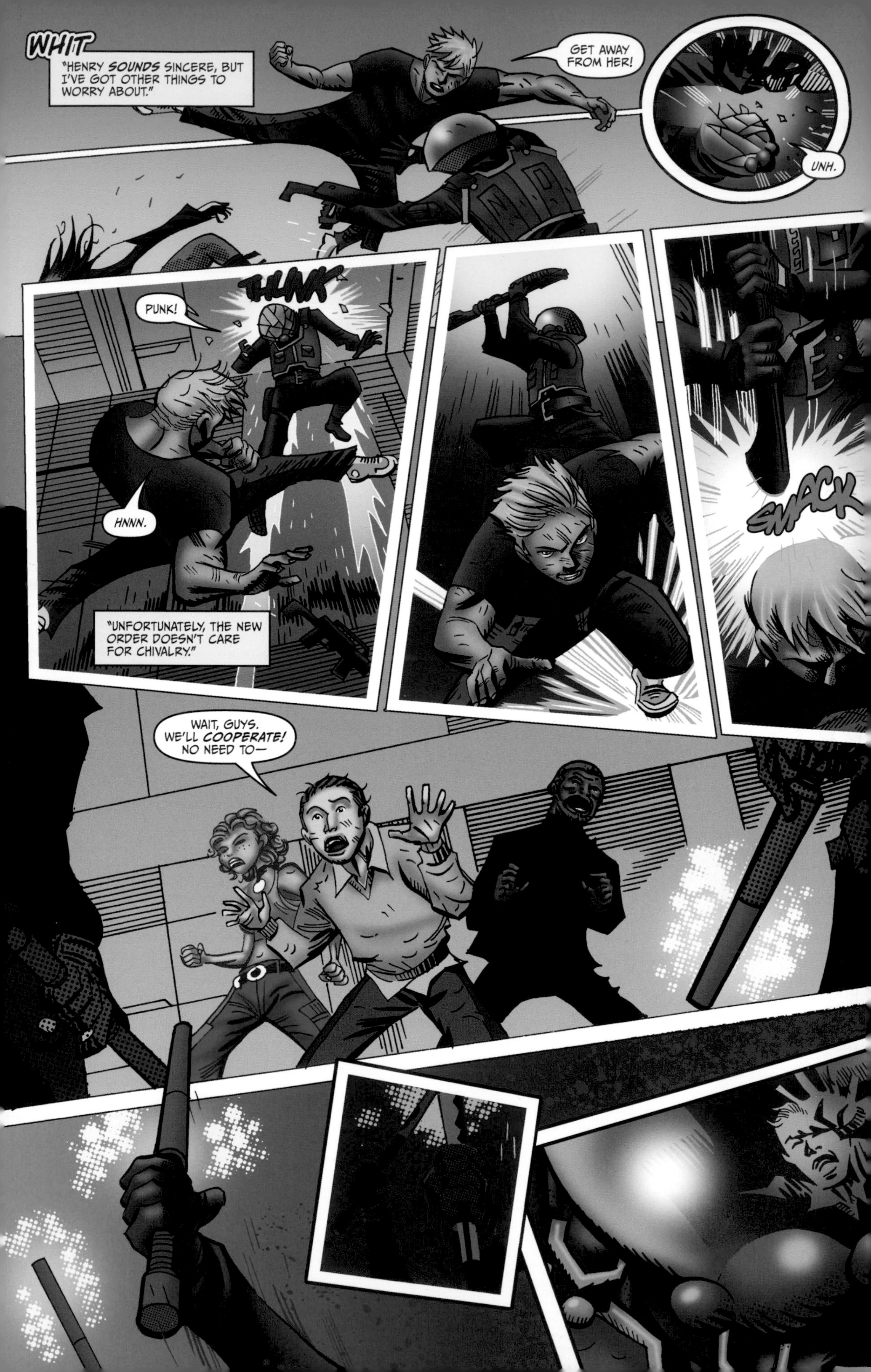
WHIT
"HENRY SOUNDS SINCERE, BUT I'VE GOT OTHER THINGS TO WORRY ABOUT."
GET AWAY FROM HER!
UNH.
THUNK
PUNK!
HNNN.
"UNFORTUNATELY, THE NEW ORDER DOESN'T CARE FOR CHIVALRY."
SMACK
WAIT, GUYS. WE'LL COOPERATE! NO NEED TO—

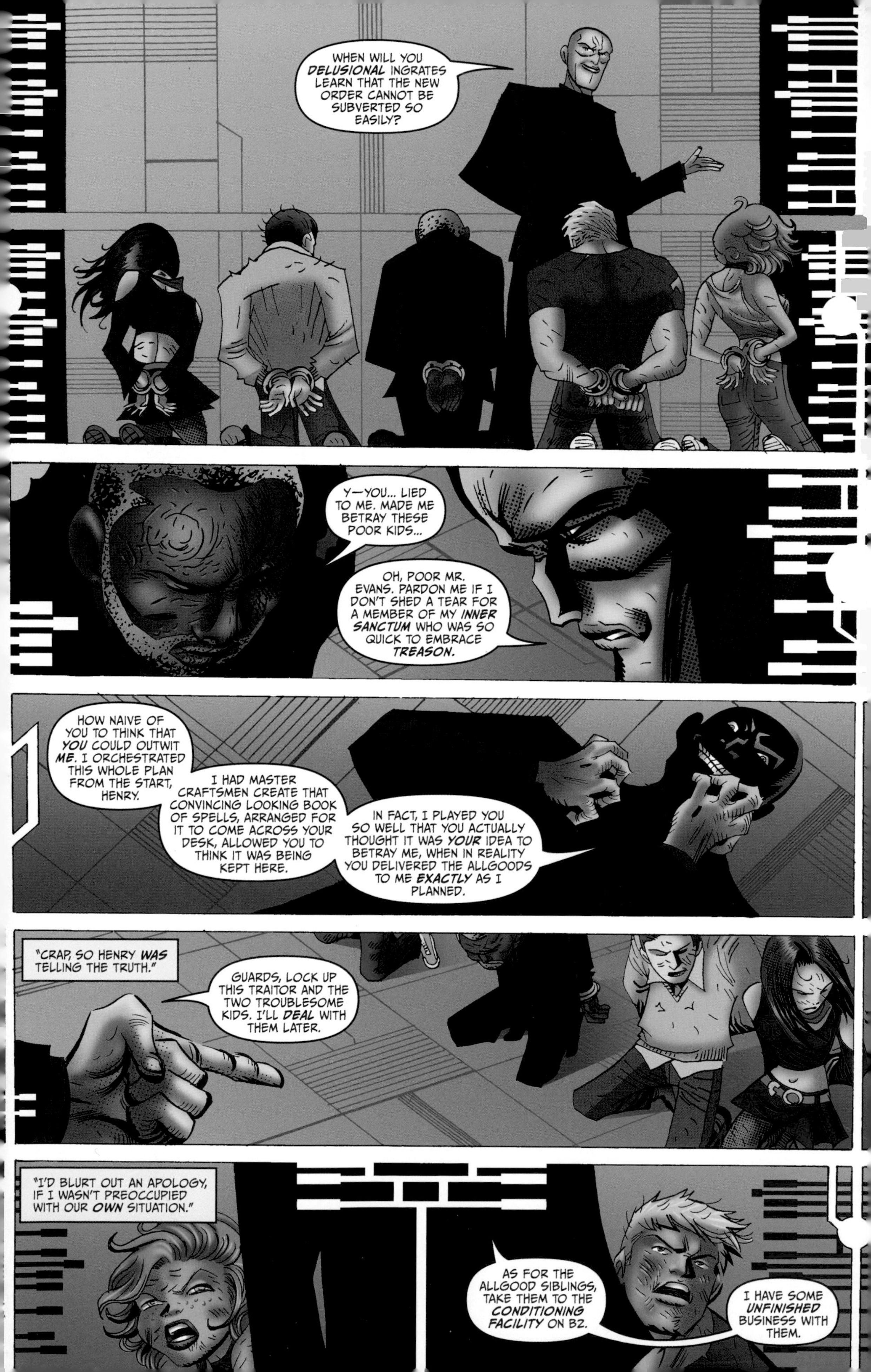
WHEN WILL YOU DELUSIONAL INGRATES LEARN THAT THE NEW ORDER CANNOT BE SUBVERTED SO EASILY?
Y—YOU... LIED TO ME. MADE ME BETRAY THESE POOR KIDS...
OH, POOR MR. EVANS. PARDON ME IF I DON'T SHED A TEAR FOR A MEMBER OF MY INNER SANCTUM WHO WAS SO QUICK TO EMBRACE TREASON.
HOW NAIVE OF YOU TO THINK THAT YOU COULD OUTWIT ME. I ORCHESTRATED THIS WHOLE PLAN FROM THE START, HENRY.
I HAD MASTER CRAFTSMEN CREATE THAT CONVINCING LOOKING BOOK OF SPELLS, ARRANGED FOR IT TO COME ACROSS YOUR DESK, ALLOWED YOU TO THINK IT WAS BEING KEPT HERE.
IN FACT, I PLAYED YOU SO WELL THAT YOU ACTUALLY THOUGHT IT WAS YOUR IDEA TO BETRAY ME, WHEN IN REALITY YOU DELIVERED THE ALLGOODS TO ME EXACTLY AS I PLANNED.
"CRAP, SO HENRY WAS TELLING THE TRUTH."
GUARDS, LOCK UP THIS TRAITOR AND THE TWO TROUBLESOME KIDS. I'LL DEAL WITH THEM LATER.
"I'D BLURT OUT AN APOLOGY, IF I WASN'T PREOCCUPIED WITH OUR OWN SITUATION."
AS FOR THE ALLGOOD SIBLINGS, TAKE THEM TO THE CONDITIONING FACILITY ON B2.
I HAVE SOME UNFINISHED BUSINESS WITH THEM.

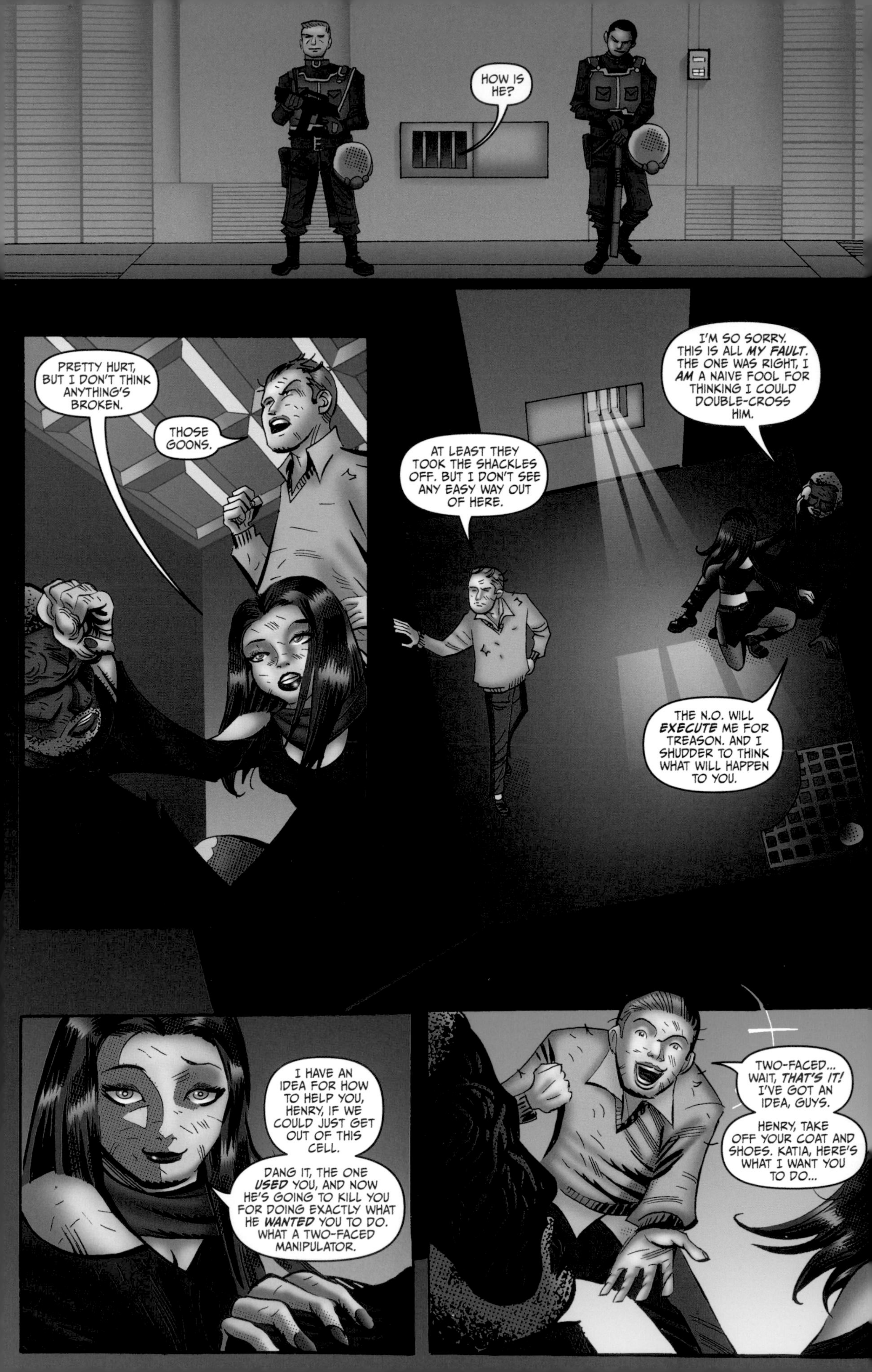
HOW IS HE?
PRETTY HURT, BUT I DON'T THINK ANYTHING'S BROKEN.
THOSE GOONS.
AT LEAST THEY TOOK THE SHACKLES OFF. BUT I DON'T SEE ANY EASY WAY OUT OF HERE.
I'M SO SORRY. THIS IS ALL *MY FAULT*. THE ONE WAS RIGHT, I *AM* A NAIVE FOOL FOR THINKING I COULD DOUBLE-CROSS HIM.
THE N.O. WILL *EXECUTE* ME FOR TREASON. AND I SHUDDER TO THINK WHAT WILL HAPPEN TO YOU.
I HAVE AN IDEA FOR HOW TO HELP YOU, HENRY, IF WE COULD JUST GET OUT OF THIS CELL.
DANG IT, THE ONE *USED* YOU, AND NOW HE'S GOING TO KILL YOU FOR DOING EXACTLY WHAT HE *WANTED* YOU TO DO. WHAT A TWO-FACED MANIPULATOR.
TWO-FACED... WAIT, *THAT'S IT!* I'VE GOT AN IDEA, GUYS.
HENRY, TAKE OFF YOUR COAT AND SHOES. KATIA, HERE'S WHAT I WANT YOU TO DO...

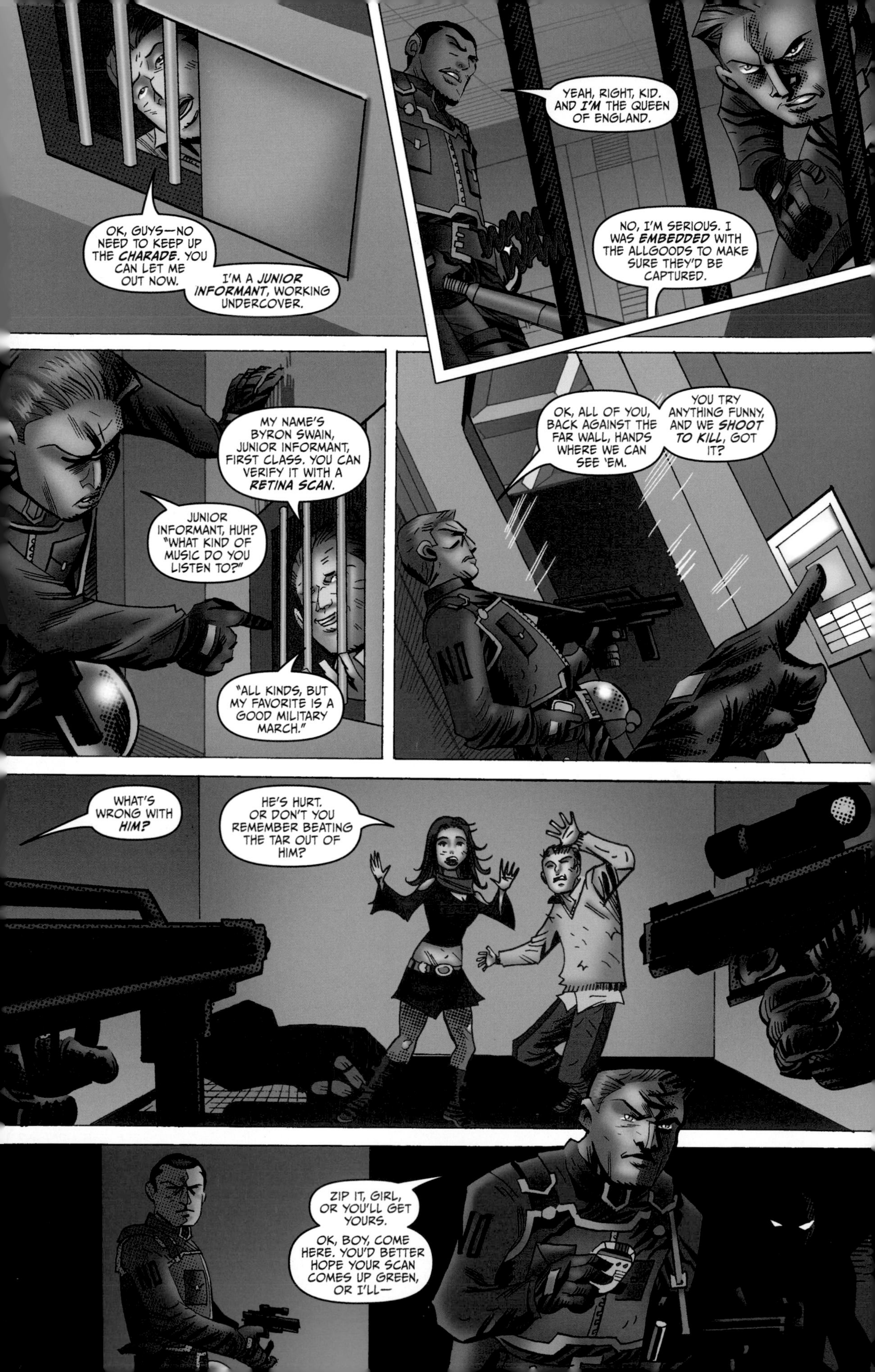
OK, GUYS—NO NEED TO KEEP UP THE *CHARADE*. YOU CAN LET ME OUT NOW.
I'M A *JUNIOR INFORMANT*, WORKING UNDERCOVER.
YEAH, RIGHT, KID. AND *I'M* THE QUEEN OF ENGLAND.
NO, I'M SERIOUS. I WAS *EMBEDDED* WITH THE ALLGOODS TO MAKE SURE THEY'D BE CAPTURED.
MY NAME'S BYRON SWAIN, JUNIOR INFORMANT, FIRST CLASS. YOU CAN VERIFY IT WITH A *RETINA SCAN*.
JUNIOR INFORMANT, HUH? "WHAT KIND OF MUSIC DO YOU LISTEN TO?"
"ALL KINDS, BUT MY FAVORITE IS A GOOD MILITARY MARCH."
OK, ALL OF YOU, BACK AGAINST THE FAR WALL, HANDS WHERE WE CAN SEE 'EM.
YOU TRY ANYTHING FUNNY, AND WE *SHOOT TO KILL*, GOT IT?
WHAT'S WRONG WITH *HIM?*
HE'S HURT. OR DON'T YOU REMEMBER BEATING THE TAR OUT OF HIM?
ZIP IT, GIRL, OR YOU'LL GET YOURS.
OK, BOY, COME HERE. YOU'D BETTER HOPE YOUR SCAN COMES UP GREEN, OR I'LL—

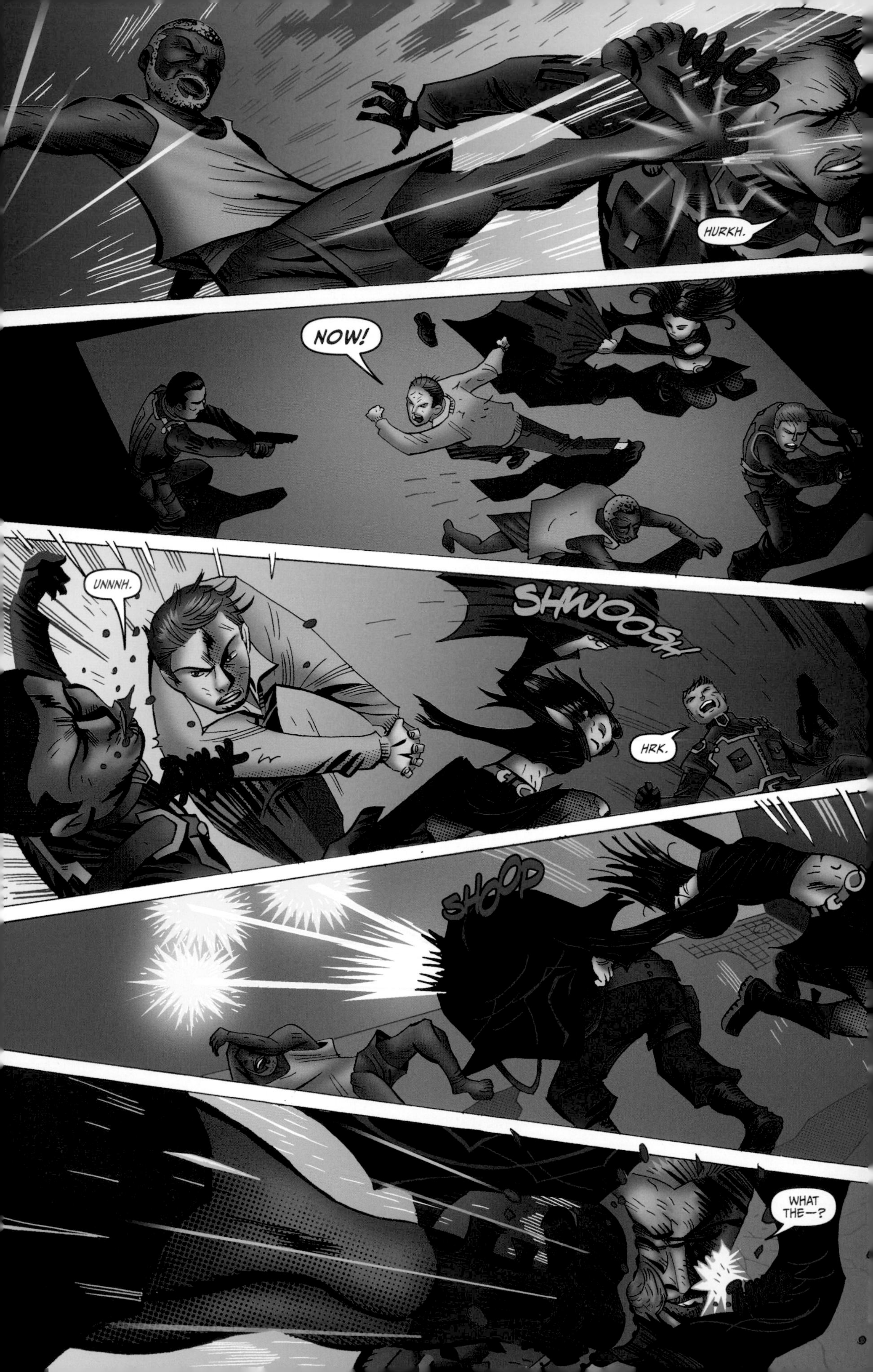
WHSD
HURKH.
NOW!
UNNNH.
SHWOOSH
HRK.
SHOOP
WHAT THE—?

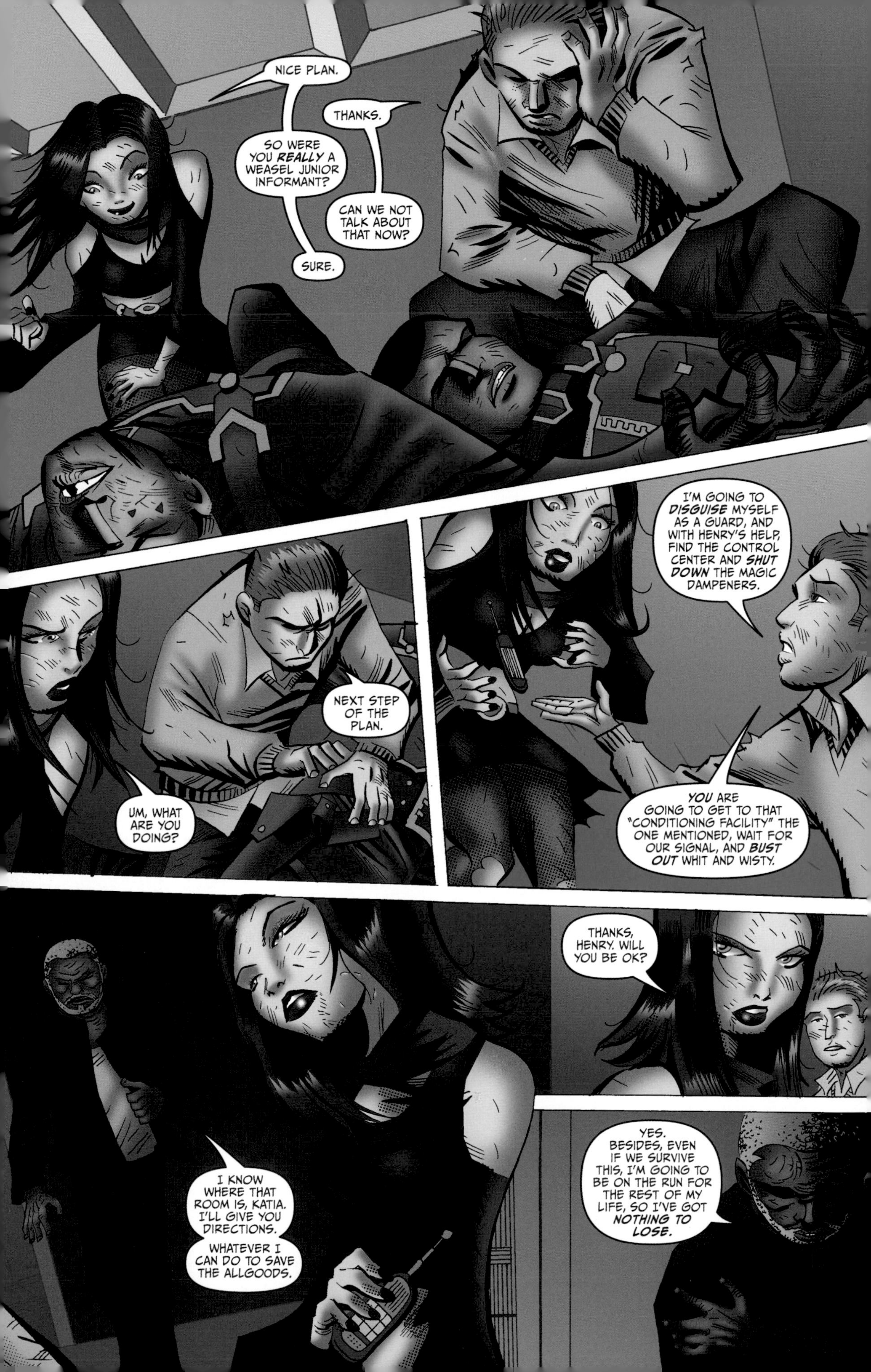
NICE PLAN.
THANKS.
SO WERE YOU REALLY A WEASEL JUNIOR INFORMANT?
CAN WE NOT TALK ABOUT THAT NOW?
SURE.
UM, WHAT ARE YOU DOING?
NEXT STEP OF THE PLAN.
I'M GOING TO DISGUISE MYSELF AS A GUARD, AND WITH HENRY'S HELP, FIND THE CONTROL CENTER AND SHUT DOWN THE MAGIC DAMPENERS.
YOU ARE GOING TO GET TO THAT "CONDITIONING FACILITY" THE ONE MENTIONED, WAIT FOR OUR SIGNAL, AND BUST OUT WHIT AND WISTY.
I KNOW WHERE THAT ROOM IS, KATIA. I'LL GIVE YOU DIRECTIONS.
WHATEVER I CAN DO TO SAVE THE ALLGOODS.
THANKS, HENRY. WILL YOU BE OK?
YES. BESIDES, EVEN IF WE SURVIVE THIS, I'M GOING TO BE ON THE RUN FOR THE REST OF MY LIFE, SO I'VE GOT NOTHING TO LOSE.

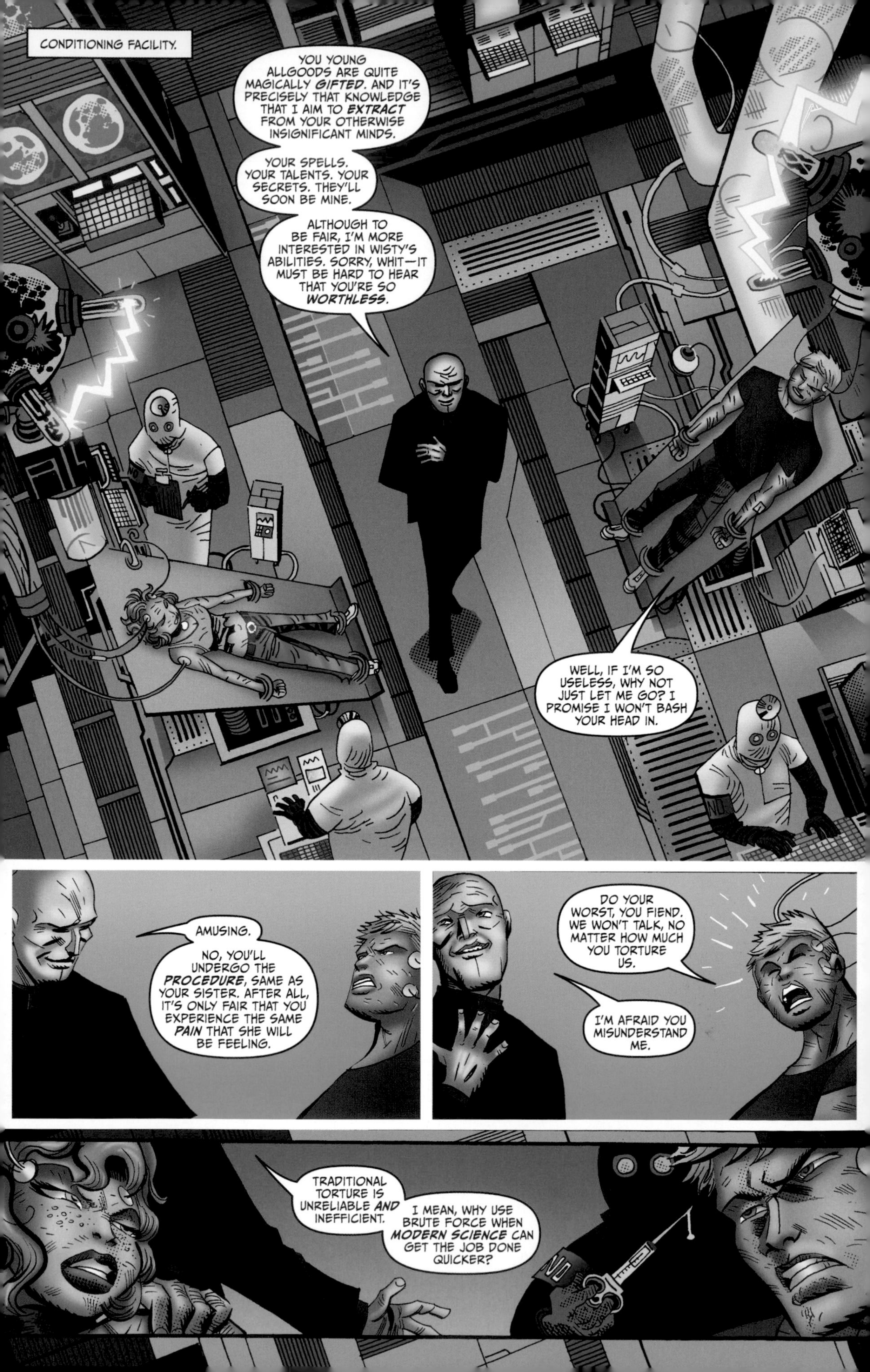
CONDITIONING FACILITY.
YOU YOUNG ALLGOODS ARE QUITE MAGICALLY GIFTED. AND IT'S PRECISELY THAT KNOWLEDGE THAT I AIM TO EXTRACT FROM YOUR OTHERWISE INSIGNIFICANT MINDS.
YOUR SPELLS. YOUR TALENTS. YOUR SECRETS. THEY'LL SOON BE MINE.
ALTHOUGH TO BE FAIR, I'M MORE INTERESTED IN WISTY'S ABILITIES. SORRY, WHIT—IT MUST BE HARD TO HEAR THAT YOU'RE SO WORTHLESS.
WELL, IF I'M SO USELESS, WHY NOT JUST LET ME GO? I PROMISE I WON'T BASH YOUR HEAD IN.
AMUSING.
NO, YOU'LL UNDERGO THE PROCEDURE, SAME AS YOUR SISTER. AFTER ALL, IT'S ONLY FAIR THAT YOU EXPERIENCE THE SAME PAIN THAT SHE WILL BE FEELING.
DO YOUR WORST, YOU FIEND. WE WON'T TALK, NO MATTER HOW MUCH YOU TORTURE US.
I'M AFRAID YOU MISUNDERSTAND ME.
TRADITIONAL TORTURE IS UNRELIABLE AND INEFFICIENT.
I MEAN, WHY USE BRUTE FORCE WHEN MODERN SCIENCE CAN GET THE JOB DONE QUICKER?

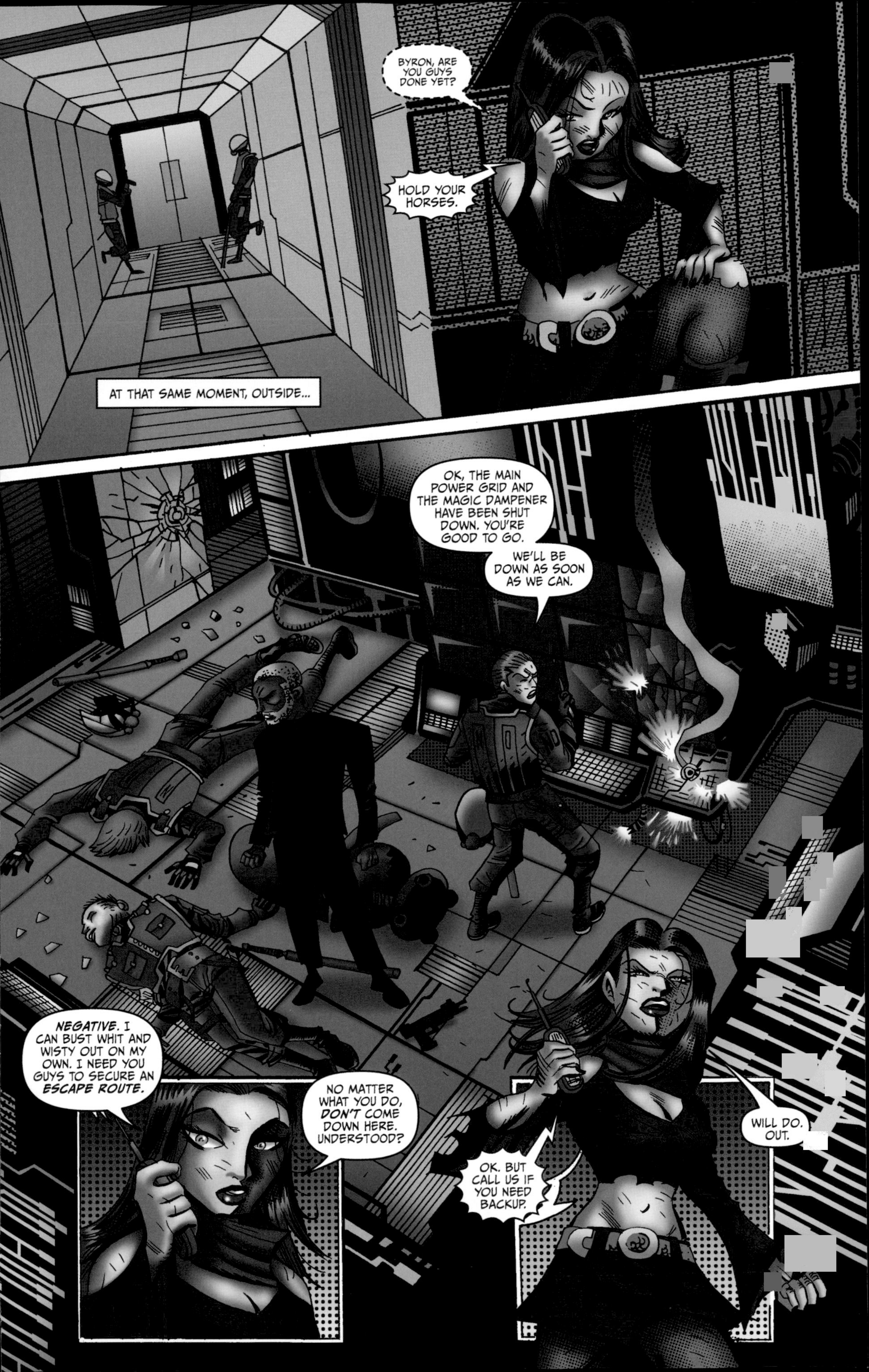
BYRON, ARE YOU GUYS DONE YET?
HOLD YOUR HORSES.
AT THAT SAME MOMENT, OUTSIDE...
OK, THE MAIN POWER GRID AND THE MAGIC DAMPENER HAVE BEEN SHUT DOWN. YOU'RE GOOD TO GO.
WE'LL BE DOWN AS SOON AS WE CAN.
NEGATIVE. I CAN BUST WHIT AND WISTY OUT ON MY OWN. I NEED YOU GUYS TO SECURE AN ESCAPE ROUTE.
NO MATTER WHAT YOU DO, DON'T COME DOWN HERE. UNDERSTOOD?
OK. BUT CALL US IF YOU NEED BACKUP.
WILL DO. OUT.

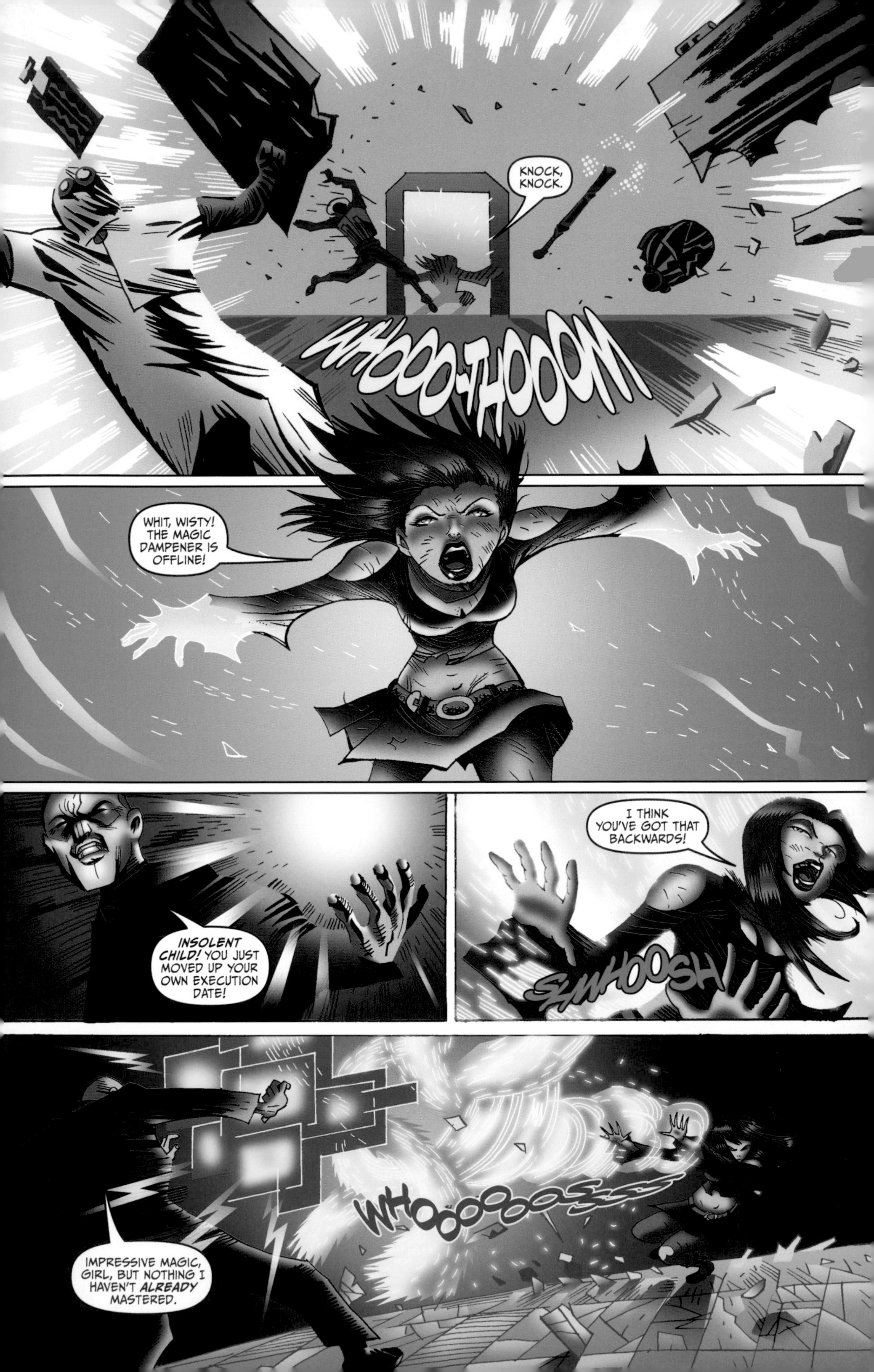
KNOCK, KNOCK.
WHOOO-THOOOM
WHIT, WISTY! THE MAGIC DAMPENER IS OFFLINE!
INSOLENT CHILD! YOU JUST MOVED UP YOUR OWN EXECUTION DATE!
I THINK YOU'VE GOT THAT BACKWARDS!
SHWHOOSH
WHOOOOOOSSSS
IMPRESSIVE MAGIC, GIRL, BUT NOTHING I HAVEN'T ALREADY MASTERED.

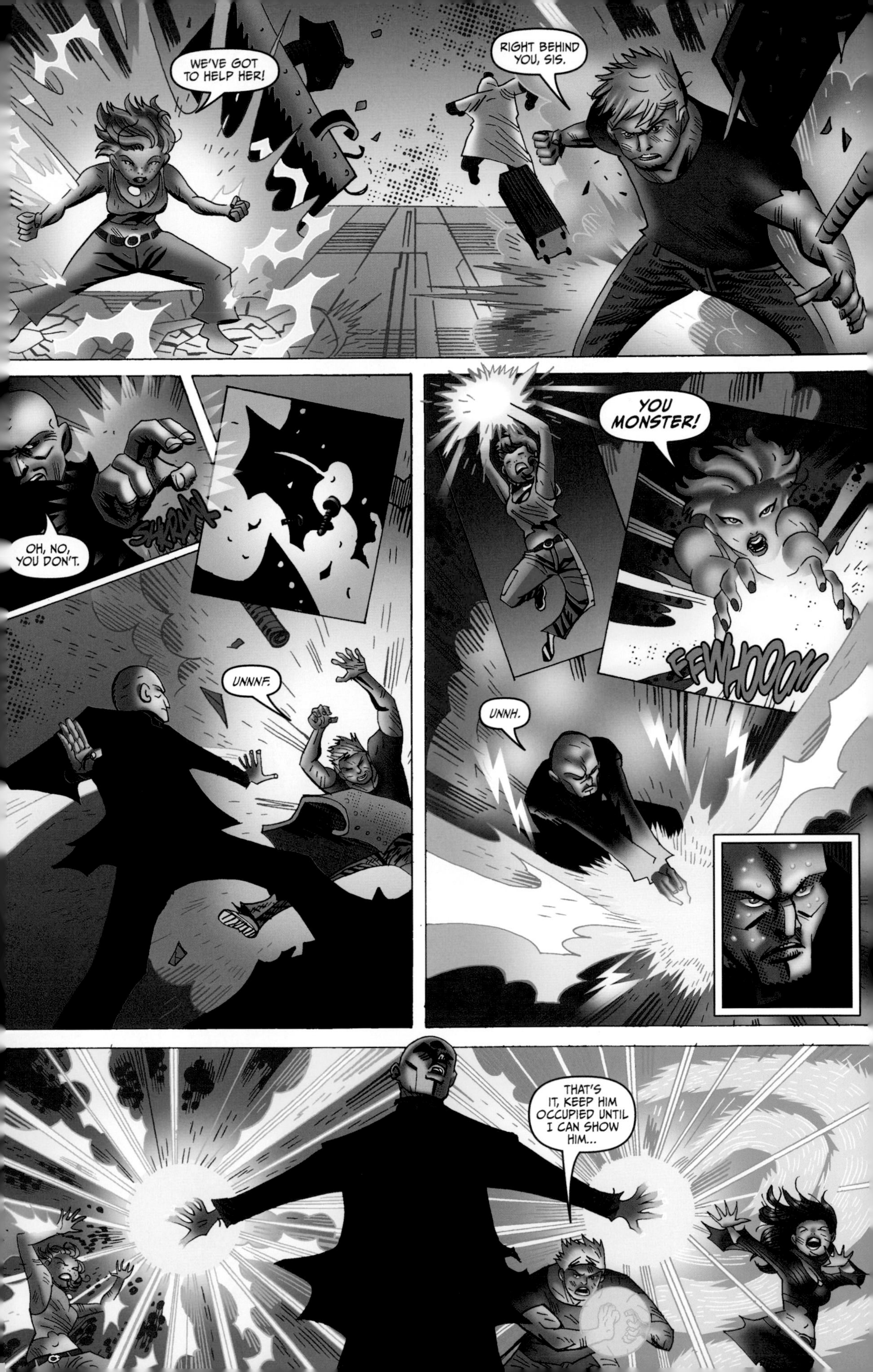
WE'VE GOT TO HELP HER!
RIGHT BEHIND YOU, SIS.
OH, NO, YOU DON'T.
SHRAK!
UNNNF.
YOU MONSTER!
FFWHOOOM
UNNH.
THAT'S IT, KEEP HIM OCCUPIED UNTIL I CAN SHOW HIM...

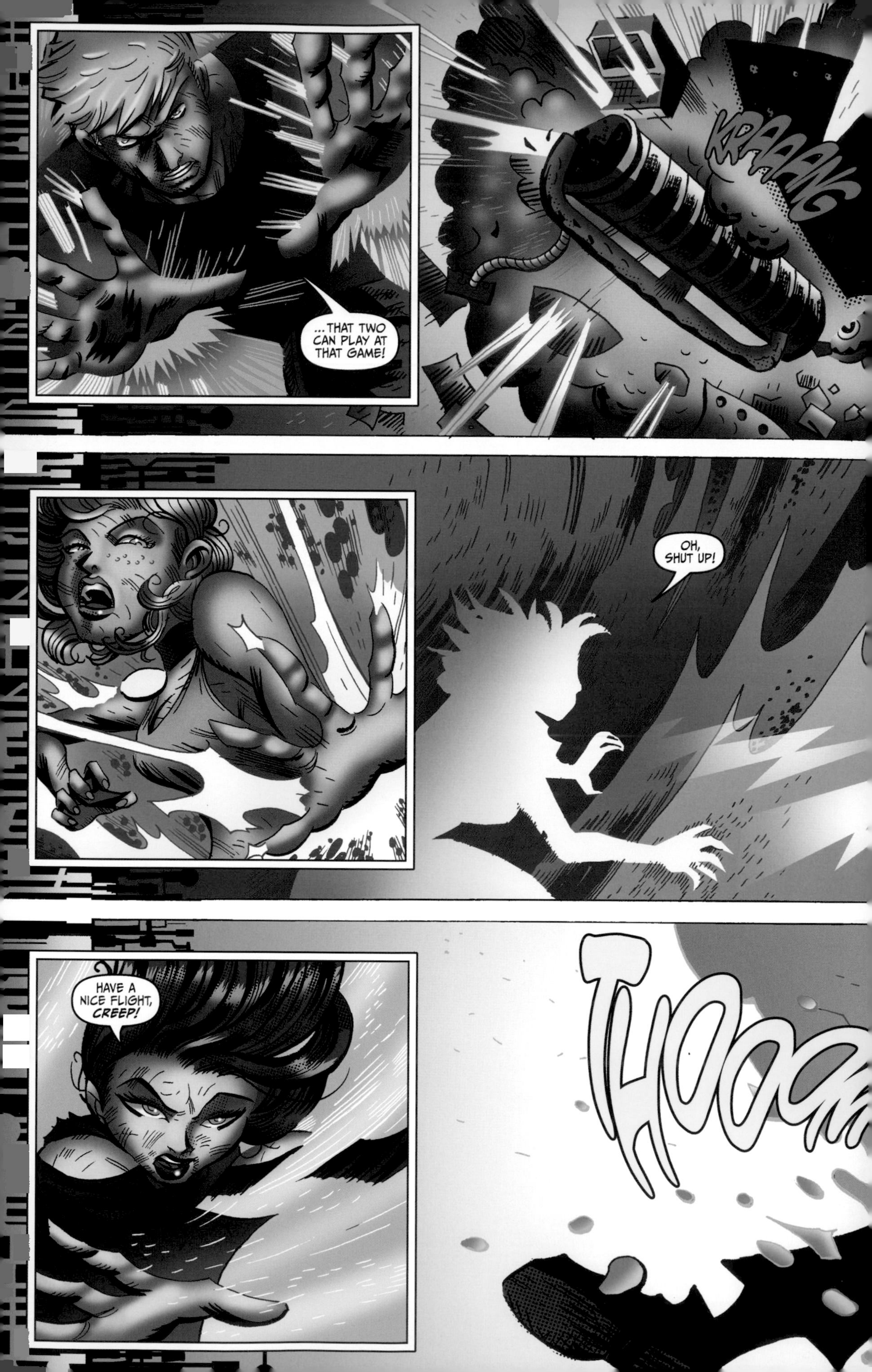
...THAT TWO CAN PLAY AT THAT GAME!
KRAAANG
OH, SHUT UP!
HAVE A NICE FLIGHT, CREEP!

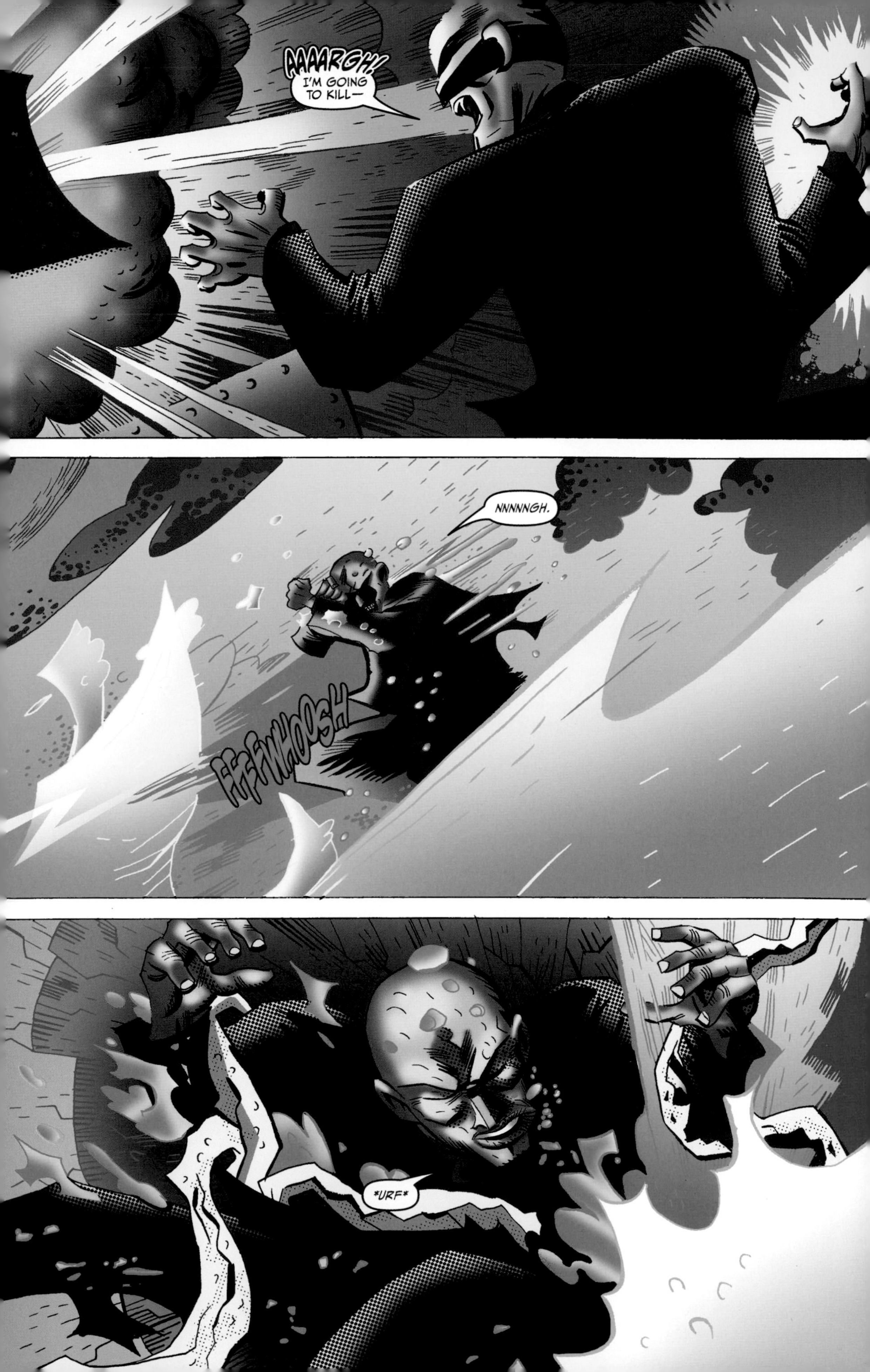
AAAARGH! I'M GOING TO KILL—
NNNNNGH.
FFFFWHOOSH
URF

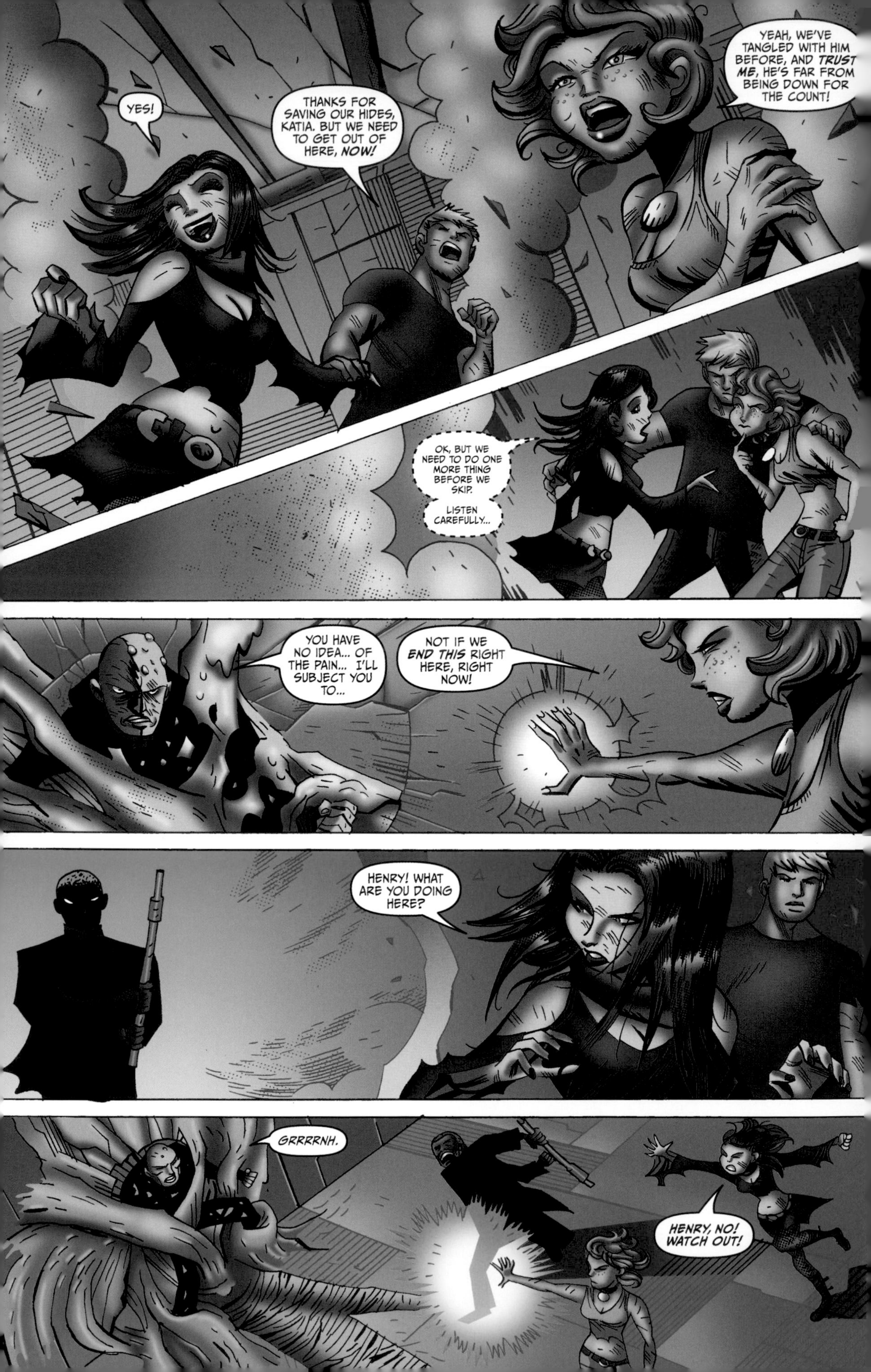
YES!
THANKS FOR SAVING OUR HIDES, KATIA. BUT WE NEED TO GET OUT OF HERE, NOW!
YEAH, WE'VE TANGLED WITH HIM BEFORE, AND TRUST ME, HE'S FAR FROM BEING DOWN FOR THE COUNT!
OK, BUT WE NEED TO DO ONE MORE THING BEFORE WE SKIP.
LISTEN CAREFULLY...
YOU HAVE NO IDEA... OF THE PAIN... I'LL SUBJECT YOU TO...
NOT IF WE END THIS RIGHT HERE, RIGHT NOW!
HENRY! WHAT ARE YOU DOING HERE?
GRRRRNH.
HENRY, NO! WATCH OUT!

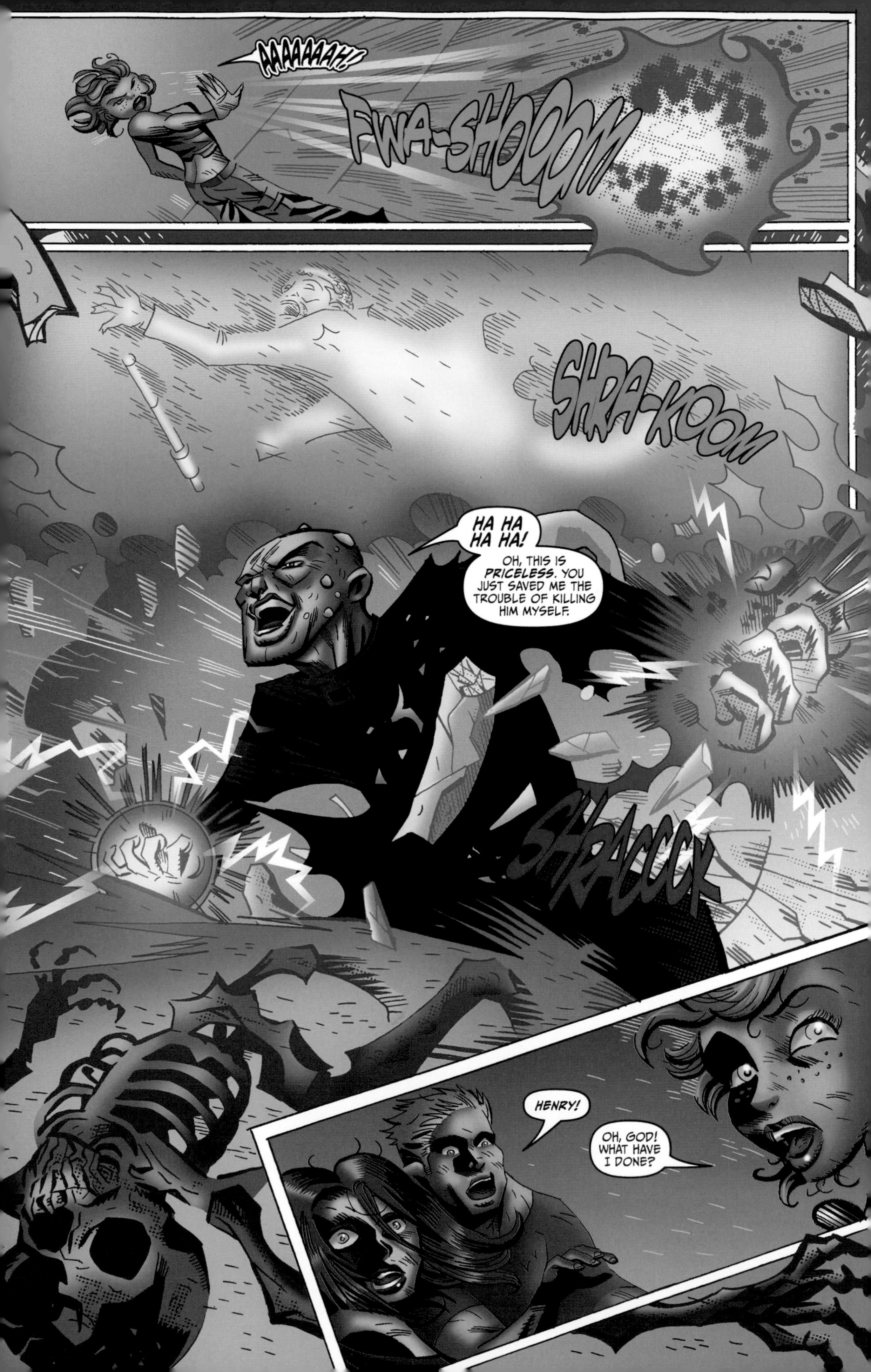
AAAAAAAH!
FWA-SHOOOOM
SHRA-KOOOM
HA HA HA HA!
OH, THIS IS *PRICELESS*. YOU JUST SAVED ME THE TROUBLE OF KILLING HIM MYSELF.
SHRACCCK
HENRY!
OH, GOD! WHAT HAVE I DONE?

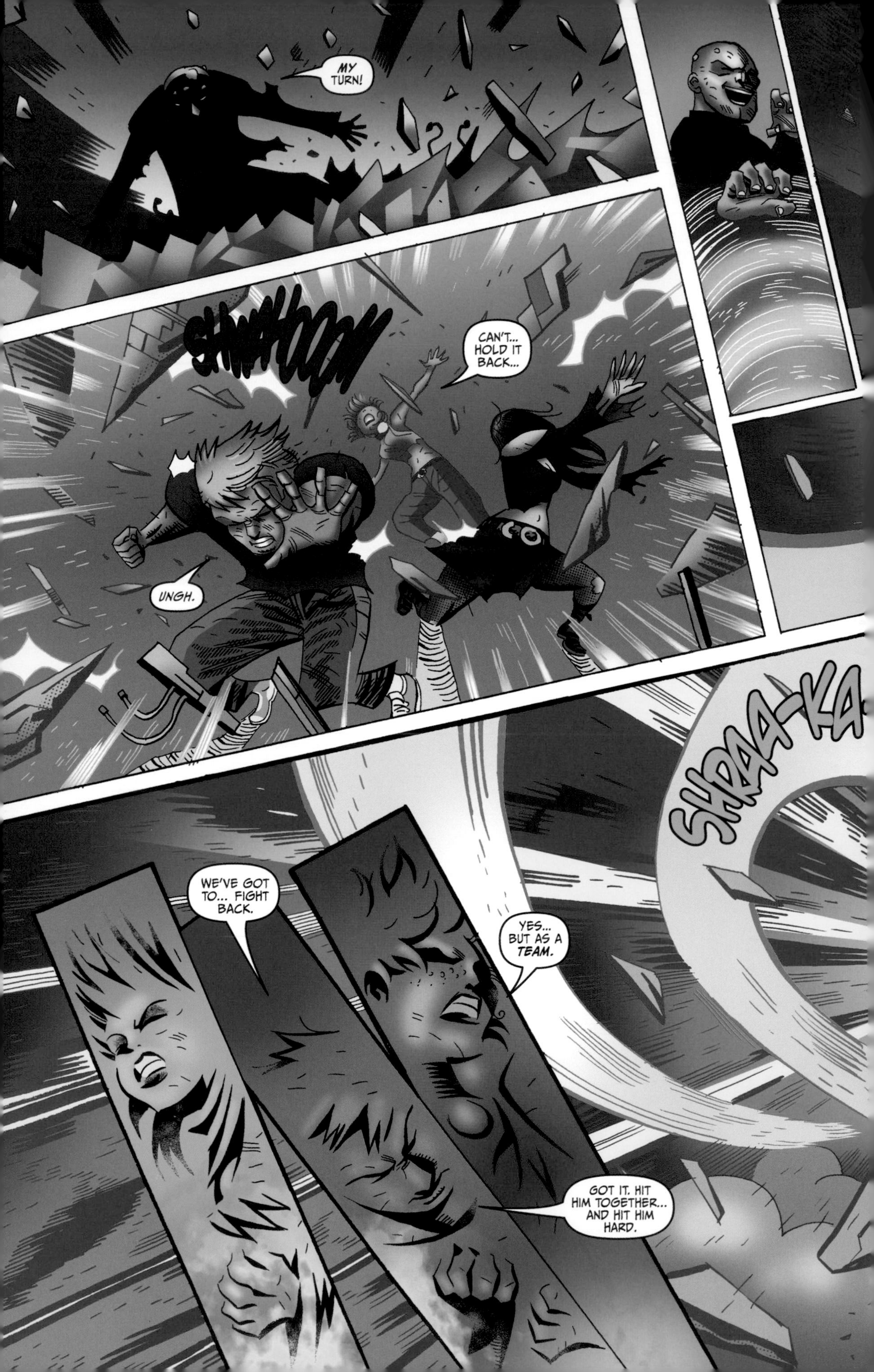
MY TURN!
SHWHOOOM
CAN'T... HOLD IT BACK...
UNGH.
SHRAA-KA
WE'VE GOT TO... FIGHT BACK.
YES... BUT AS A *TEAM*.
GOT IT. HIT HIM TOGETHER... AND HIT HIM HARD.

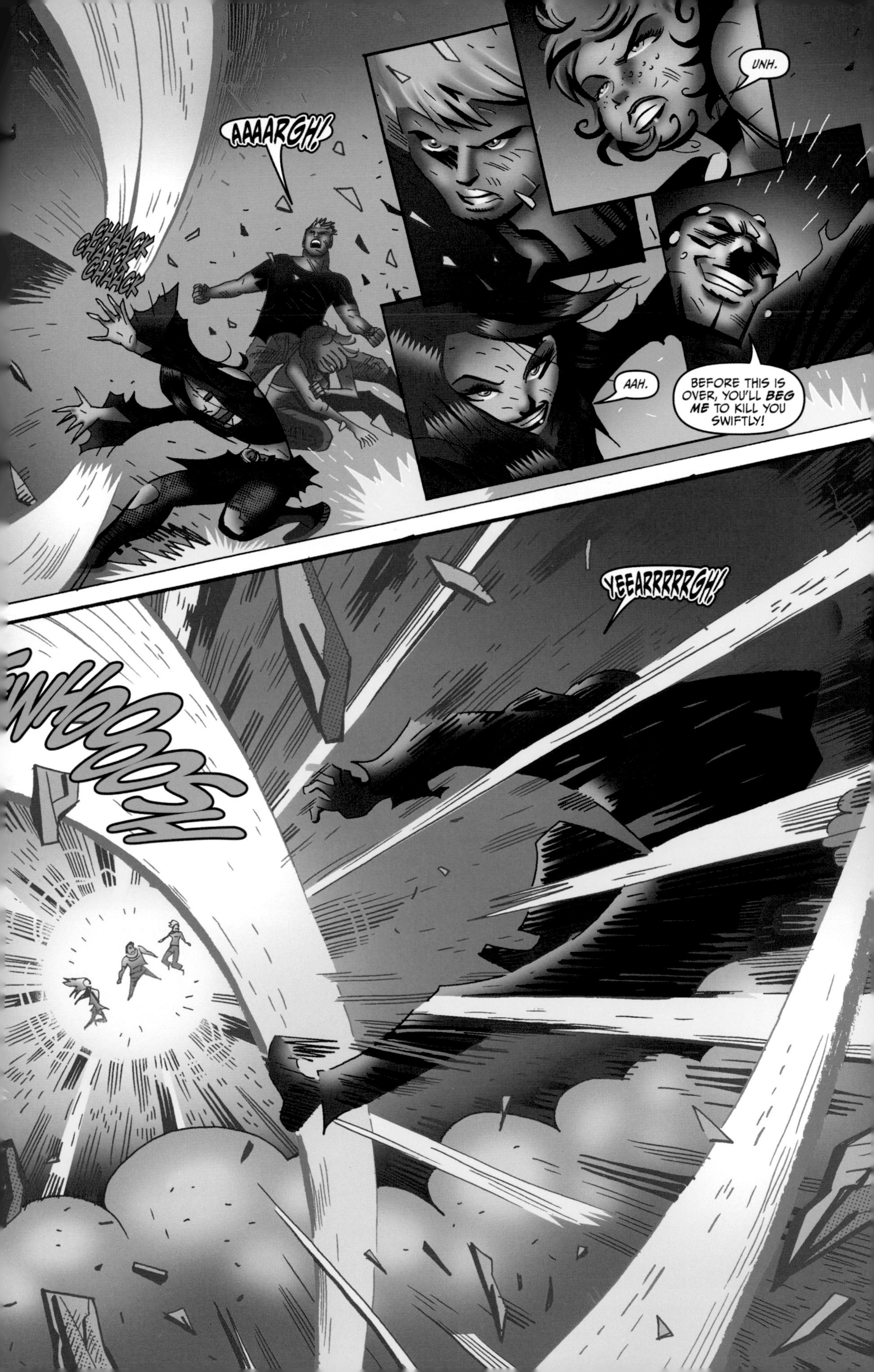
AAAARGH!
CHAACK CHAACK CHAACK
UNH.
AAH.
BEFORE THIS IS OVER, YOU'LL **BEG ME** TO KILL YOU SWIFTLY!
YEEARRRRRGH!
FWHOOOOSH

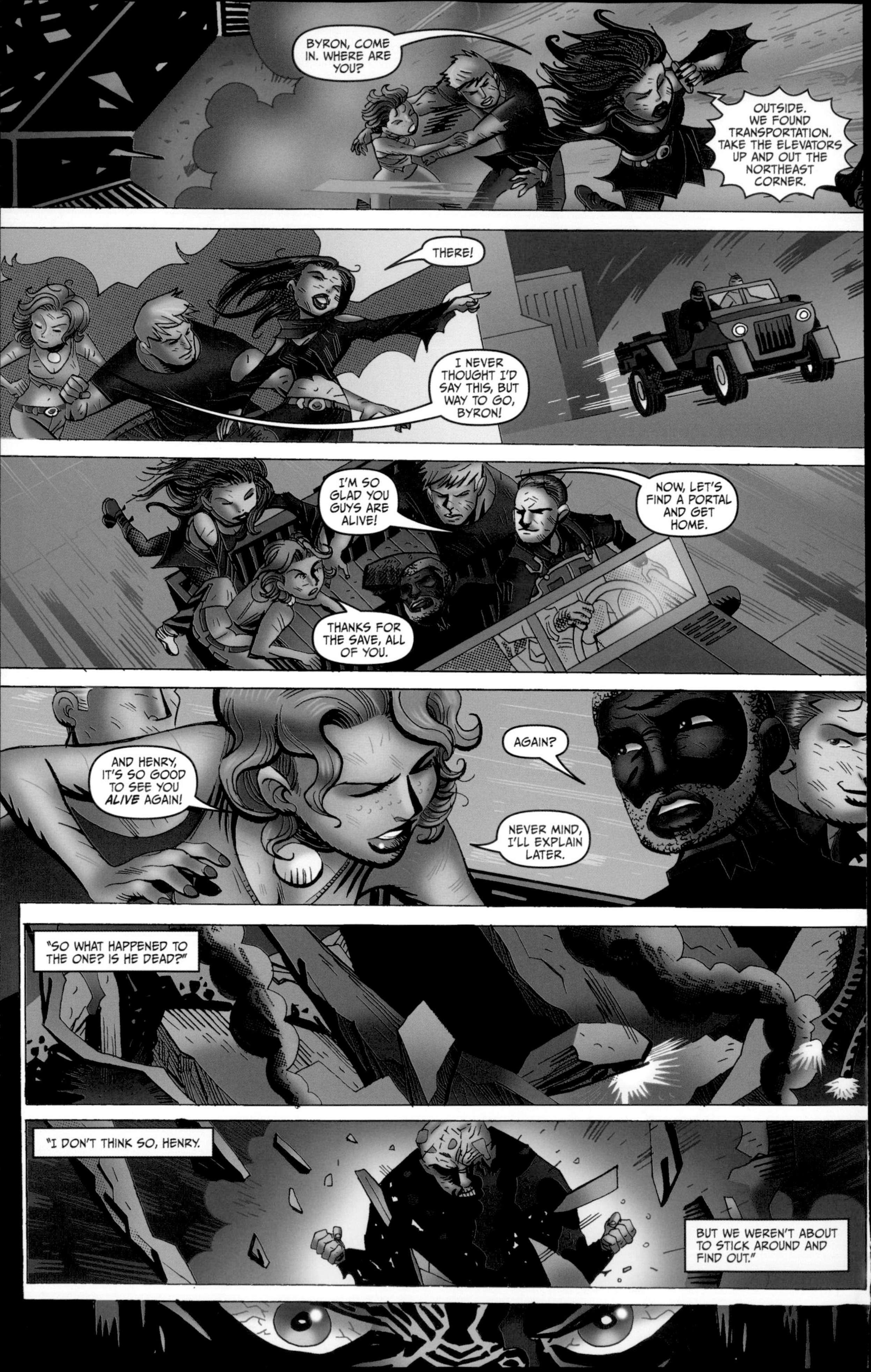
BYRON, COME IN. WHERE ARE YOU?
OUTSIDE. WE FOUND TRANSPORTATION. TAKE THE ELEVATORS UP AND OUT THE NORTHEAST CORNER.
THERE!
I NEVER THOUGHT I'D SAY THIS, BUT WAY TO GO, BYRON!
I'M SO GLAD YOU GUYS ARE ALIVE!
NOW, LET'S FIND A PORTAL AND GET HOME.
THANKS FOR THE SAVE, ALL OF YOU.
AND HENRY, IT'S SO GOOD TO SEE YOU *ALIVE* AGAIN!
AGAIN?
NEVER MIND, I'LL EXPLAIN LATER.
"SO WHAT HAPPENED TO THE ONE? IS HE DEAD?"
"I DON'T THINK SO, HENRY.
BUT WE WEREN'T ABOUT TO STICK AROUND AND FIND OUT."

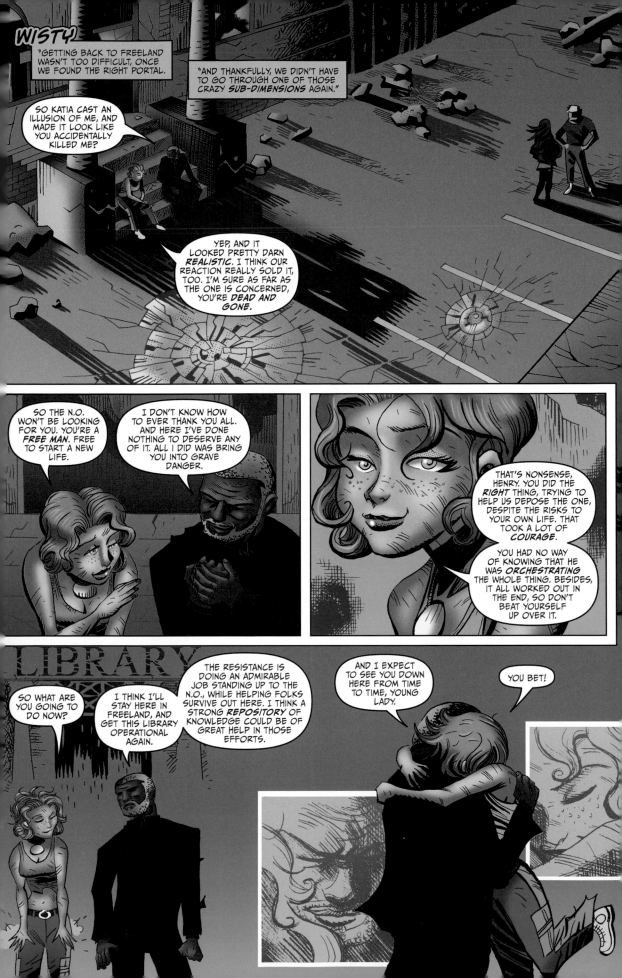

WISTY

"GETTING BACK TO FREELAND WASN'T TOO DIFFICULT, ONCE WE FOUND THE RIGHT PORTAL.

"AND THANKFULLY, WE DIDN'T HAVE TO GO THROUGH ONE OF THOSE CRAZY *SUB-DIMENSIONS* AGAIN."

SO KATIA CAST AN ILLUSION OF ME, AND MADE IT LOOK LIKE YOU ACCIDENTALLY KILLED ME?

YEP, AND IT LOOKED PRETTY DARN *REALISTIC*. I THINK OUR REACTION REALLY SOLD IT, TOO. I'M SURE AS FAR AS THE ONE IS CONCERNED, YOU'RE *DEAD AND GONE*.

SO THE N.O. WON'T BE LOOKING FOR YOU. YOU'RE A *FREE MAN*. FREE TO START A NEW LIFE.

I DON'T KNOW HOW TO EVER THANK YOU ALL. AND HERE I'VE DONE NOTHING TO DESERVE ANY OF IT. ALL I DID WAS BRING YOU INTO GRAVE DANGER.

THAT'S NONSENSE, HENRY. YOU DID THE *RIGHT* THING, TRYING TO HELP US DEPOSE THE ONE, DESPITE THE RISKS TO YOUR OWN LIFE. THAT TOOK A LOT OF *COURAGE*.

YOU HAD NO WAY OF KNOWING THAT HE WAS *ORCHESTRATING* THE WHOLE THING. BESIDES, IT ALL WORKED OUT IN THE END, SO DON'T BEAT YOURSELF UP OVER IT.

LIBRARY

SO WHAT ARE YOU GOING TO DO NOW?

I THINK I'LL STAY HERE IN FREELAND, AND GET THIS LIBRARY OPERATIONAL AGAIN.

THE RESISTANCE IS DOING AN ADMIRABLE JOB STANDING UP TO THE N.O., WHILE HELPING FOLKS SURVIVE OUT HERE. I THINK A STRONG *REPOSITORY* OF KNOWLEDGE COULD BE OF GREAT HELP IN THOSE EFFORTS.

AND I EXPECT TO SEE YOU DOWN HERE FROM TIME TO TIME, YOUNG LADY.

YOU BET!

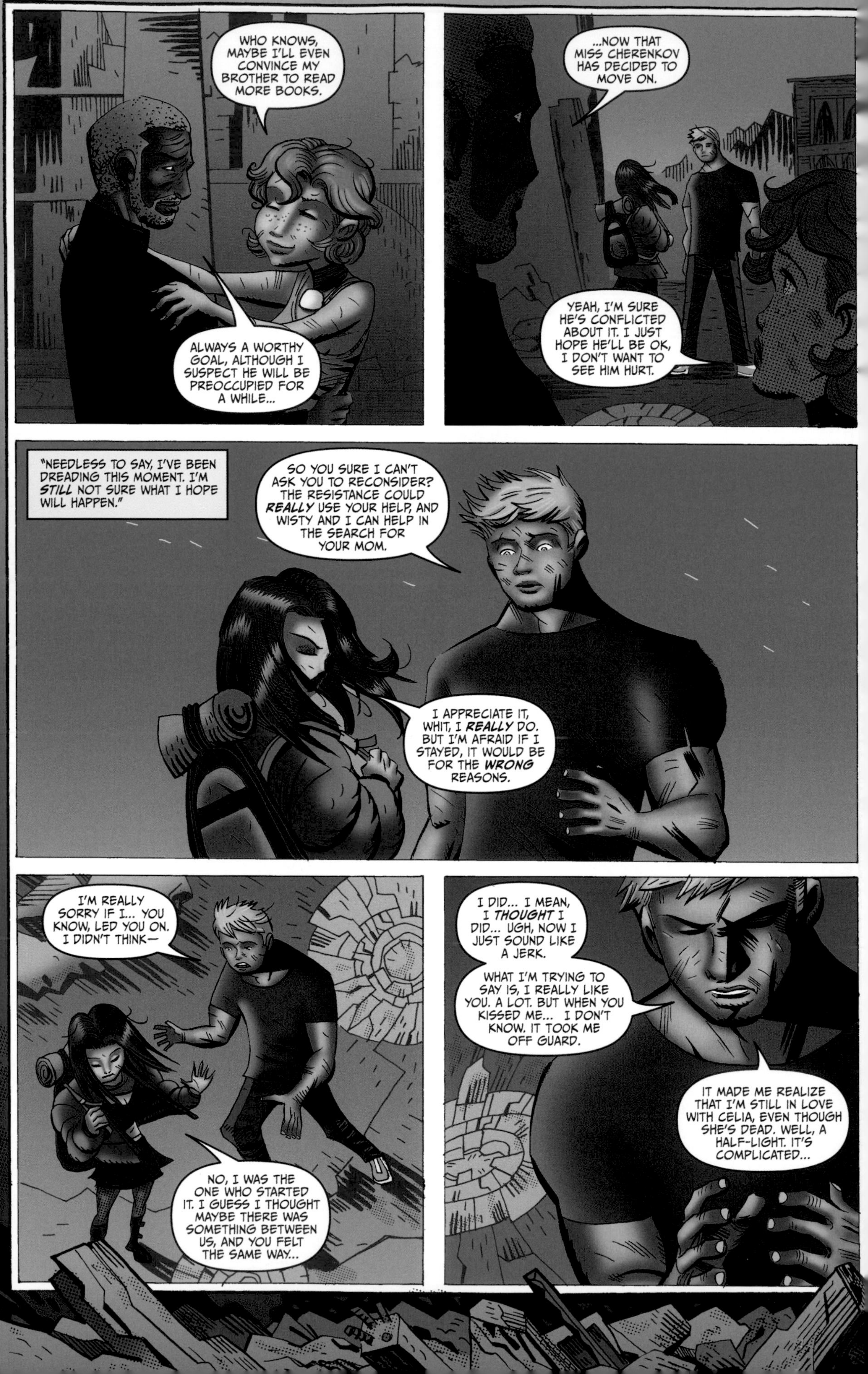
WHO KNOWS, MAYBE I'LL EVEN CONVINCE MY BROTHER TO READ MORE BOOKS.
ALWAYS A WORTHY GOAL, ALTHOUGH I SUSPECT HE WILL BE PREOCCUPIED FOR A WHILE...
...NOW THAT MISS CHERENKOV HAS DECIDED TO MOVE ON.
YEAH, I'M SURE HE'S CONFLICTED ABOUT IT. I JUST HOPE HE'LL BE OK, I DON'T WANT TO SEE HIM HURT.
"NEEDLESS TO SAY, I'VE BEEN DREADING THIS MOMENT. I'M STILL NOT SURE WHAT I HOPE WILL HAPPEN."
SO YOU SURE I CAN'T ASK YOU TO RECONSIDER? THE RESISTANCE COULD REALLY USE YOUR HELP, AND WISTY AND I CAN HELP IN THE SEARCH FOR YOUR MOM.
I APPRECIATE IT, WHIT, I REALLY DO. BUT I'M AFRAID IF I STAYED, IT WOULD BE FOR THE WRONG REASONS.
I'M REALLY SORRY IF I... YOU KNOW, LED YOU ON. I DIDN'T THINK—
NO, I WAS THE ONE WHO STARTED IT. I GUESS I THOUGHT MAYBE THERE WAS SOMETHING BETWEEN US, AND YOU FELT THE SAME WAY...
I DID... I MEAN, I THOUGHT I DID... UGH, NOW I JUST SOUND LIKE A JERK.
WHAT I'M TRYING TO SAY IS, I REALLY LIKE YOU. A LOT. BUT WHEN YOU KISSED ME... I DON'T KNOW. IT TOOK ME OFF GUARD.
IT MADE ME REALIZE THAT I'M STILL IN LOVE WITH CELIA, EVEN THOUGH SHE'S DEAD. WELL, A HALF-LIGHT. IT'S COMPLICATED...

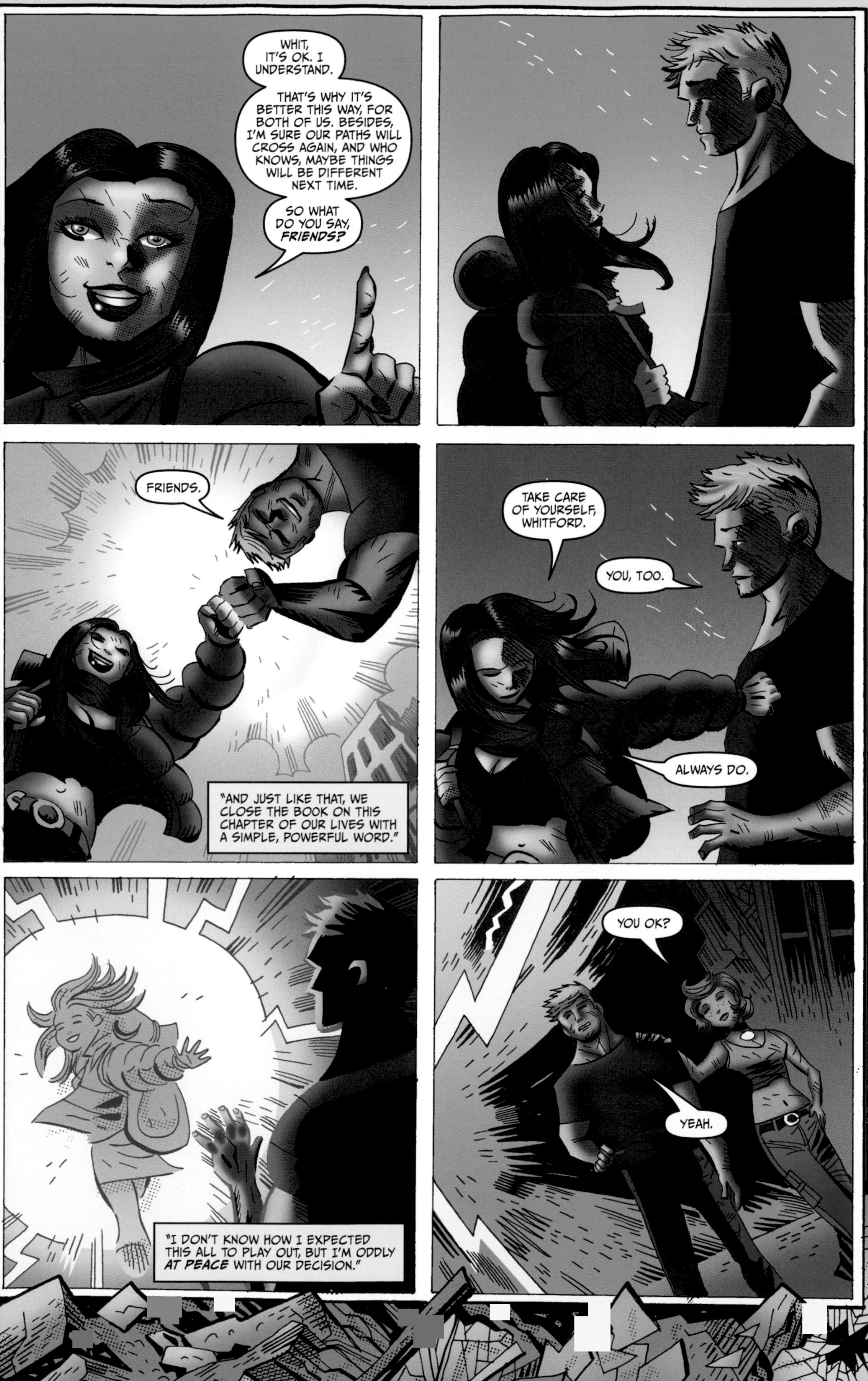
WHIT, IT'S OK. I UNDERSTAND.
THAT'S WHY IT'S BETTER THIS WAY, FOR BOTH OF US. BESIDES, I'M SURE OUR PATHS WILL CROSS AGAIN, AND WHO KNOWS, MAYBE THINGS WILL BE DIFFERENT NEXT TIME.
SO WHAT DO YOU SAY, *FRIENDS?*
FRIENDS.
"AND JUST LIKE THAT, WE CLOSE THE BOOK ON THIS CHAPTER OF OUR LIVES WITH A SIMPLE, POWERFUL WORD."
TAKE CARE OF YOURSELF, WHITFORD.
YOU, TOO.
ALWAYS DO.
"I DON'T KNOW HOW I EXPECTED THIS ALL TO PLAY OUT, BUT I'M ODDLY *AT PEACE* WITH OUR DECISION."
YOU OK?
YEAH.

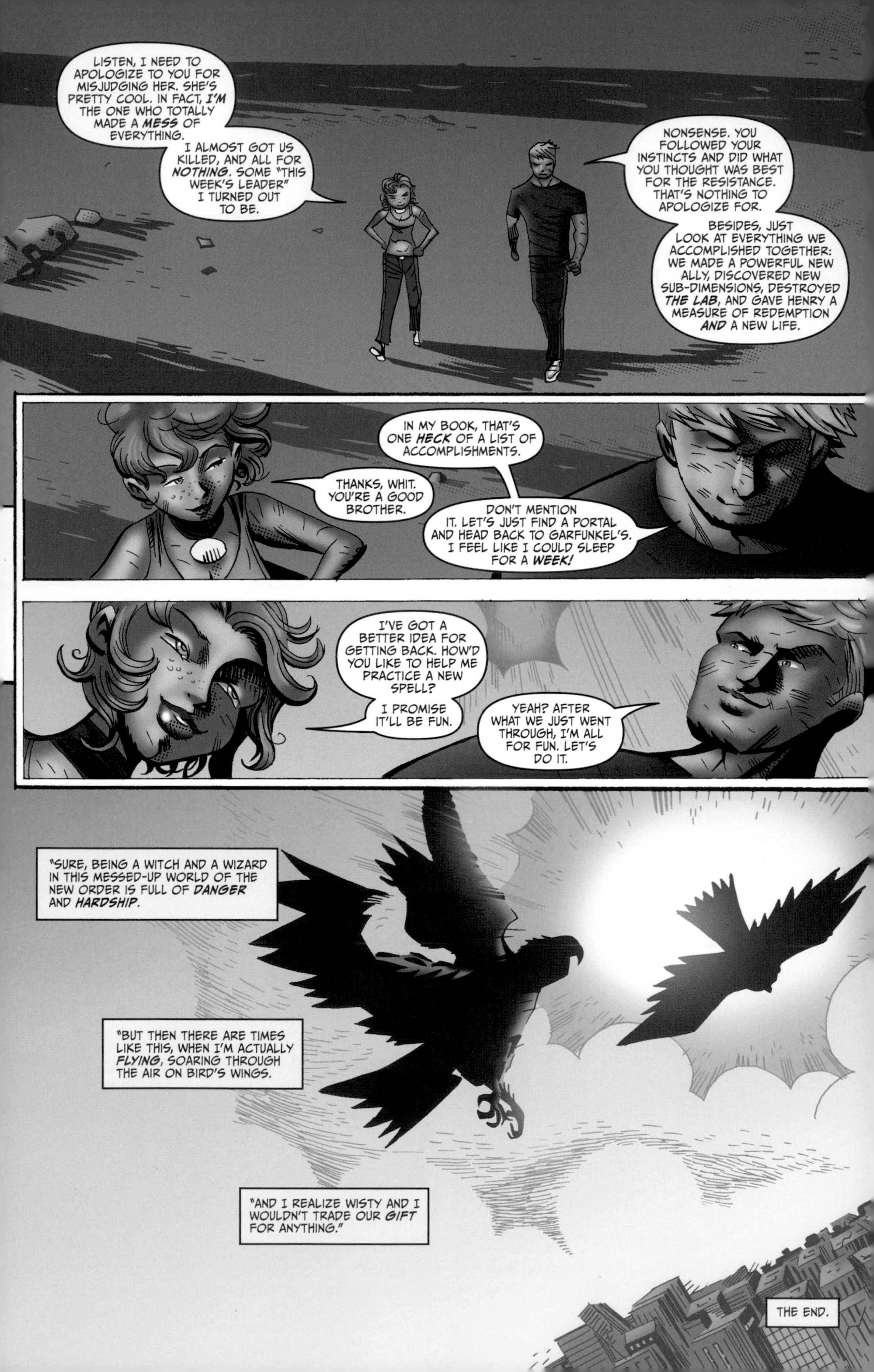
LISTEN, I NEED TO APOLOGIZE TO YOU FOR MISJUDGING HER. SHE'S PRETTY COOL. IN FACT, *I'M* THE ONE WHO TOTALLY MADE A *MESS* OF EVERYTHING.
I ALMOST GOT US KILLED, AND ALL FOR *NOTHING*. SOME "THIS WEEK'S LEADER" I TURNED OUT TO BE.
NONSENSE. YOU FOLLOWED YOUR INSTINCTS AND DID WHAT YOU THOUGHT WAS BEST FOR THE RESISTANCE. THAT'S NOTHING TO APOLOGIZE FOR.
BESIDES, JUST LOOK AT EVERYTHING WE ACCOMPLISHED TOGETHER: WE MADE A POWERFUL NEW ALLY, DISCOVERED NEW SUB-DIMENSIONS, DESTROYED *THE LAB*, AND GAVE HENRY A MEASURE OF REDEMPTION *AND* A NEW LIFE.
IN MY BOOK, THAT'S ONE *HECK* OF A LIST OF ACCOMPLISHMENTS.
THANKS, WHIT. YOU'RE A GOOD BROTHER.
DON'T MENTION IT. LET'S JUST FIND A PORTAL AND HEAD BACK TO GARFUNKEL'S. I FEEL LIKE I COULD SLEEP FOR A *WEEK!*
I'VE GOT A BETTER IDEA FOR GETTING BACK. HOW'D YOU LIKE TO HELP ME PRACTICE A NEW SPELL?
I PROMISE IT'LL BE FUN.
YEAH? AFTER WHAT WE JUST WENT THROUGH, I'M ALL FOR FUN. LET'S DO IT.
"SURE, BEING A WITCH AND A WIZARD IN THIS MESSED-UP WORLD OF THE NEW ORDER IS FULL OF *DANGER* AND *HARDSHIP*.
"BUT THEN THERE ARE TIMES LIKE THIS, WHEN I'M ACTUALLY *FLYING*, SOARING THROUGH THE AIR ON BIRD'S WINGS.
"AND I REALIZE WISTY AND I WOULDN'T TRADE OUR *GIFT* FOR ANYTHING."
THE END.

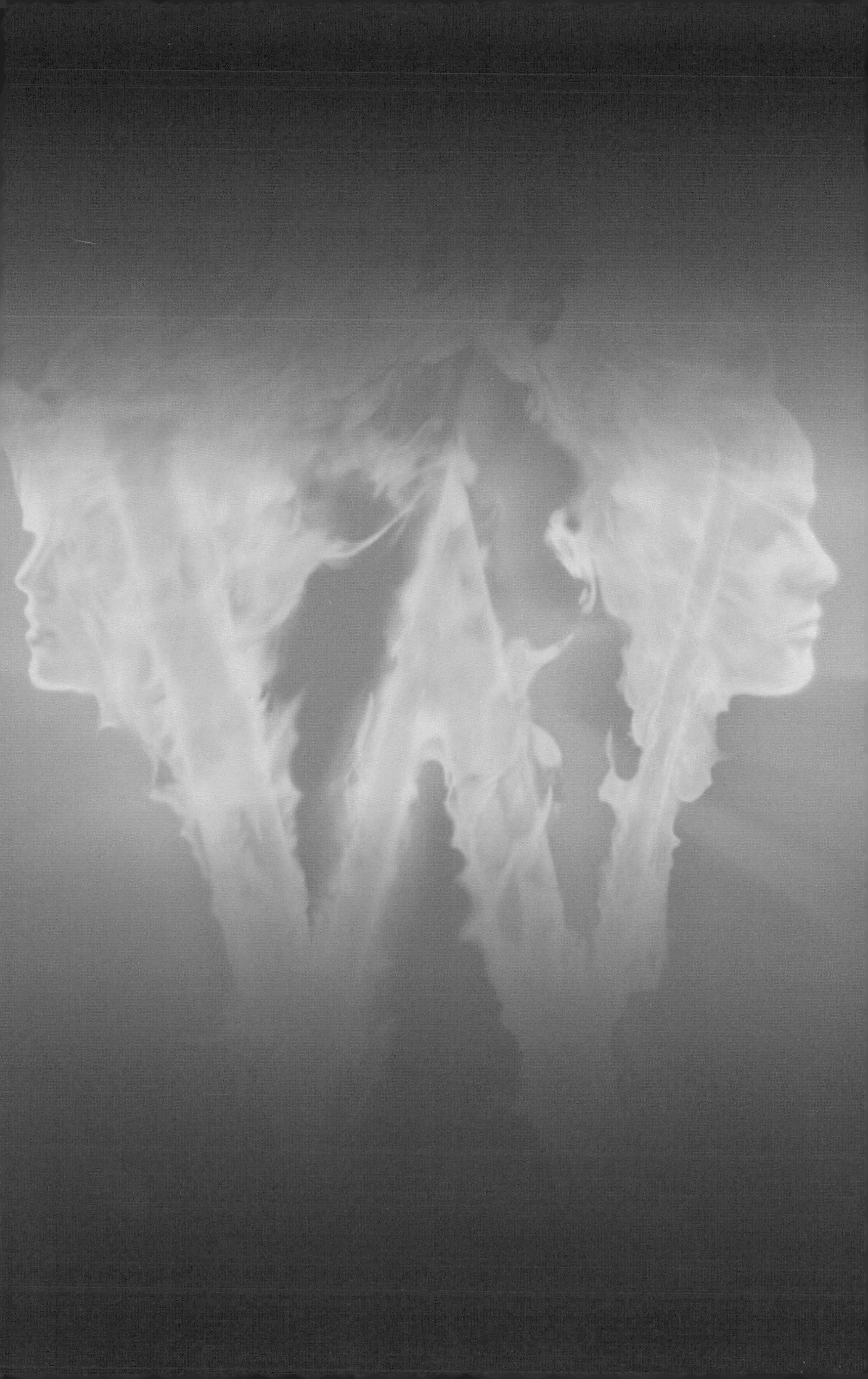

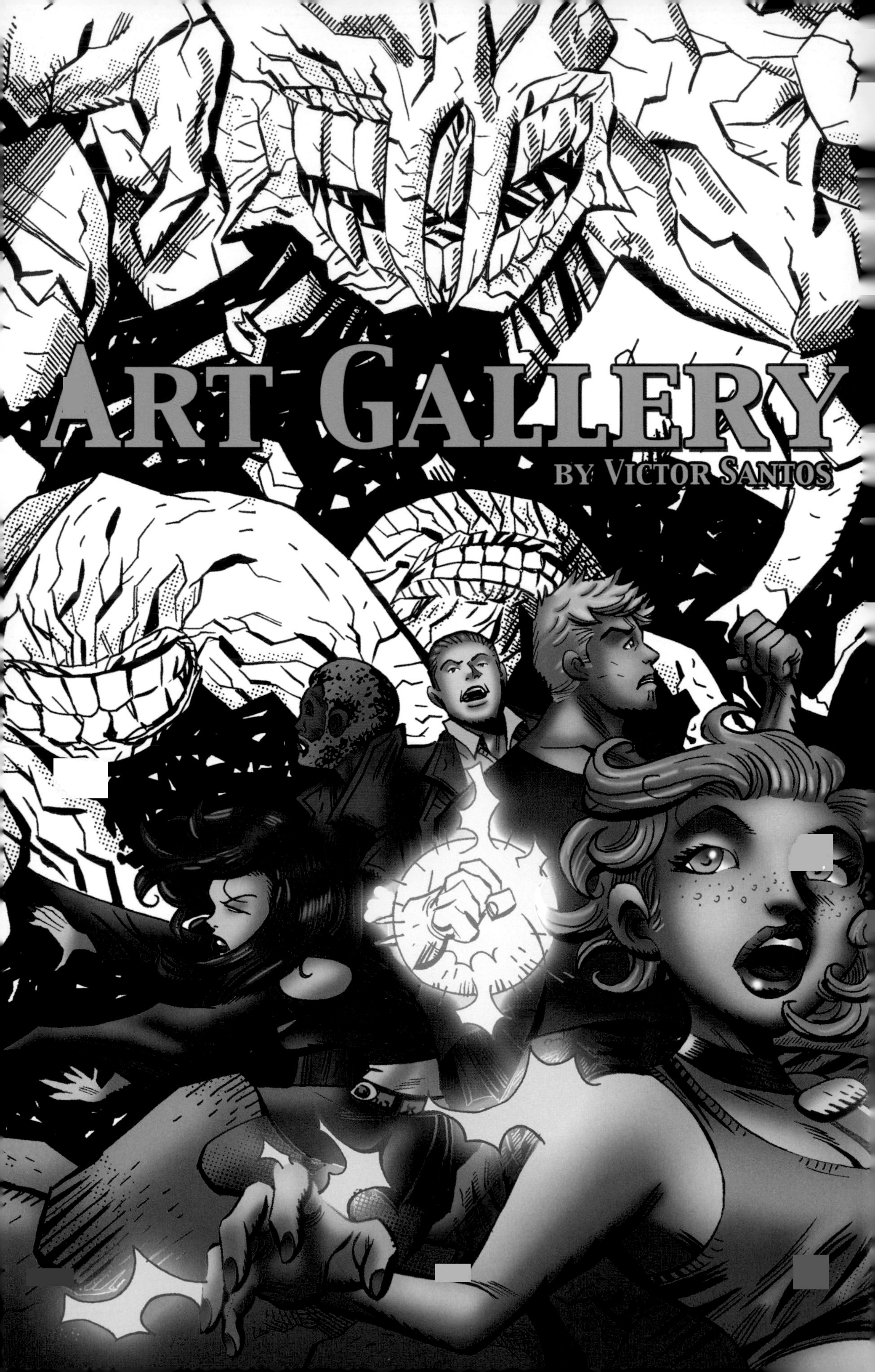
ART GALLERY
BY VICTOR SANTOS

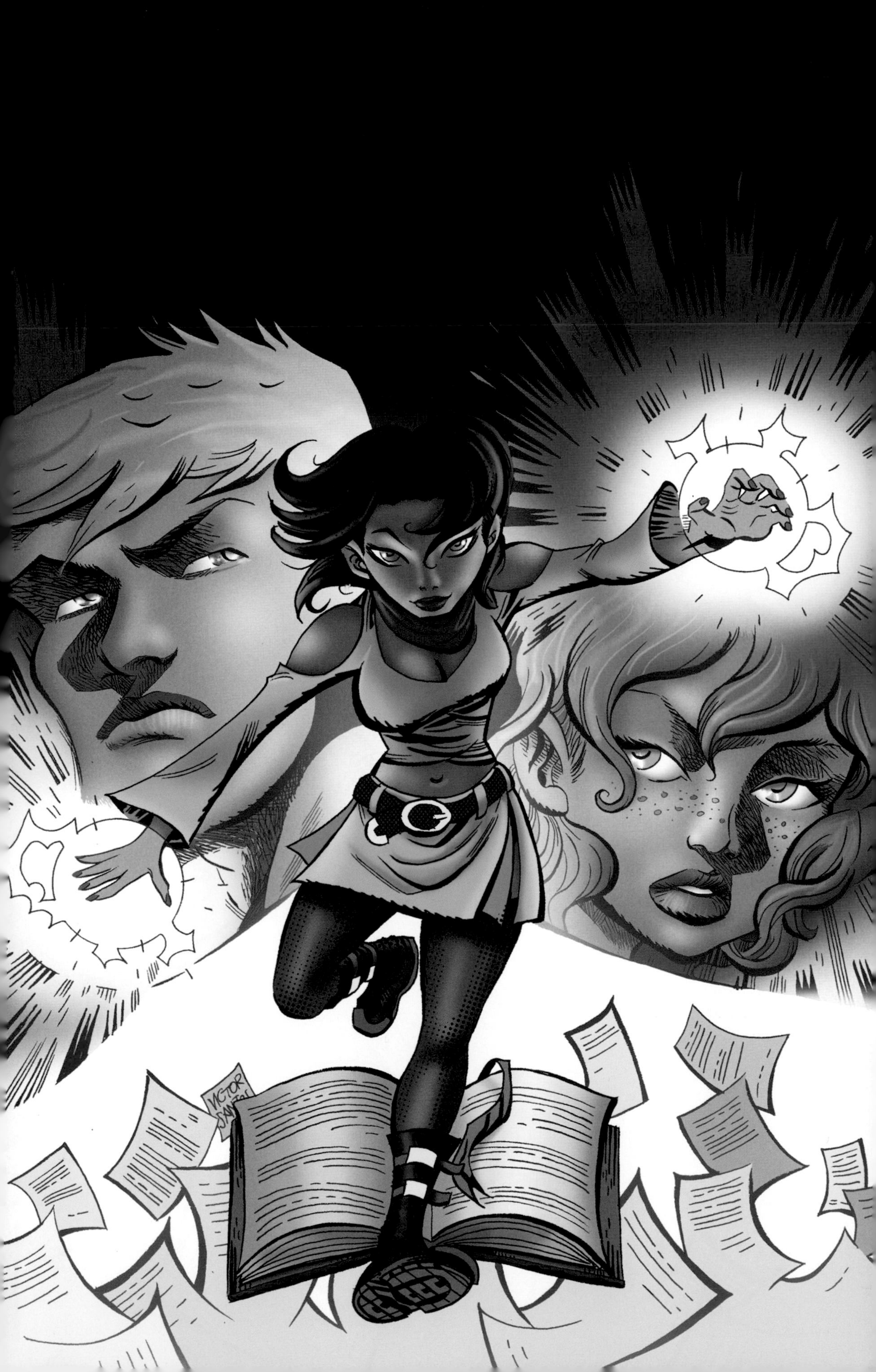

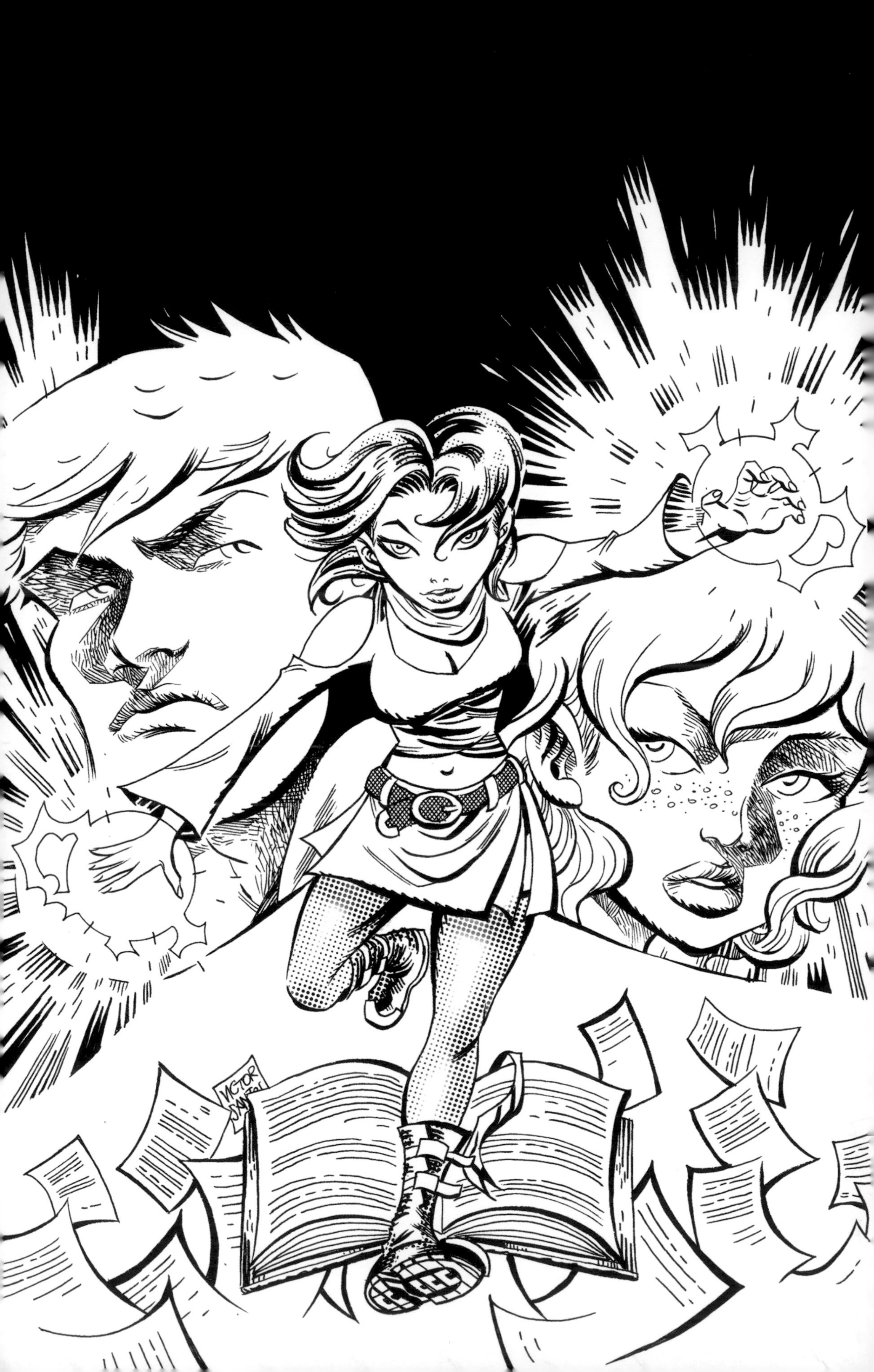
VICTOR

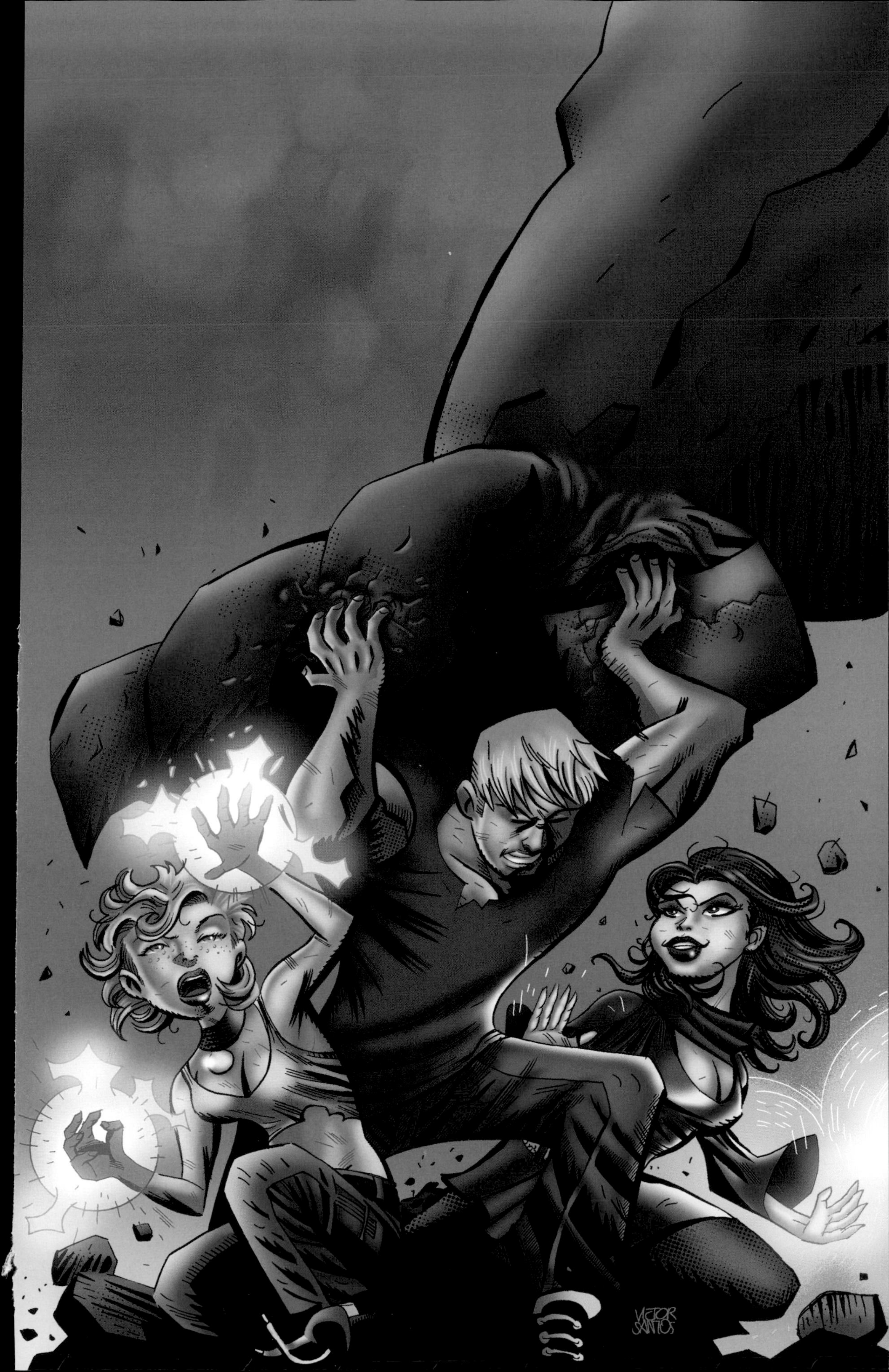
VICTOR SANTOS

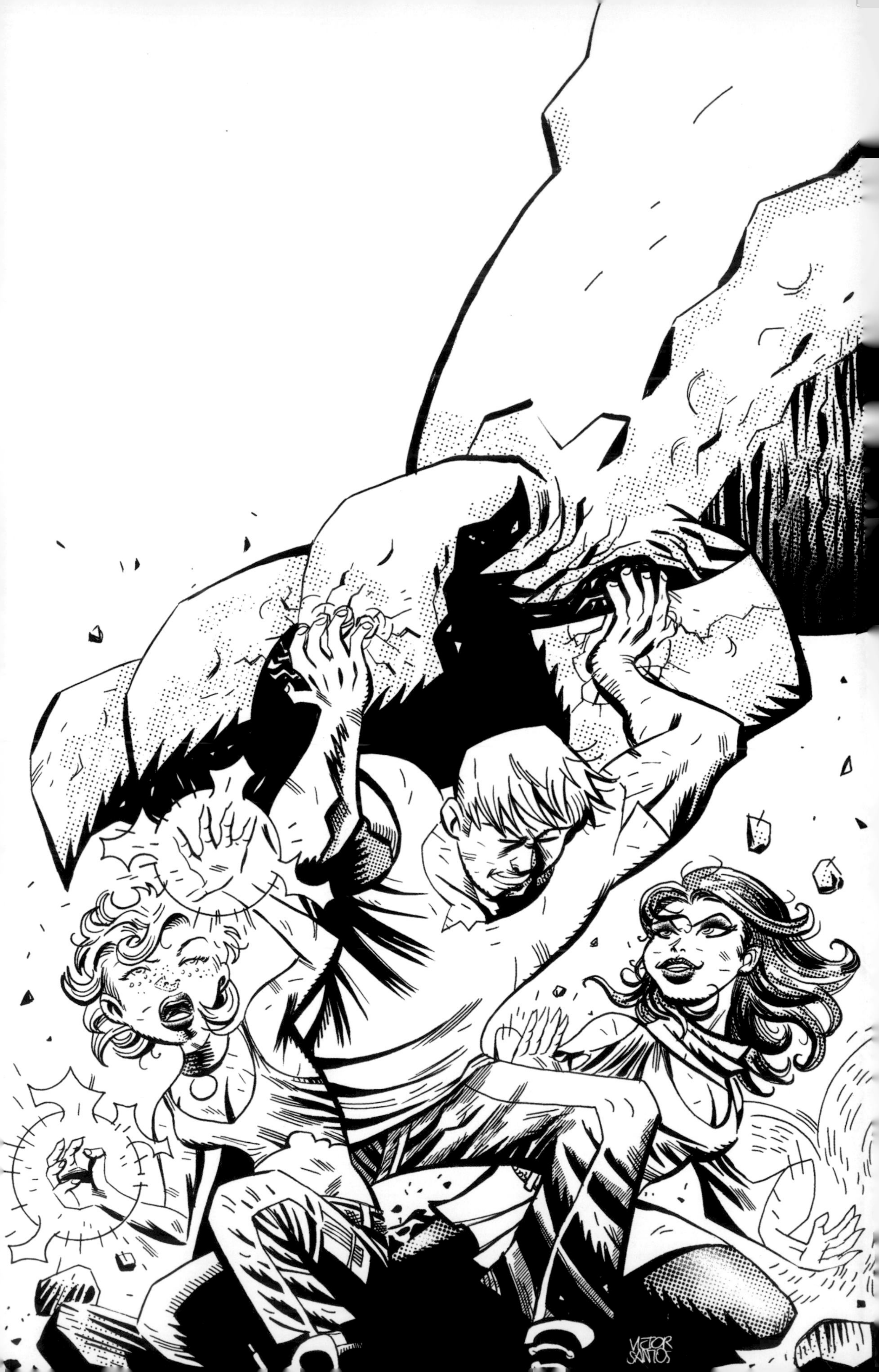
VICTOR SANTOS

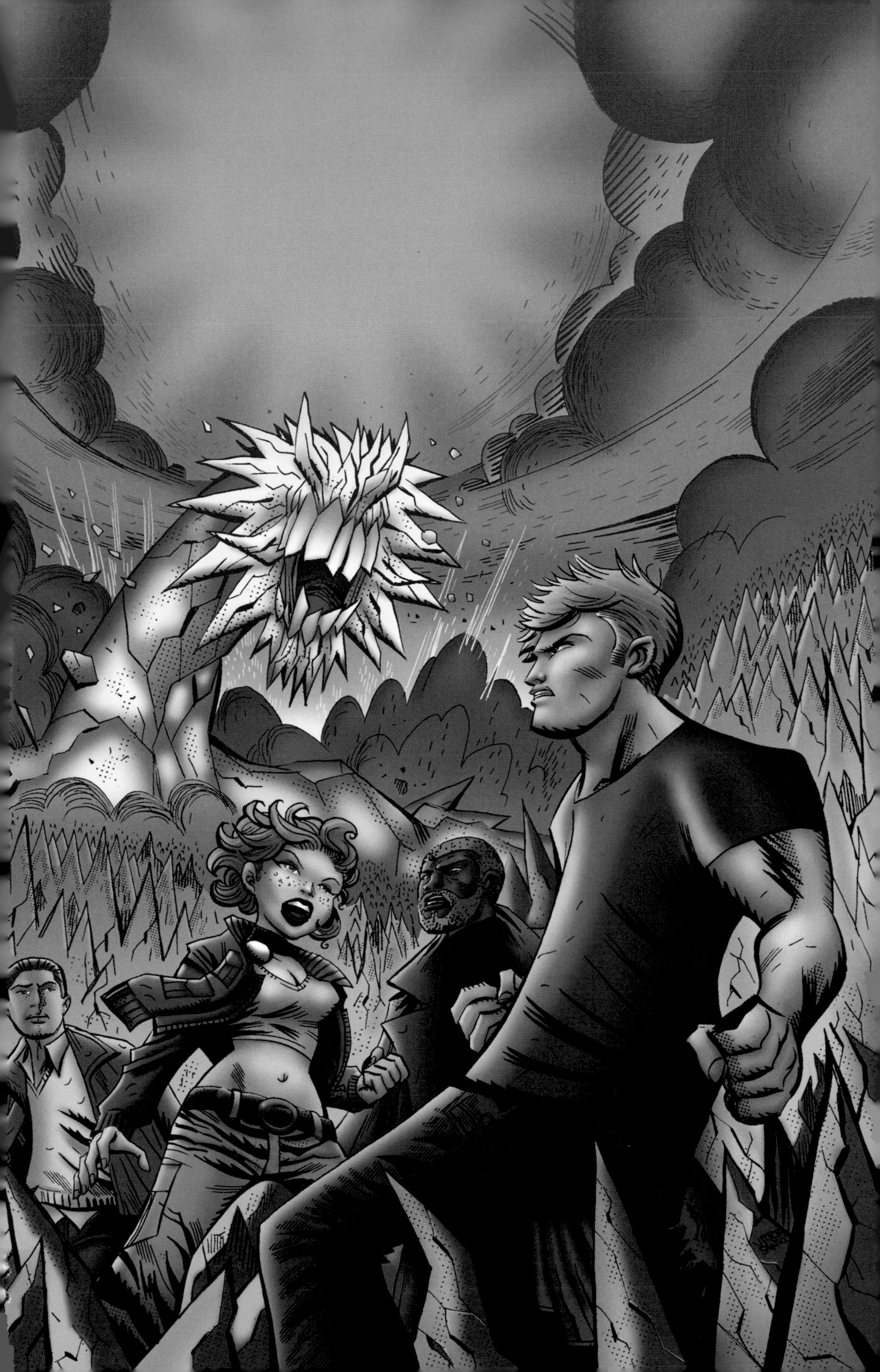

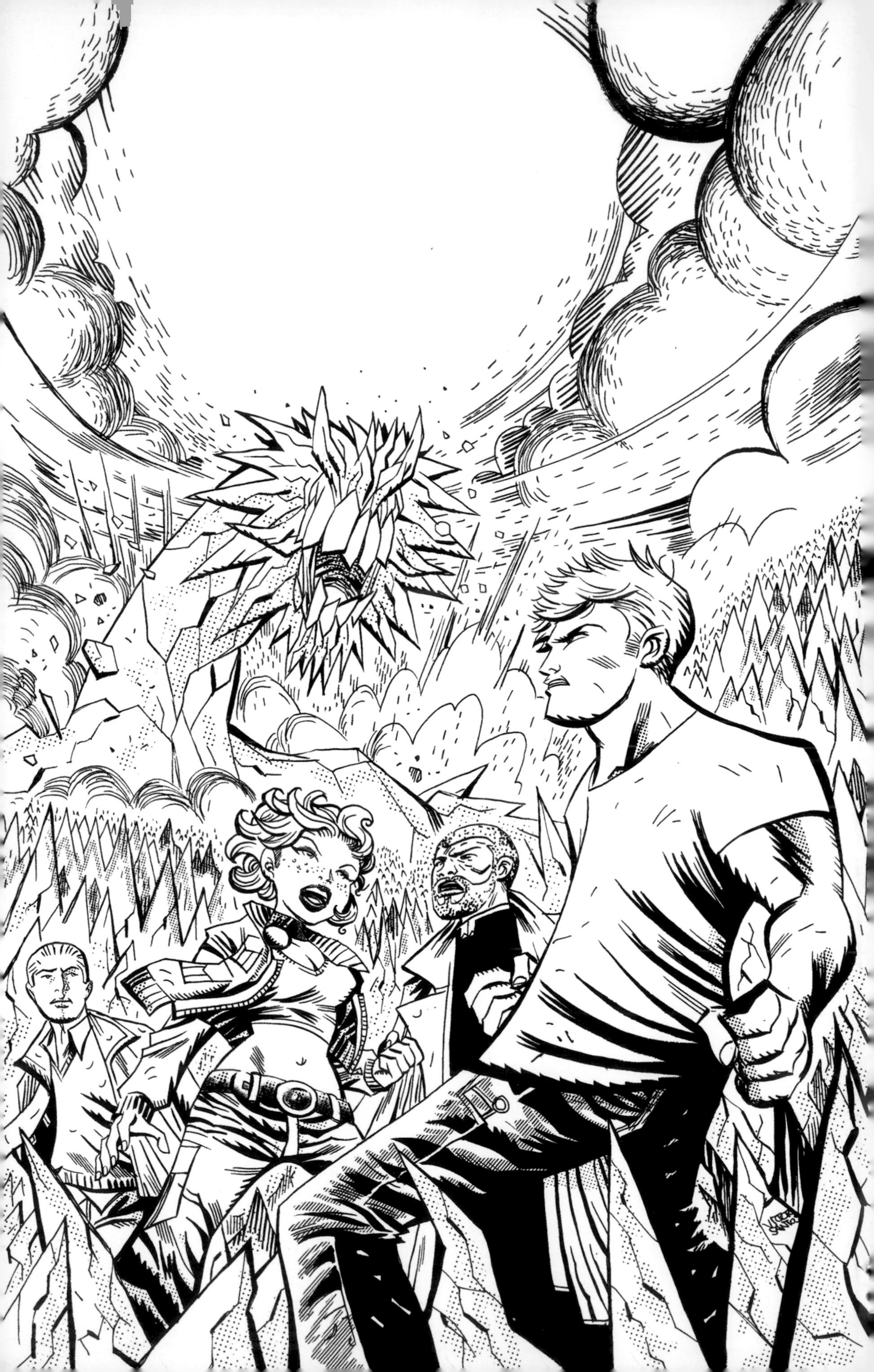

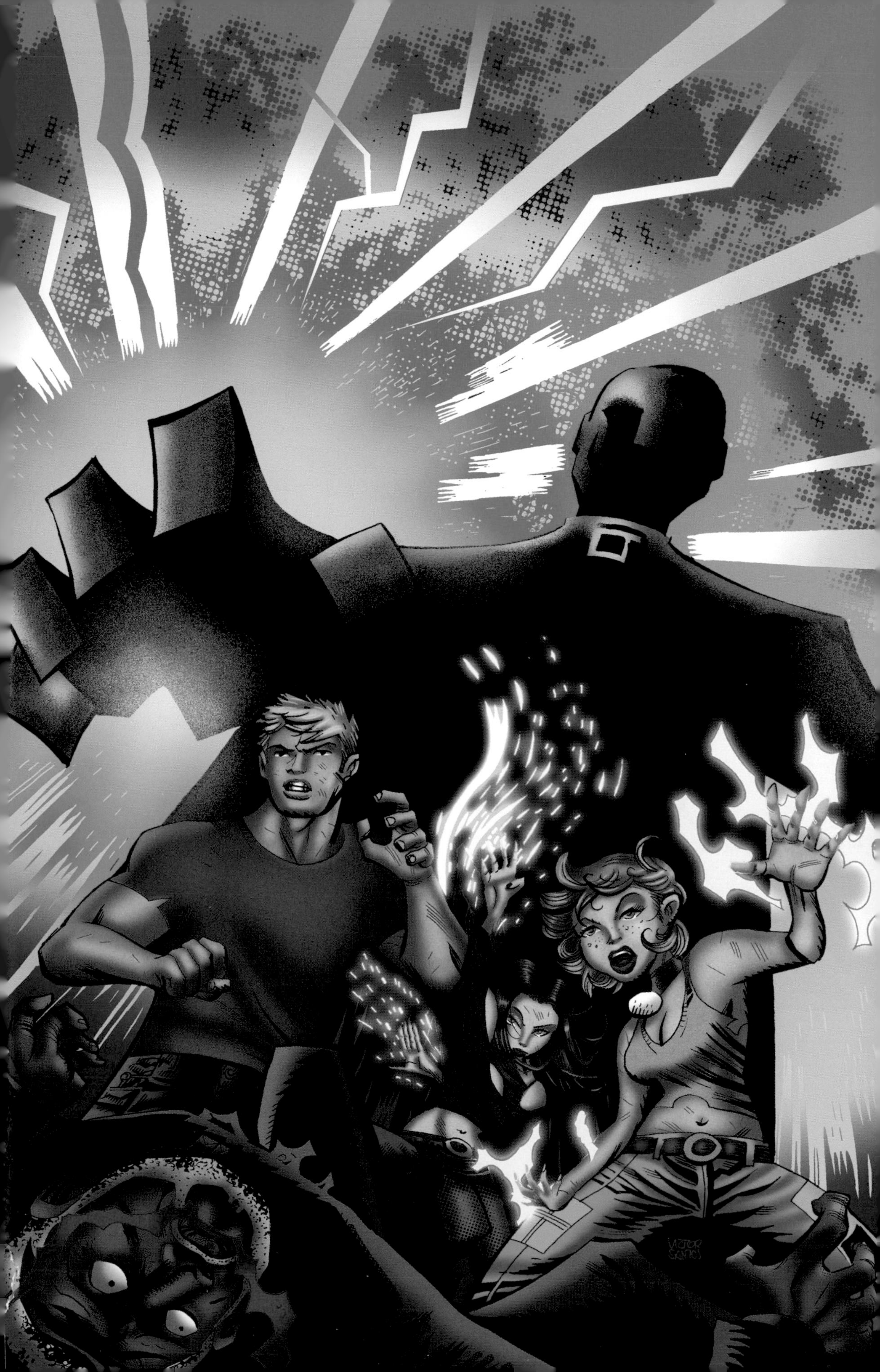
VICTOR SANTOS

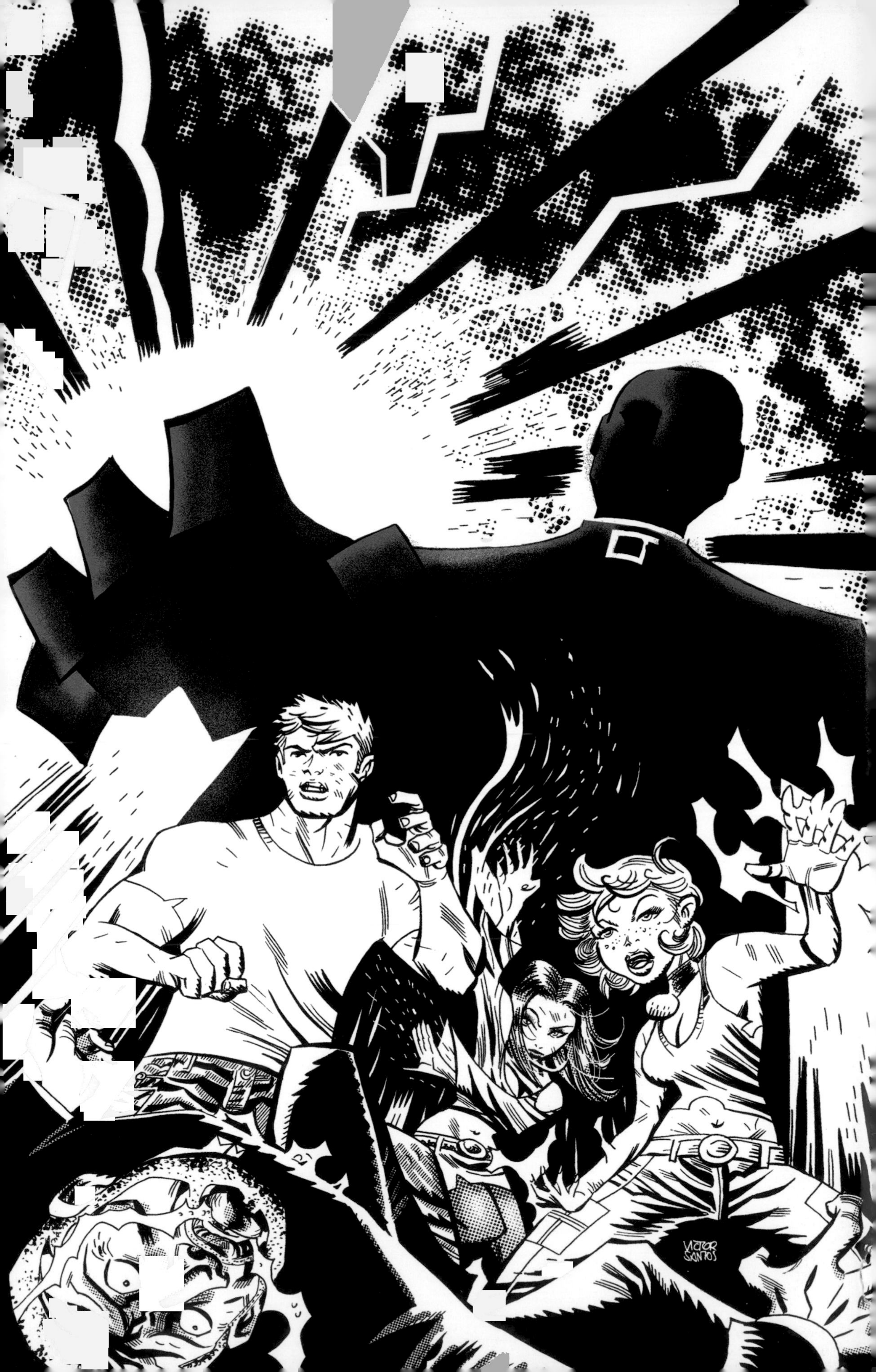
VICTOR SANTOS

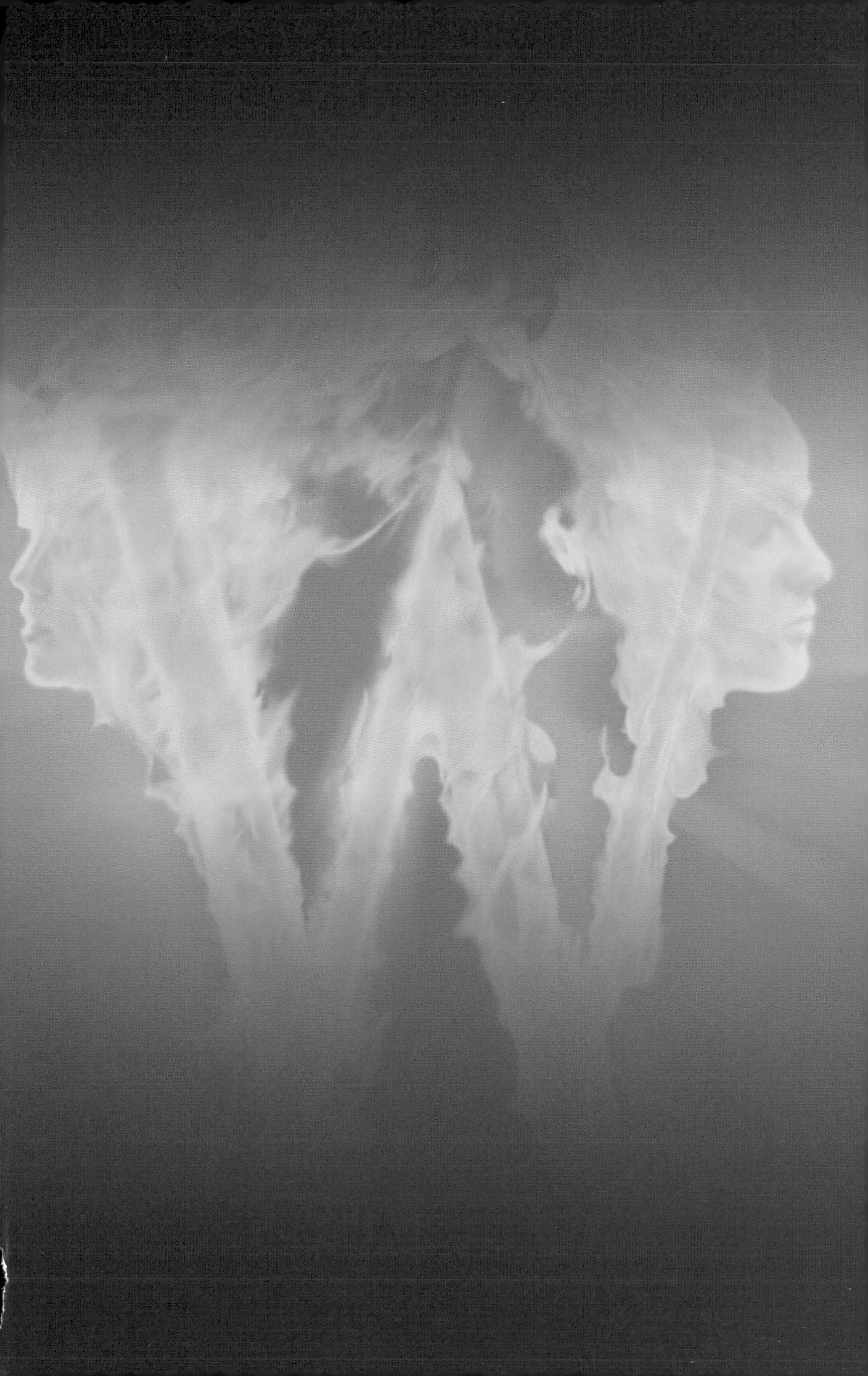

JAMES PATTERSON

WITCH & WIZARD

OPERATION ZERO

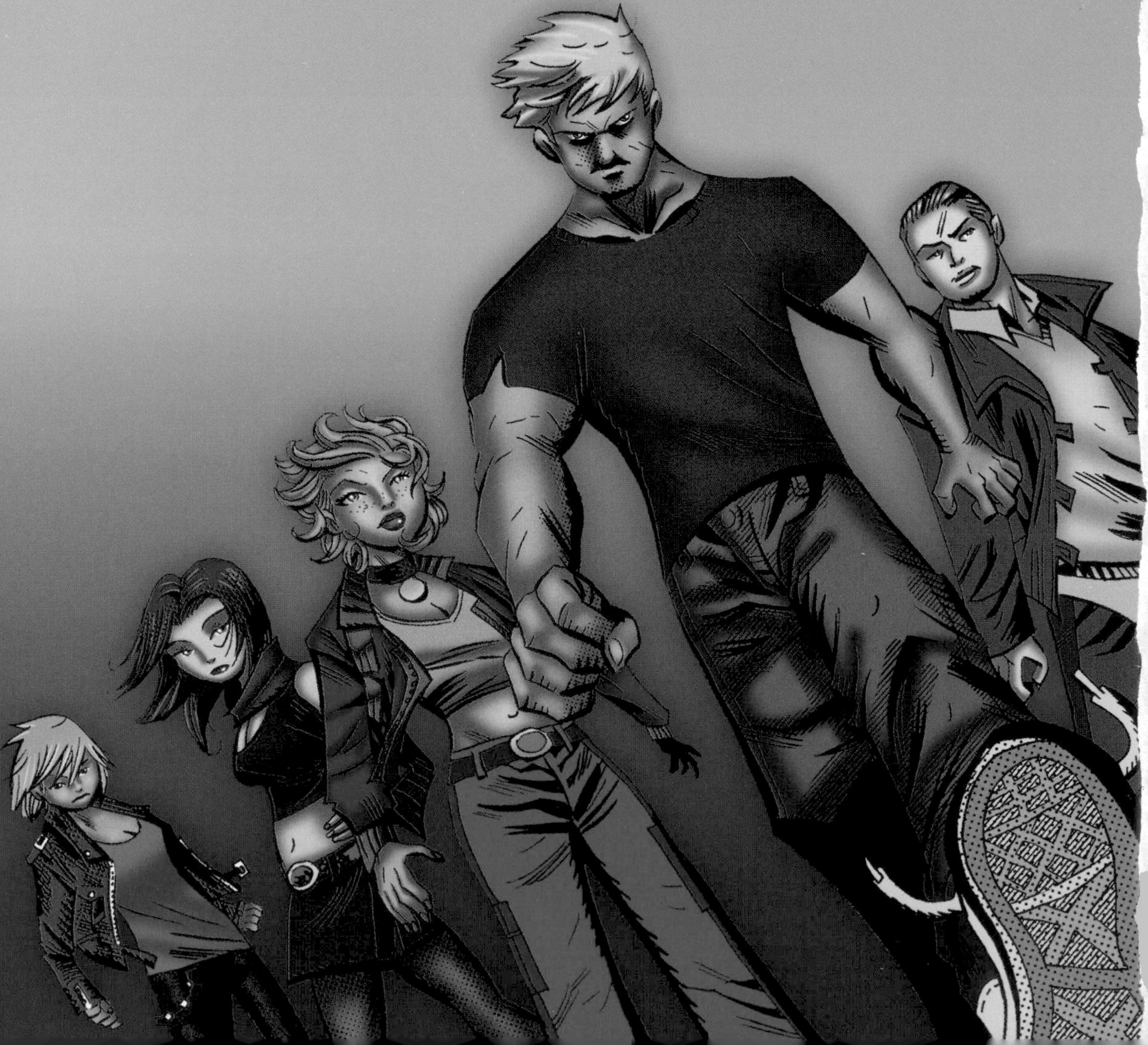